A YEAR
IN PALM BEACH

A YEAR
IN PALM BEACH

LIFE IN AN ALTERNATE UNIVERSE

PAMELA ACHESON
RICHARD B. MYERS

Two Thousand Three Associates
TTTA

Page 7: Excerpt from "The Country Life"
© 2007, 2010 Peter Cincotti and SonyATV Music Publishing, Inc.
Used with permission.
Permission given to authors to change the words "country life" to "Palm Beach life."

Page 315: Excerpt from "One More Moment"
Music by Johnny Rodgers, Lyrics by Johnny Rodgers and Lina Koutrakos.
© Melody Thread Music (ASCAP)/Plynerpublishing (ASCAP). Used by permission.

Two Thousand Three Associates
4180 Saxon Drive, New Smyrna Beach, FL 32169

www.twothousandthree.com
www.ayearinpalmbeach.com

Cataloging-in-Publication Data is on file with the Library of Congress

ISBN: 978-1-892285-15-7

Printed in the United States of America

First Edition: August 2011
10 9 8 7 6 5 4 3 2 1

A YEAR IN PALM BEACH
LIFE IN AN ALTERNATE UNIVERSE

"Let's go back and find
The simple world we knew
'cause I still wanna live again
The Palm Beach life with you

Don't let it be another thing
We always meant to do
Just let me live again
The Palm Beach life with you"

—Adapted from "Country Life"
by Peter Cincotti

CONTENTS

A Word about Palm Beach 11

"How Did Yesterday Get So Far Away from Today?" 13

"You Guys Are in for an Adventure." 19

"We'll Be Fat and Broke in a Month." 31

"Perhaps We Could Hunt Benjamin Down and Beat Him with a Stick." 39

"What Are You Guys, Hillbillies?" 61

"I See, That Would Make Us the Town DOPES." 87

"What's That? We Must Be Under Attack." 111

"I Feel Like Tony Soprano When the Ducks Left." 137

"They've Ordered Piggy Pie Freckles to Leave." 155

"I'm Looking Around for a Wood Chipper." 179

"Maybe It's Time to Start Throwing Paint Around." 203

"You Don't Have the Bulge." 227

"Chardonnay, and a Bowl of Chilled Evian for My Puppy, Please." 247

"We Finally Just Stopped Counting at Ninety-Six." 271

"It's a Perfect Example of the Law of Unintended Consequences." 289

Epilogue 311

A WORD ABOUT PALM BEACH

The Town of Palm Beach occupies a barrier island that is sixteen miles long and about a half-mile wide, just off the east coast of Florida. The quiet, well-manicured town has a population of about 10,000 that expands to 30,000 or more during the winter months. Arguably more millionaires and billionaires own residences in this town than in any other town in the country. More than two dozen of the Forbes top 400 billionaires own homes here. That is billionaires with a "b."

Palm Beach is known for its magnificent mansions, its exclusive and expensive clubs, grand hotels and resorts, world-class dining, and dozens and dozens of high-profile charity balls. Palm Beach is also known for Worth Avenue shopping. The three blocks of galleries and shops are among the most expensive and exclusive in the world. It would not be at all unusual to find a $60,000 lady's handbag or a $600,000 man's watch, or to discover that many of the cars parked along the avenue cost more than the average American house.

Lake Worth separates the island Town of Palm Beach from its decidedly different mainland neighbor, the City of West Palm Beach, with a population of 130,000. It only takes about thirty seconds to drive across the bridge from the mainland to the island, but the two are light-years apart. Palm Beach is truly an alternate universe.

one

"HOW DID YESTERDAY GET SO FAR AWAY FROM TODAY?"

We are very, very wet. Our oversize, supposedly windproof umbrella is no match for this melee of wind and rain. Water is dripping from our hair, and our clothes are glued to our bodies.

What was once a street is now a shallow rushing river, and our shoes are soaked. Streaks of lightning rake across the eerily dark afternoon sky, silhouetting palm trees bending in the wind. Deafening thunder shakes the ground. Conversation is difficult.

We get the car door open and slip into the back seat of this stranger's Mercedes. "It's nothing to worry about, just a typical August thunderstorm," Bob the real estate agent assures us. He's about as wet as we are, his tailored suit and expensive-looking shoes trashed, but he appears unperturbed.

We apologize for getting the leather seats of his car so wet, but Bob just smiles. "There's one more house, then we'll stop for the day," he says, handing us some paper towels.

We make feeble attempts to mop ourselves off.

How can we walk into this next house when we are so wet? And even more worrisome, how did yesterday get so far away from today?

Yesterday we left our New Smyrna Beach, Florida home and drove three hours south to The Chesterfield Hotel in Palm Beach for a brief romantic escape. We've been doing this several times a year for ten years. Each trip, we window-shop, take a whirlwind tour of our favorite bars and restaurants, dance the nights away, and then head happily back home.

But last night, walking back to our hotel for a dance or two after a romantic dinner, we started playfully imagining what fun it would be to live in Palm Beach. Walking along these beautiful, quiet streets. Eating at elegant restaurants. Dancing every night. A fantasy of indulgence quickly forgotten once we got on the dance floor.

Then this morning, out walking, we laughed at our silliness, our imagining we could live in Palm Beach. The trips are an escape, not real life. We couldn't afford to live here, anyway. Palm Beach property's way too expensive.

We found ourselves in front of a real estate office and looked at the pictures posted in the window. A mansion for $8 million. A bigger one for $10.7 million. An even bigger one for $33 million. Right. Not for us.

At the bottom of the window was an ad for rentals. On a lark, we went in to check them out. The real estate agent said he had some little cottages available as annual rentals. Cottages? On the exclusive, ritzy island of Palm Beach? We couldn't imagine what he was talking about but, mildly curious, we asked to see some. It sounded like a pleasant, harmless way to spend an hour or two.

That was back when the sun was shining, six houses ago. Now we're drenched and bedraggled, and the properties have blurred together in our minds. But there is no doubt we're hooked. This has gone from a few hours of idle fun to an intense scrutiny of possible living spaces.

Some of the places we saw were houses, not cottages, and way too big and way too expensive. But others were small and actually affordable to rent, although we could never afford to buy one.

In each house, we found ourselves refining what we could and couldn't live without. Definitely would like a fireplace. Winter nights can be in the forties, even this far south. One bathroom is not enough. Need at least three bedrooms, even if two are really tiny, so we can each have an office. Must have a pool.

As we approach the seventh and last house, the rain lets up and the skies lighten. This turns out to be a cottage, the best one so far. The kitchen is tiny, the third bedroom is minuscule, and the walls are painted wild colors. But the little yard is private, and there's a charming pool.

"So, what do you think?" Bob asks.

"We need to go back to The Chesterfield, we don't know what we think, a year might be too long, we could be crazy," we say, all in a jumble.

Bob drives us to our hotel. We promise to call him in the morning, rush up to our room, pull off our wet clothes, wrap ourselves in hotel robes, and raid the minibar.

Settled now with health food (two cold beers, cashews, and a can of Pringles), it's time to talk. How did we move from an idle afternoon's amusement to seriously considering renting a Palm Beach cottage for a year? How did we make such a gigantic leap?

The day before yesterday, staying where we were was definitely our plan. After all, we just planted rows of tomatoes and English peas and red peppers. It seems alarming that we could so easily switch gears.

We remind ourselves we're writers and can live almost anywhere. We've lived in big cities, small towns, Caribbean islands, and even on a boat. It's got to be easier to write in Palm Beach than it was on that boat.

We talk about our house in New Smyrna. We love it. Why would we leave it? But then, time is passing. We're getting older.

Alex, our real estate agent, is always telling us our house would rent in an instant. And moving to Palm Beach would be an adventure.

For a decade, we could never consider leaving New Smyrna for more than a week or two because we were responsible for a relative whom we loved dearly. But she recently passed away. For the first time in ten years, we're actually free to come and go as we please.

But still. Changing plans this radically in just a few hours seems more than a bit hasty. What about the practical aspects, such as seeing if we actually *can* rent our New Smyrna house? Shouldn't we go back home and think about all this?

Our heads are bursting. We decide to shower, go out on the town, and forget all this nonsense, at least for the night.

But this is not to be. We talk all evening. We go over the pros and cons. The idea is exciting. We must do it. What fun to rent and let other people take care of the problems.

We go over the details of the various cottages but get everything mixed up. "Was that the cottage on Hibiscus with no closets?" "Was it the place on Australian with the bizarre wallpaper?" "Do you think we could really live in that tiny one with no driveway?"

We sleep badly, give up, get up at dawn, and restlessly pace until a decent hour when we can call Bob. We go over the properties on the phone, ask to see two of them again.

He meets us in the hotel lobby, and we head out for a second inspection. Both cottages have pluses and minuses, but there is no question the small cottage right in town, the wildly colorful one, is our choice.

We discuss the specifics of the lease, agree to terms, and write a check for the deposit. The lease will begin in three weeks, on September 1. Bob will mail it to us.

It's noon and we're ready to go for it, a year in Palm Beach. We'll figure out the details later. We have no idea what an effect this whimsical decision will have on the rest of our lives.

two

"YOU GUYS ARE IN FOR AN ADVENTURE."

Bob drives us back to The Chesterfield and we quickly pack up.

"My clothes are still wet from yesterday," Dick says.

"Mine, too," I say. I look in a drawer and find a plastic laundry bag. "Here, we can put the wet stuff in this." I collect our soggy shoes and put them in a second bag. They look ruined.

We check out, get in the car. Dick's behind the wheel. In just a few minutes, we're driving over the bridge to the mainland.

I think of how symbolic this bridge is for me. Driving down from New Smyrna, crossing this bridge always means we're really here, the escape's beginning. Going home, it's the passage back to real life. Yet I don't know if we're going back to real life this time. It seems unreal that the next time we drive over this bridge, we'll be moving here.

Soon, Dick pulls onto I-95 and we begin our way north. We're both quiet for a long time.

Finally, Dick says, "Well, that was an interesting two days."

"You mean Friday morning we hadn't thought of moving anywhere, and now it's Sunday afternoon and we have a cottage in Palm Beach? It's bizarre." We both laugh. "I can't quite get my head around what we did," I say. "It seems normal one minute, and the next minute I think I must have dreamed it."

We both go quiet again. I watch the mile markers whiz by. I think back over our life together.

When I met Dick, I was working in New York and grieving over a loss. He was grieving over a lost marriage. I was living in a small apartment, trying to remake my life. He was living in his office, doing the same, and painfully adjusting to life as an every-other-weekend dad. He has a daughter, Samantha, grown now and living and working in New York. I never had a child.

When Dick and I met, I had no interest in getting into a relationship. Neither did he. But apparently our lack of interest was irrelevant. Though we both fought it in the beginning, we fell in love, spent our first month mostly outside of time, doing things like meeting for lunch at noon and finding ourselves at the same table in the same restaurant at eight at night, still talking nonstop.

Since then, we've had our ups and downs and crossed a lot of bridges, but our life together, at least for me, has been a wonderful adventure. We've moved many times, and every move has been exciting. I thought we'd never move again and I feel giddy at this change of plan.

We reach our exit and drive over another bridge, this one leading to New Smyrna, a barrier island like Palm Beach, but different in all other ways. New Smyrna's a laid-back T-shirt-and-surfboard beach town. Driving over this bridge always means we're home. I wonder if I'll miss it.

We coast down our driveway, pull up in front of the house, get out of the car. Our house is in the middle of two acres of oak and palm trees. We've planted flower gardens here and there. The only sounds I hear are birds singing. Two red cardinals frolic in the birdbath.

"I can't believe we've decided to leave this place," Dick says, looking around.

"Crazy, huh? Wonder what'll happen to the vegetable garden we just planted."

"The rabbits will be happy."

We take our overnight bags and wet clothes into the house. Our cockatiels, Duckie and Blanco, greet us, chirping wildly. I go let them out of their cage. They climb to the top, and Blanco hops on my shoulder. "You guys are in for an adventure," I tell them.

Dick and I unpack, go through the mail, water the plants around the pool, and generally busy ourselves with returning-home rituals. Palm Beach fades away as the evening arrives.

Around seven o'clock, Dick asks, "How about pasta tonight?"

"Sounds delicious," I say. "I'll make a salad."

We go into the kitchen. Dick puts the iPod in a dock and sets it to Peter Cetera who, years ago, for reasons unknown, became our standard background music for cooking together. I like to cook. My mom taught me early, and by the time I was nine I knew how to fry an egg over easy, make béchamel sauce and vinaigrette dressing, and stuff a turkey. I think Dick likes to cook even more than I do, and although we prepare dinner together, he usually creates the main course.

I designed this kitchen just for us. Everything has a place and there's plenty of counter space. Tonight, Dick scrambles some sausage, adds onion and garlic, chops up some tomatoes, and gets a sauce going.

I cut up vegetables and wash some arugula; make a dressing of mustard, garlic, balsamic vinegar, and olive oil; then go set the table out by the pool.

Dick comes to the door, holding a bottle of wine. "How about an Amarone, to celebrate?" he says.

We dine outside, savor the Amarone, and have a brief swim after dinner.

"I'm exhausted," Dick says.

"Me, too." We carry the dishes in, put them in the sink to soak, and fall into bed.

But I don't fall asleep right away. Instead, my thoughts turn to Aunt Jane. She was my father's older sister, one of five children, the last to die. I got to know her well when I moved to an apartment near hers in Manhattan soon after college. We'd been close ever since. In her later years, she asked me to take care of her, and moved into a nursing home near our house when she could no longer live in New York alone.

That was over ten years ago. For a decade I saw her, or Dick did, almost every day. Earlier this year she turned one hundred, still happy and healthy. She recently died peacefully in her sleep. Even though she was a hundred years old, it was a shock to have her go. I miss her a great deal. But now Dick and I are completely free to go just about anywhere, for as long as we want. The freedom feels good. I drift off to sleep.

An unsettling dream wakes me, but I can't remember it. The room is dark. My bedside clock tells me it's five, way too early to get up. I turn over, pull the covers around me. As I close my eyes, the memory of renting a Palm Beach cottage jolts me awake. Yikes! What have we done? Anxiety replaces yesterday's thrill. What if we can't rent this house? Do we want strangers living here? Can we just pick up and leave? Palm Beach is fine for a vacation, but for a year? What if we hate living there? I start to sit up, and Dick says, "You awake, too?"

"Yeah. I feel kind of panicked."

Dick laughs. "You mean because strangers are going to live in this house? And we won't like living in Palm Beach? And we don't want to go anywhere for a whole year? That kind of thing?"

"In a nutshell."

He sits up and turns on his light. "Are we crazy?"

"I don't know. We were awfully impulsive." I turn on my light, fluff the pillows so I can sit comfortably. "The thing is, well, I mean, there are so many things."

"Might as well get up," Dick says. "Tea or espresso?"

"This morning I need tea. Something calming."

Dick goes off to the kitchen. I slip into a robe and follow him, put some biscotti and slices of banana and apple on a plate.

We settle in the corners of the living room couch. It's beginning to get light outside, and I can just begin to see the flowers planted around the pool.

"This all seemed so frivolous and fun yesterday," I say.

"That's because it was frivolous and fun yesterday. Today it's buyer's remorse. Or actually renter's remorse."

I look around. "The space here is wonderful. Do we really want to leave the house we remodeled to be our dream house to live in a tiny cottage?"

"And do it for a year?" Dick says.

"I don't know. That seems like an awfully long time to live in something so small."

"And a year could be way too long a time to live in Palm Beach," Dick says.

I think about this. All we really know about Palm Beach are the bars and restaurants. We don't know what the town is like. We have no friends there.

"You mean, like, what would we do day to day?" I say.

"Right."

"How do you feel about renting this house, letting strangers live here? There's a lot of nice stuff they could wreck," I say.

"You mean like the Rookwood pottery," Dick says. "Or all the plates you like. Or the pool table. Or the art on the walls."

"We could put the good stuff away."

"I suppose." Dick says.

"Also, what about leaving our friends for a year?"

Suddenly, the idea is becoming more and more unappealing. I think of our relationships here, all our friends, our dentist, our doctors, Priscilla at the bank. We could come back to see friends or for doctors' appointments, I suppose, but we couldn't stay here if our house is rented.

"Have we made a mistake?" I say.

"I don't know," Dick says. "I'm getting something to write on." He goes into his office and comes back with a notepad and a pen.

Duckie and Blanco start chirping. "I guess we woke the birds," I say. "I'll go get them." I go into my office, where they sleep, uncover their cage, and open the door. They both hop onto my shoulders, and we all head into the living room. Dick has made more tea and drawn a two-column chart.

"Negatives on the left," he says. "Positives on the right." Duck hops off my shoulder, walks over to Dick's lap, and starts preening. We start by listing pros and cons. Dick fills in the columns as we talk.

"How're we doing?"

Dick makes a quick count. "It's about three to one we shouldn't go."

"Wow. That's depressing. Let me see." I move next to him to take a look. The chart is heavy on the negative side. It makes clear the move is impractical, impulsive, perhaps even foolish. The cottage is too small, the risk of renting out our furnished house is too big, and we have absolutely no idea whether we'd like living day to day in Palm Beach. Not to mention that having three weeks to simultaneously move and handle our work commitments is a ridiculously short amount of time.

"Well, yuck," I say. "They must have put something in the water down there."

Dick says, "Let's take a walk."

I put the birds back in their cage, and we head over to the beach. The surf's up, and surfers are paddling out to catch the next big one. A platoon of pelicans swoops low and flies just barely above the waves, looking for breakfast. The wind is fairly strong, coming right off the ocean, and the distance is a haze of salty air. I love this beach. We walk about a mile north along the water. Neither of us says a word.

"Head back?" Dick says.

"Okay." We turn around and make our way south, still silent.

I've been turning things over and over in my mind. Each time I come to the conclusion we shouldn't rent the cottage in Palm Beach, the decision feels wrong. The truth is, I want to go, no matter what.

Finally, I say, "I don't care if the move is impractical; I want to go."

"Mrs. Practical wants to go even if it's totally impractical?"

"It doesn't feel right not to go."

"Well, I want to go, too," Dick says. "We're too young to just write books and tend to our vegetable garden."

"And we're too old not to do this. Plus, it'll be fun in a year to come back to our dream house."

"I'd better call Alex, see if he really can rent this house," Dick says.

We leave the beach and walk toward our house.

"So, we're going to do it," I say.

"Yup, it's going to be fun," Dick says. "And scary."

"I like fun and scary."

Dick calls Alex as soon as we get home. Alex is confident he can rent the house, probably for a little more than we were expecting. I start making lists of all the things we need to do, forwarding the mail, setting up a phone in Palm Beach, and so forth. Dick walks around the house, making a list of what we need to bring. The cottage is partially furnished. We'll need to fill in the blanks with stuff but leave enough so this house is adequately furnished for renters.

I know some people hate to move but I love it. Packing up isn't my favorite activity, but I like the experience of living somewhere that is new to me, adjusting to the inside of the house, the unfamiliar rooms, and exploring the neighborhood, finding out where to do errands, the best routes for long walks. I feel the thrill of the unknown, just as I have every single move in my life.

"Shall I call Michele and Henry, give them the news?" Dick says. Henry and Michele are good friends who we met when they opened the Spanish River Grill in New Smyrna a decade ago.

"Yes," I say. "Actually, see if they want to have dinner tonight here or at Spanish River. We can tell them then."

We get to the restaurant around eight and relax at the bar while Henry and Michele take care of restaurant business. Around eight thirty, the four of us settle in at a table. Henry orders a bottle of red, pours each of us a glass.

We hold up our glasses and say "Sim Sala Bim" in unison. It's been our standard toast since we first met, although none of us can remember why.

Dick tells them of our impending move, with me adding details, and Henry and Michele asking question after question. Once they get over being astonished, Henry insists if we're leaving town for a year, he's going to be the one to move us.

"The truck I have for the restaurant," he says. "It'll be perfect. Everything will fit." He laughs. "I'll make it fit."

"Henry, you can't do that; you've got a restaurant to run. Your plate's full already," Dick says. "Excuse the expression."

"No, no, no, I'm doing this," Henry says. "Besides, I want to check on our sleeping quarters. Don't think we won't be regular visitors down there."

Michele says, "I want to come, too. I want to see the cottage, see just how crazy you guys are."

Driving home, Dick says, "We can't let them do that."

"I'm not sure we can stop them," I say.

The next several weeks are a blur. Days are divided into working time and packing and planning for the move. The lease comes in the mail, and we both sign it. Because Alex is showing the house to renters, we have to keep everything neat. I pile things that we're taking by the front door, and Dick takes the stuff to the garage and packs it up.

We go to the dentist and the doctor, get haircuts, have the cockatiels clipped. We don't have these connections in Palm Beach and we suspect everything will be much more expensive there. We get up earlier to write and stay up later to pack. It's hectic, but I feel excited, like a little kid, and Dick says he does, too. One morning, Dick answers the phone, and it's the miracle call from Alex. A couple wants our house for ten months. Close enough. The days speed past.

Two days before we're destined to leave, Henry drops his truck off, and by late afternoon on the last day of August, the truck is packed. In the early evening, Henry and Michele arrive.

They're going to spend the night here so we can get an early start. They want to get back tomorrow before their restaurant opens.

"Let's go to the double deck," Dick says. He hands Henry two chilled beer mugs. "If you would fill these, I'll carry the champagne for the ladies." He picks up the ice bucket. Henry goes to the kegerator.

"What can I do?" Michele says.

"Just get two champagne glasses," I say. She reaches into the cupboard, and I pick up a plate of cheese and crackers. We all walk out to the end of the property and up to the second floor of our two-story open deck. It looks out over thousands of acres of wetlands.

We settle in chairs. Dick pours Michelle and me champagne, and then we all raise our glasses.

"Sim Sala Bim."

The sun is setting. The owl that lives in one of our oak trees swoops out over the marshes in search of dinner.

"So, Henry," Dick says, "I need another favor."

"Uh-uh, I just helped you fill the truck. Tomorrow's drive is it," Henry says.

"I need you to watch over my kegerator. I can't let strangers use it."

"I guess I can do that," Henry says. "But once I put in a Heineken keg, it's never going back to Miller Light."

"Mmm, cold beer on tap at our house. Sounds good," Michele says.

"We'll pick it up tomorrow, on the return trip," Henry says.

"So, tomorrow's the day," Michele says to me. "Are you still excited?"

"Yeah," I say. "And scared."

"You mean good scared, right?" Michele says.

"Yeah. It's fun to be scared like this. But we're going to miss you guys."

"We're going to miss you. But we'll be down," Michele says.

We're all silent for a few minutes, looking out at the view. A great blue heron takes off from the marshy grasses. We watch the bird fly up, propelled by its huge wings. The bird makes an improbable landing in a mangrove bush.

"Won't you guys miss this?" Michele says.

"Yeah," I say. "But we'll be back."

"And our renters can enjoy it in the meantime," says Dick.

After an hour or so, we walk back to the house, grill dinner out by the pool, then linger at the table, talking.

"One last game of pool before you guys go," Henry says.

"Partner, you want to risk it?" Dick says to Michele. "We're the champs."

"No," Henry says, "your wife and I are the champs. Pam and I always win. At least that's how I remember it."

"I'm willing to risk it," Michele says.

"You guys obviously are mixing things up," I say. "But Henry and I will put our championship on the line."

"Doesn't matter," Dick says. "Whatever team wins tonight is the champ for the next year."

Henry opens another bottle of wine and sets up the balls. After six games, we're tied. "This is it," says Dick, as we start the seventh game. It's a heated battle but Dick and Michele win. Dick looks at his watch. "Good thing you guys came over so we could get an early start," he says. "It's almost two. We're supposed to be on the road in five hours."

three

"WE'LL BE FAT AND BROKE
IN A MONTH."

Tuesday, September 1

It's eight o'clock, and although the four of us are moving slowly, we're actually ready to go. I'm closing up Henry's truck, and Pam is closing up the house. The four-year-old Audi is full, and our Corvette is stuffed from stem to stern. We aren't the Beverly Hillbillies, exactly, but pretty close. No chickens or goats in the car, but the two cockatiels, Duckie and Blanco, are in their cage wedged somewhere in the backseat of the Audi.

Henry and Michele drive the truck. I drive the overstuffed Audi, Pam the Corvette filled with file folders. The three-hour drive, usually a blip, seems to be taking forever. I'm like a kid. I want to know, "Are we there yet?" Finally, our caravan pulls off I-95 and heads east toward the island. Then, just as we're about to cross over the Intracoastal Waterway, the light turns red and the drawbridge goes up.

While we're waiting, I'm thinking the town fathers (and mothers) will have to let the Audi over the bridge, and I'm pretty sure they have to let Henry's truck over, but the Corvette? Very un-Palm Beach, very déclassé. Palm Beach is home to expensive, exotic Italian, German, and English automobiles, not two-seater drop tops made by Chevrolet.

I have visions of Pam crossing the bridge and being pulled over by the police. "Madam, please, we can't have people bringing Corvettes onto The Island. What would be next? Dodge Vipers?"

Finally, the drawbridge is back down and the light turns green. All three vehicles, even the Corvette, make it over the bridge, on to South Ocean Boulevard and to the cottage.

Henry parks the truck on the street in front, and Pam and I pull the two cars into the narrow driveway. The keys are in the mailbox as promised. The four of us have been unloading for about forty minutes when a blue and white Palm Beach police cruiser pulls up behind the truck.

"That was quick," Henry says.

A rather large police officer unfolds himself from the driver's side. Here to impound the Corvette? Ticket the moving truck? Send us back over the bridge where we belong?

"This your truck?"

"Yes, officer. Well, actually it's his," I say, and nod toward Henry.

The officer looks at Henry and then says to me, "You moving into this house?"

"Yes, sir, that's the plan. Is there a problem?"

He smiles and says, "No problem. It's a cool house; hope you enjoy it." He hands me his card, says to call if we ever need him.

As he is starting to leave, he turns around and says, "Sweet looking 'Vette."

Henry's truck is empty in about an hour, and Henry and Michele have to leave.

"We're out of here," Henry says, "but if you can find out what drug the guy was on who painted the inside of this place, let me know. Those colors are wild. And if that giant cop gives you any trouble, don't call me."

As they're getting into the truck, Michele says, "I see what you mean about the size. Your living room in New Smyrna is probably the same size as this whole cottage. But you guys will make it work. You're going to have fun."

Pam and I hug and thank them, and as they are pulling away, Henry yells out the window, "We'll be back to haunt you, probably in about six weeks."

Pam looks at me and says, "To quote Joyce, 'Friends, like food and beauty, are essential.'" Joyce, one of Pam's closest and dearest friends, recently died, and I know Pam misses her. I do, too.

I look at my watch, and it's way past lunchtime. "I'm starving," I say. "I'm going out to look for some food. If I'm not back in a day or two, call that cop we just met."

Just a few blocks from the cottage I discover Sandwiches by the Sea. I want everything on the menu. They've got chili, white bean soup, homemade chicken salad, meatball subs, hot pastrami, Italian combos. I'm thinking meatball here, but remember I'm splitting it with Pam. She's not big on meatballs, so I settle on a turkey sub with Swiss and coleslaw and some white bean soup to go.

On the way back, I pass Scotti's Liquor store (nice to have neighbors) and stop in to pick up a few essentials and I meet Joe and Vinnie and John. As I'm turning into the yard, loaded down with several brown bags, Pam is by the front door.

"I'm back with soup and a sub," I say, "and some grapefruit juice, a wedge of cheddar cheese, crackers, two sixes of beer, and a bottle of Chianti Classico, all the essentials."

Pam comes over and takes two of the bags and gives me a kiss. "Well, maybe not all the essentials, but a good start."

Later, as evening approaches, I remember our bed is supposed to be delivered this afternoon. We called and ordered it when we were back in New Smyrna, and the store promised it would be delivered to the cottage today. Promised. I'm about to find Pam and share the bedless bad news when the doorbell rings. Yes, it's the Bed Man.

He carries everything into our bedroom and goes to work. This is quite obviously not his first day on the job. This man knows exactly what he is doing, and it looks like he is doing it in fast forward. Bed Man bolts the frame together, lifts the mattress on to the frame, and leaves—bolts, lifts, and leaves, in about twenty minutes.

It is definitely time to put the birds to bed, shower, and have a nice night. The boxes, cartons, and mess will still be there for us in the morning.

As she is drying her hair, Pam says, "What do you want to do for our first date? We can easily walk to over ten different restaurants and ten bars."

"Ten?" I say. "I could maybe do nine. Well, maybe six. Actually, it's been a long day. How about a drink at Taboo, dinner at Renato's, and if we're still standing, a dance at The Chesterfield?"

"Perhaps ambitious, but perfect. Taboo, Renato's, and the Chesterfield's Leopard Lounge," Pam says.

The truth is, I'm feeling a little disoriented. The bathroom seems weird, I'm getting dressed in a bedroom I've never slept in, and Pam is drying her hair in front of a tiny mirror.

But outside, it is a breezy, summery evening, and the streets are quiet. Pam looks beautiful in a blue dress and high-heeled sandals. We walk hand in hand along Worth Avenue, and when we get to Taboo things seem normal again.

Taboo is what a bar should be. It's classy, dark, and long. It feels like you could settle in here. There's a large tank of tropical fish in the middle of the back wall. Two small, silent televisions are discreetly built in at each end, and the Yankees are up by two in the fourth. Bobby, a bartender's bartender and world traveler, is working tonight. Over the years, the three of us have shared many stories about our trips around the U.S. and various Caribbean islands.

"Dick, Pam, you guys back already?" he asks.

"Should we leave?"

He laughs. "No, but weren't you two down just last month?"

Pam recounts the story of our madcap move and warns, "You'll be sick of us in no time."

"Never," Bobby says.

"We'll see. It's going to be a test," I say.

We finish our drinks, say goodbye, and walk along Worth Avenue to Renato's. The maître d', Brad, all six feet five of him, is by the door, elegant as always in a double-breasted pinstriped suit. Luciano, Renato's longtime captain, is next to him. Luciano began his life in the restaurant business at a very young age, serving cocktails to Princess Grace in Monaco. He speaks Italian, Portuguese, French, Spanish, German, and English.

"Mr. and Mrs. Myers, back so soon?" Brad says.

"You're stuck with us for a year. We've rented a cottage on the island," I say.

"Then please allow me to buy libations to welcome Palm Beach's newest residents."

Luciano shakes his head and says, "It may be time for me to look for a job in another city."

At the table, Pam and I choose a Banfi Chianti Classico Riserva and Luciano describes the evening specials. While waiting for dinner, we sip our wine and talk. We're in a dark, romantic corner table, and I'm looking out at the equally romantic candlelit terrace. The setting is perfect, and as always, Luciano takes care of us like family.

Our dinner arrives, and as we're eating, Pam says, "I can't believe Renato's is so close to where we live."

"I can't, either. We'll be fat and broke in a month."

"Then we better finish up and go dance the night away while we can."

We finish our espressos and walk over to The Chesterfield Hotel's Leopard Lounge. It is a quiet night. The multi-talented Adam Austin is at the piano. Lou, who (it is rumored) was banished from Boston for telling bad jokes, and Michelle, a stunning blonde, are behind the bar. We have known Adam, Michelle, and Lou for years.

The three of them give us a strange double take. Lou brings us a cocktail and, as always, an old joke. "This penguin walks into a bar and asks the bartender, 'Have you seen my brother?' The bartender says, 'I don't know, what does he look like?'"

After a drink and a few dances, it is time to call it a night.

I say, "Michelle, can we cash out and we'll leave you guys alone?"

"I'll just put it on your room," she says.

"That would be fine, but we're not staying here."

"You're not? Then where are you guys staying?"

"We moved here for a year, to a cottage."

Michelle says, "Well, that's a surprise. Good for you."

"I think you're right," Pam says. "I think it is going to be good for us."

For a dozen or more years, we would now walk through the lobby to the elevator and up to our room. But tonight we are walking through the lobby and out the front door to our cottage in Palm Beach. As we get to our front walk, Pam says, "What a thing."

We'll sleep in our new bed for the first time. Maybe tomorrow I'll believe we're really here.

four

"PERHAPS WE COULD HUNT BENJAMIN DOWN AND BEAT HIM WITH A LARGE STICK."

Wednesday, September 2

Pam and I are up early, and yes, I'm surprised to be here, but very happy. We go out for a walk to explore our new neighborhood. The ocean is less than a block away, and the Lake Worth Lagoon, part of the Intracoastal Waterway, about four blocks. After almost an hour of walking, we're back home to continue unpacking, setting up the rooms, moving furniture, hanging photos, and filling a few cabinets. Getting settled is going to take a while, but I love our first walk around the neighborhood.

From the outside, our new house is a small, one-story Bermuda-style cottage with white stucco walls, a black roof, and a large chimney. A twelve-foot ficus hedge shields the small front yard, and the east, west, and north sides of the property are also bordered by trees and hedges.

Inside we are surrounded by colorful walls, and the entire cottage has white wooden floors. The living room, painted bright coral, has a fireplace, built-in bookcases, and a tray ceiling. Interior French doors open into another, less-formal, soft yellow family room. From the family room, more French doors open out to the pool area.

We have two small bedrooms and three tiny bathrooms. We claim the slightly larger, sky-blue bedroom for ourselves. I put the electric "wood-burning" stove in the corner. The second bedroom, pale green, becomes our office and Duckie and Blanco's room. Pam and I have been working in the same house on a daily basis for over a decade, but we have always each had our own office. This room looks smaller than I remembered. Much smaller. We'll see.

The kitchen is like our first New York apartment kitchen. It's small but functional. An empty doorway off the kitchen leads to what is supposed to be the third bedroom, which measures about six feet by eight feet. For the time being, we are storing boxes there.

The pool and pool area are way out of proportion to the cottage. The twenty-by-forty-foot pool has a generous coquina deck and is completely and privately enclosed by giant seagrape, palm, umbrella, and ficus trees. Bathing suits will not be necessary.

Our small cottage has an even smaller guest cottage. This is, after all, Palm Beach. It houses a compact washer-dryer and its own tiny full bathroom, and I think there will be just enough room for a futon for guests, a bureau, an iPod dock, and some books. But at the moment it, too, holds still-unpacked boxes.

Thursday, September 3

Along with unpacking and settling in, we are waiting, the expected waiting that comes with a move, not my favorite activity. The cable people and the phone people are both supposed to arrive today. The man from the phone company arrives at ten o'clock as promised. In my experience, this is the exception to the rule. He puts on little booties, walks around inside, and finds six phone/internet jacks.

"Looking good," he assures us. "I'll be right back."

About ten minutes later, he is back at the door. His expression indicates that things are not looking good.

"There are no phone lines to this house," he says.

Pam turns her head and points to one of the phone jacks. "What are those?"

He shakes his head. "I know," he says, "you have phone jacks inside the house, but there are no wires attached to anything outside. Someone cut all the lines coming in. I can't hook you up, but I called it in. Someone will be here tomorrow between three and five. I'm sorry."

"Cut lines? What's that about?" Pam says.

About four o'clock, Pam says, "Some guy is wandering around out back. I think it might be the cable guy."

I go to the French doors, open them up, and say, "Good afternoon."

"Hey, how ya doing?" he says, and walks over. The name on his shirt is actually Larry. "Buddy, I think we have a problem here," he says.

By now Pam has joined us by the door.

"Can I come in?" he says.

"Of course," Pam says, and the three of us step inside the yellow room.

Larry the Cable Guy looks around, spots a cable coming out of the east wall, walks over, and gives it a tug. It pulls right out of the wall and swings in the air.

"Someone cut all the cables coming into the house," he says. "This is a big problem."

Larry goes on to explain we need a special service team to come out and evaluate the situation. He can't do anything. He gives us a phone number to call and wishes us luck.

After he leaves, Pam says, "What is this cut wires and cables stuff about? Why would anyone want to cut all the cables?"

"I have no idea. Maybe we should call the property manager. His name and number are clipped to the lease."

"Okay, but let's wait until tomorrow and see what the other phone guy says. At least by then we'll have a little more information," Pam says.

Friday, September 4

I am realizing that the cottage offers some interesting challenges. There is only one medicine cabinet, the kitchen cabinets are missing shelves, there are very few hooks or towel racks, no toilet tissue holders, two of the showers don't have curtain rods or curtains, and two of the toilets are not attached solidly to the floor.

Each day we make a new discovery. This afternoon I am quite sure the pool has a leak, and Pam thinks the sprinkler system may not be working. I start a punch list.

Unfortunately, I can't make a punch list to correct the inherent smallness of the cottage. I am an off-the-rack 44 long, six three, one ninety. There are doorways I have to turn sideways to get through. One of the bathrooms I cannot stand up in, and I've already hit my head on the slanted ceiling in the guest cottage several times.

Then there are the other oddities, like I can't open my closet door without closing the bedroom door, and no one can get into the kitchen if the icebox is open. But the cottage isn't going to adjust to me, so I guess I'll be adjusting to the cottage.

The good news is that at ten to five the new phone man arrives and by six thirty the cottage has a working landline and internet service. Pam and I decide to live without TV for a while and don't even bother to call the number Larry the Cable Guy gave us.

Saturday, September 5

The list of problems is growing. This morning our pool man confirms the pool does have a leak, but he needs the property manager to okay the repair. I call Benjamin, who is listed as the property manager. Benjamin's machine picks up. I leave him a message and our number.

In the meantime, to make the cottage more livable, we need towel racks, tools, shower curtain rods, shelves, light bulbs, and several other items. Neither of us has a clue where to find these things in Palm Beach.

I discover a copy of the *Palm Beach Guide and Phone Book* in a kitchen drawer. Leafing through it, I say to Pam, "This is extremely helpful. I just counted over thirty entries for jewelry stores, and there are several dozen designer boutiques, ladies' shoe stores, and art galleries listed, but absolutely nothing resembling a hardware, houseware, or office supply store anywhere on the island."

Pam laughs. "This is Palm Beach. People need Ferragamo and Armani, not light bulbs and screwdrivers." After consulting her iPhone, she reports, "All the necessities of life are available over the bridge, strung out along Okeechobee Boulevard. Office Depot, Lowe's, Bed Bath & Beyond, Staples, Target, Restoration Hardware, and Pottery Barn."

I get it. Real stuff is on the mainland. The stores in West Palm have everything a person might need. The stores in Palm Beach have nothing a person might need, but everything they might possibly want.

Sunday, September 6

It's time to find a grocery store. We have been existing quite well on grapefruit juice from Scotti's for breakfast, and salads and sandwiches from Sandwiches by the Sea for lunch, and just wandering out for dinner. So far we have walked to cocktails or dinner at Taboo, Bice, The Chesterfield, Renato's, Trevini, Amici, and Café Boulud.

The evenings have been wonderful, but I actually miss cooking. It is time to start normal life here. It dawns on me I have no idea where the grocery store might be or even if there is one on the island.

"Pam, do you know if Palm Beach even has a grocery store?" I say.

"There must be one. I'll Google 'Palm Beach groceries' on my cell," she says. "Looks like there's a Publix Super Market about a mile north on the island."

I must admit that Pam's iPhone comes in handy from time to time, but I really hate cell phones. Or maybe just the way some people use them. I don't have one and don't want one. My daughter Samantha assures me that this fact alone makes me a weird old man, but she helpfully points out the list does not stop there.

I drive us to Publix, pull the car into the parking lot, and am greeted by a valet parker. Valet parking at the local grocery store. Welcome to Palm Beach. We skip the valet, park and go in, load up, and then head home.

Tonight, with cupboards, freezer, and icebox stocked, we stay home and have our first cookout. It is a balmy night, a sip and dip night. Pam marinates a flank steak, I shuck a few ears of white corn and toss a salad together, and then the two of us head out for a cocktail in the pool. I put the iPod in its dock and decide Don McLean should join us.

Having just confessed to hating cell phones, I must now confess to loving my iPod. I've got thousands of songs to choose
from, literally hundreds of artists, and dozens of playlists. Making music a part of our life is very easy with the iPod. I am not a
total dinosaur.

We wallow in the peace and privacy of the (leaking) pool. I
start the coals and get back in the pool. Eventually, Pam goes into
the kitchen and brings out the rest of the food. I put the steak
and corn on the grill and then start a wood fire in our fire pit.
"Are those birds watching us?" I say

"The ones on the guest cottage?" Pam says. "I think they're
doves."

"Whatever they are, they've been sitting there watching us
for quite a while."

"Maybe they want to meet Blanco and the Duck," Pam says.

After dinner, Pam and I walk over to the beach. There is no
one else around. Walking back home, for maybe the first time, I
feel like we really live here.

Monday, September 7

Today it is pouring rain, so we work around the house, thinking Benjamin will be returning our call from last Saturday. Pam
has discovered the clothes dryer in the little guest cottage is not
vented. When the dryer is on, the hot exhaust just fills the room.
Even with the air conditioner on, the temperature is about 100
degrees in there. We've also discovered the disposal doesn't work.
I call Benjamin. Again. This morning he actually answers. He
doesn't seem to really know who we are or what he should do, but
he agrees to come over and meet with us at two o'clock.

A little after three o'clock, Benjamin is at our front door.
Benjamin, it turns out, is a college student who looks like he just

stepped out of *The Preppy Handbook* or perhaps a surfer dude magazine. He does not inspire confidence, but he's a nice kid and seems sincere, so we go over our typed list of problems. I politely point out that many of them were outlined in an attachment to the lease and supposed to be taken care of before we moved in.

Benjamin agrees we "should fix some of these things up." He takes a copy of our list and promises to be back tomorrow morning, before ten. As he's leaving, he explains, "You can always leave a message, but I'm mostly available on Saturday and Sunday." A strange bit of information.

Tuesday, September 8

Pam and I are on an early morning walk exploring our mostly empty neighborhood. We're on Peruvian Avenue near the lake when I hear a man yell, "Honey, which car are you taking?"

After a second or two, a woman says, "I'm not sure; I guess I'll take the blue one," and they both start laughing. As we pass the driveway, I see there are two Bentleys parked side by side, exactly the same blue, except one is a coupe and the other's a convertible. I guess she could have just as easily answered "the Bentley."

Two Bentleys. Welcome to Palm Beach.

Benjamin was supposed to show up this morning before ten, but he didn't. I call him at noon. I get his machine. I don't know if people are supposed to be here today, but it seems wise to stick around on the off chance someone actually comes and tries to fix something. The cottage has never been professionally cleaned as outlined in the lease. Pam and I decide to tackle the cleaning ourselves and spend all day going at it.

About seven thirty, Pam says, "It's been a long, dirty day. Let's have a hot shower and a civilized evening."

"Café L'Europe?" I say. "That's one place we haven't been since we moved."

"Perfect. I'll be out of the shower in five," she says.

"Or maybe ten," I say, "but we're not in a rush."

I'm getting the birds new food and water when Pam appears in the office wrapped in a towel. "There is no hot water," she says.

"Oh crap. Let me take a look." Two minutes later, I walk out of the bathroom and say, "There's no hot water."

Pam laughs. "The guest cottage has its own hot water heater. I'll sneak out there and shower. You can try to call our surfer dude property manager."

Benjamin's machine picks up. Again. I leave a short message and then inspect the water heater. It seems to be gas powered. I don't do water heaters, but there is a phone number pasted on the side. I call and leave another message. I'm getting quite good at leaving messages.

Pam's out of the guest cottage shower (in ten) and I'm into it. Then it is time to escape the cottage and try dinner at Café L'Europe. We haven't been there in almost a year. The owners Norbert and Lidia have made this place a Palm Beach legend for thirty years. Bruce, the dining room manager, greets us at the door. Bruce has been with this restaurant for almost its entire thirty years. I look at him and think he must have started here around age five.

We settle into barstools and admire the scene. The wall across from the bar is a shimmering mosaic of shiny bottles, mirrors, carved woodwork, and two huge displays of fresh flowers. David is at the piano.

After a few minutes, Bruce takes us to a table, and I order a bottle of Veuve Clicquot. This is a tradition we started when we moved out of Manhattan. At the time I, declared, "A big move deserves a bottle of Veuve." Since then, any big move in our life calls for a bottle of Veuve.

Rainer is the restaurant's knowledgeable and amusingly crazy sommelier. He is tall, thin, and boyishly handsome. On our last visit here, he mentioned a new lady friend, so Pam gave him a book we had written on romantic Florida escapes.

As he is opening our champagne, Pam says, "Rainer, you won't remember—"

Rainer says, "I remember you two. You are the romantic people. I love your book. Got rid of the woman."

Pam and I laugh, I taste the champagne, we talk to Rainer for a minute or two. We order, and after dinner, we finish the last of our champagne while listening to David play his *West Side Story* medley.

Full and happy and forgetting our cottage problems, we stroll home along the Atlantic. The waves are sounding on the shore, there are warm ocean breezes, and the moon is lighting up the night sky. "This is wonderful," Pam says.

"I couldn't agree more," I say. And I couldn't.

Friday, September 11

I find Pam in the kitchen this morning cutting up vegetables. "I just thought I'd roast some stuff to have in the icebox," she says. Pam and I may be the last two people on the planet who still say icebox.

"Why don't you just give me the vegetables? I'm going to put some stuff in the dryer, and if I leave the vegetables anywhere near it, they'll cook in no time."

"Very funny," Pam says.

The phone rings, and I pick up.

"Benjamin," I say, "I told you never to call me here."

There is a long pause.

"Benjamin, I'm just kidding. Where the hell have you been?"

Old Ben explains there have been problems, but that a plumber will be over today to look at the revolving toilets, the dryer vent, and the disposal. "The plumber will be there definitely no later than four," Benjamin assures me.

We work and wait until almost six. No plumber. I call Benjamin. Get his machine. "Let's get out of the house, walk to the beach or something," Pam says.

"Or we could hunt Benjamin down and beat him with a large stick," I suggest.

"The beach is a better idea, I think," Pam says.

The sky is clear. Large waves are breaking against the sand, and the water looks turquoise and tropical, almost like Caribbean water.

"The cottage is not without its problems," Pam says.

I laugh. "Who are you tonight, the Mistress of Understatement? The cottage is driving us crazy. It really sucks."

"Remember when we said what fun it would be to rent? Any problems, we'd just pick up the phone and someone else fixes them," Pam says. "It's been almost two weeks; I'm just about done."

"I am too. It's really stupid, but let's sleep on it. First thing tomorrow morning I'll call Benjamin, scream at him a little, and try to set up a reasonable, but specific, schedule. He said Saturday is a good day to get him. We'll see."

As Pam and I reach our front door, there is a note from the plumber, that's the plumber who was to be here no later than four o'clock but still wasn't here at six. The note says simply: "Sorry to have missed you."

Sunday, September 13

The hot water heater, which we thought was fixed, has stopped working again. That and many other inside problems have driven Pam and me outside, where we are decked out in gardening clothes, working in the little front yard. I'm planting hibiscus and Pam is spreading mulch. "Don't look now," Pam says. "An angry-looking man is marching towards us on the sidewalk."

The neighborhood garden patrol, I wonder. Although he has a black shoe polish dye job, this chap has to be in his eighties. He does not look at all happy with us.

Pam and I glance at each other. "What now?" Pam whispers.

I'm thinking red mulch may be illegal. Maybe we can't work outside on Sundays or we need a gardening license.

He stops about four inches from me and almost steps on my foot. "What do you two think you're doing?" the old guy says. "I'm going to have to lodge a complaint."

I am about to answer when he laughs and adds, "You two are making the place look too damn good."

He introduces himself as Barney. We chat and he invites us to visit him for a cocktail sometime, explains which house is his, and marches on his way around the corner.

Monday, September 14

Today, the deluge. Two guys from the gas company come to check the water heater, followed by a plumber and an air conditioner guy. Progress is being made, I think, but our cottage is getting trashed. The entire afternoon we spent cleaning was a waste of time. The white wood floors look like someone hurled vanilla fudge ice cream all over them.

Pam is close to losing it. Actually, so am I, but we have an unspoken rule that only one of us can lose it at a time. So I am pretending to be a patient, understanding adult.

It's almost seven o'clock. "I think we should go to The Chesterfield for a drink, or maybe three, and some dancing, perhaps dinner at the bar," I say.

"Sounds good to me."

We shower and change. As we walk out the door, Pam says, "Yikes, it's raining. Actually, it's pouring. We'll get soaked if we walk all the way to The Chesterfield."

"Well, we've got to get away from this cottage. We'll go to Amici. It's much closer," I say. I grab an umbrella. "Hold my hand, it's really slippery."

We walk into Amici, a bit wet but laughing because we made it through the rain. It is lobster night so we order grilled lobsters. I'm not a big lobster eater, but once a year or so, either at a restaurant or at home, Pam and I have a lobster dinner together.

Early in our relationship, we took a five-day trip to Anguilla with some friends. Six of us stayed in an island shack with no hot water and no real kitchen, so we ate lunch and dinner out all five days, ten meals.

Pam had lobster all ten times: cold lobster, grilled lobster, lobster salad, you name it. About the third night, the Jimmy Buffett lyrics about eating her own weight up in crab meat started echoing in my head. Only with Pamela it was lobster, not crab. To commemorate that first trip and give ourselves an excuse to reminisce, we're doing our lobster dinner tonight.

Later, after finishing our lobsters, we're having an espresso and listening to beautiful live guitar music. The rain has let up a bit, and now it is falling softly on the awning above us. Occasionally, there is the sound of distant thunder, and lightning brightens the night sky.

"This is some setting," Pam says. "What a simple, relaxing,

romantic night. I could sit here with you until dawn."

"I agree. Our nights in Palm Beach seem magical," I say, "even if the days are still a bit of a pain in the ass."

Wednesday, September 16

I love the hedge in front of our house for many reasons. I like looking out at it. I like that people can't look in. I like that I can sneak out in my boxers to get today's papers.

This morning our first copy of the *Palm Beach Daily News*, known affectionately on the island as the Shiny Sheet, has arrived in our driveway. We have subscribed for the year. The newspaper covers only the island of Palm Beach, and it's called the Shiny Sheet because it's printed on coated paper: the ink will not smudge the fingers, white gloves, or cashmere robes of its readers. Or in my case, boxer shorts.

After enjoying our new paper along with *The New York Times* and *The Wall Street Journal*, we settle in at our desks, a bird on each of us. No one is scheduled to come to the cottage today, which should give us one of the few uninterrupted workdays since we moved. At about ten thirty, the birds start chirping. I look out the office window and see three men wandering about by our pool. I go out to see what's happening.

"Can I help you, gentlemen?"

"No, we're good, thanks," one of them says.

"Ah, well I'm glad," I say, walking towards them. "Perhaps then you could help me."

"Sure, whaddya need?"

"I don't need anything, but I'd like to know who you guys are and what you are doing on my pool deck."

They look a little startled. "No one told you we'd be here this morning?" one of them says.

"No one did," I say.

"Sorry. We're here to pressure wash the pool deck, the awning, and the side walkway. That okay?"

"Yes, that's quite okay. Wish we had known you were coming."

Time to go. I put the birds in their cage and move them to the living room, away from the noise and mess of the pressure washers. Pam and I gather up our folders, red pens, and laptops and head out the door to find someplace quiet to work. There are three peaceful parks within a few blocks of the cottage. This morning Pam chooses Pan's Garden, which is next to and actually part of The Preservation Foundation of Palm Beach.

We enter and follow a pine needle path to a shady seat near the pond. "What a beautiful place to work," Pam says.

"You think I should write to The Preservation Foundation and see if we could set up permanent offices here?" I say. "A lot more room than the office at home."

We work for a few hours and walk home to find the pressure washing people finishing up and the birds settled down. All is quiet again.

Tonight, to escape the cottage issues, Pam suggests a romantic candlelit dinner at Renato's. Gets my vote, but when we arrive, Renato's is closed for a private party. No problem. Café Boulud, which is in The Brazilian Court Hotel, is only about a block away. Café Boulud is one of Daniel Boulud's restaurants, upscale, fancy, French.

They have room for us, and the maitre d' leads us to a table next to a windowed alcove. Soft lighting illuminates the outside planting. He says, "Tonight the chef is offering three menus, our regular menu, a prix fixe menu, and an eclectic summer menu. You have many wonderful choices." He hands us the six menus.

Pam and I begin our reading project. I'm looking over the formal menu.

Pam says, "I bet I know what you're having."

I think she's nuts because I don't see anything I really want to order: escargot, smoked salmon, warm gratin of peekytoe crab, octopus. These are not my favorites. Then I notice Pam's looking at a different menu. She seems quite amused.

"Look at the summer menu," she says.

I open up the summer menu, take a look, and then laugh. "You think I'm going to have the Niman Ranch hot dog Chicago style, with coleslaw and tomatoes," I say.

"Yes, I do," Pam says.

"And you're going to order the Cuban. Am I right?"

I'm thinking this is very funny. Pam's wearing an Armani skirt and a Tahari jacket, and I'm in a grey linen suit. We're dining in a fancy Daniel Boulud French restaurant and we're choosing a hot dog and a Cuban sandwich.

This hillbilly thing is starting to worry me.

Thursday, September 17

There are many, many things I do not understand. Near the top of the list are the people who make appointments and don't keep them. These are the people who promise to be somewhere at a certain time on a certain day but actually have no intention of being there. This is now what we're dealing with almost every day, and I hate it.

Once again we have a morning of no-shows. It's getting tedious. But we have had hot water for two days in a row, and the deck has been pressure washed. I suppose that's progress.

Miraculously, the air conditioning contractor arrives this afternoon only two hours late. He's been in the attic, and as he's coming down the attic stairs, he says, "You need a new ultraviolet light in the filtering system. Can't get you one till next week."

He folds up the attic stairs. "Also," he says, walking into the living room, "you gotta get someone to seal off these vents. And the vent in the attic doesn't have any screens. This place'll be filled with birds and squirrels and mice pretty soon."

"Birds and squirrels and mice?" Pam says.

"Maybe a snake or two," the guy says. "But you just have to put some screening there. That'll solve that problem. I'll have the office call you when the UV light comes in."

I walk the AC guy to the door and come back into the living room. Pam says, "Birds, squirrels, mice, and snakes? Next week?"

Saturday, September 19

This morning Benjamin, once again, is not here as he promised. Strike three. "I'm going to call Bob our crack real estate agent," I say. "Maybe he can help somehow."

"It's Saturday," Pam says.

"I don't care. I'll call his cell. I'll call his office. I'll find him." I do. "Bob, this kid Benjamin is a disaster. He's a nice kid, but he's a disaster." I explain what still hasn't been fixed in the cottage.

"Jesus," Bob says. "Stay where you are. I'll call you right back."

In about ten minutes, Bob calls back. "Dick, I talked to Ben. He says he had some problems this week, but everything is now scheduled to be finished this coming Thursday or Friday. Everything."

"Bob, I had the same promise from Benjamin a week ago. The kid doesn't know what he is doing. He's screwing up Pam's and my work schedules big time. He's screwing up our daily lives," I say.

"Give him one more chance," Bob says. "Everything done by next Friday, maybe Thursday."

"Bob, I doubt it, but okay, Friday, that's it." I hang up, feeling really beaten up. I know Benjamin is not going to have everything done. More likely he'll have nothing done.

Tonight, to escape, Pam and I walk over to the lake to watch the lights of West Palm Beach come on as day becomes night. Our plan is dinner and a Yankee game at Bice Ristorante. We haven't bothered to hook up cable yet.

I love Bice, but in recent years it sometimes makes me feel like a fossil. Pam and I first came here for a business lunch about fifteen years ago. I remember when Ronnie was a kid behind the bar, and now he's a real estate tycoon, married, and with two little kids of his own.

I remember when Jose was a waiter with no gray hair, and now he is a distinguished looking member of the management team. I remember when Jose's brother, Javier, was a busser who spoke almost no English. He is now the manager at Pizza al Fresco and speaks better English than I do. I'm so old I remember when Phillipe, who's behind the bar, was sane.

Jose welcomes us. We grab an empty bar table, have a cocktail, and share a chopped salad and a pizza. Pam and I love sharing meals. It's one of life's simple pleasures. The baseball game is not exciting, but the Yanks win it, and the evening is a welcome diversion from the chaos at the cottage.

Tuesday, September 22

This morning the electrician we waited for all day yesterday finally arrives. He can't fix the disposal, and he explains the three non-working plugs in the yellow room have no wiring going to them, but he says he can put switches on the outdoor lights by tomorrow or maybe Thursday. And with that, he is gone.

"This really sucks," Pam says.

"What are you talking," I say. "At this rate this place should be all fixed up by Christmas, New Year's Eve at the latest."

"Not funny, Dick. Let's take a walk."

After a few blocks of walking, I say to Pam, "Are you planning to rob these houses?"

She frowns and says, "What are you talking about?"

"You haven't said a word the last two blocks and you seem to be casing all the houses."

She smiles. "I'm just trying to figure out how many of these houses are really empty. There were nineteen out of twenty-eight on that last block."

So we both count houses on two or three more blocks and figure almost two thirds are unoccupied. As we get home, Pam says, "You know, no one lives next to us on either side, or in the house behind us, or the one across the street."

"Maybe all these places are as screwed up as our cottage and nobody wants to live in them."

"No, really," Pam says, "I never thought the town would be this empty."

Saturday, September 26

No one showed up Wednesday or Thursday or Friday. I'm going nuts. I call Bob. "This is our fourth Saturday here. This week is over and we're not even close. We're never going to be close."

"Oh hell, Dick, don't move. Let me call Ben. I'll call you right back," Bob says. Click. I'm counting to ten very slowly. Over and over again. Slowly.

He calls back. "Dick, I want you and Pam to be happy there.

We will take care of those problems," Bob says. "Benjamin absolutely promised me he can finish by Tuesday."

"Stop," I interrupt. "Here's the deal, Bob. Pam and I have book signings on the west coast. We're gone from this afternoon until Tuesday afternoon. If, when we get back, everything is not fixed, it will become a huge problem for everyone involved."

Tuesday, September 29

Pam and I get back home this afternoon. Looks like nothing has been done. Pam is just shaking her head.

"I've got a suggestion," I say.

"Suicide... murder... arson... sex... drugs... rock and roll?" Pam says.

"One or two of those sound okay, but my thought was a walk, a shower, and dinner and dancing at The Chesterfield. No talk of work, no talk of the cottage."

"Ah, the ostrich approach to life," Pam says. "I like it."

"Sometimes, the ostrich approach can be the best approach," I say.

And for one night it works.

Wednesday, September 30

When I wake up this morning, Pam is already up. I find her having tea by the pool. She has several of our cottage "lists" and is going through them carefully. She's listening to classical music, which means she is thinking.

"This whole thing is nuts, total insanity," Pam says by way of greeting.

"I guess the ostrich approach has a short shelf life."

She gets up. "I'm going in to call Bob."

"And say what?"

"I don't know. I guess that we won't live like this."

"Good," I say, "because we won't."

When she reappears, she says, "He's out of the office till Friday. I just left him a message saying we couldn't go on like this. Something has to be done, like get us a hotel room until the cottage is liveable."

"What a mess."

five

"WHAT ARE YOU GUYS, HILLBILLIES?"

Thursday, October 1

I open my eyes to early morning light filtering through the curtains. My bedside clock reads seven thirty. I roll over and see Dick still asleep. I watch him for a few minutes, feeling very much in love. On the wall are pictures we took of each other during our honeymoon in Antigua. I had a lucky night at the craps table, and in the pictures we each have a pile of casino chips in our laps, and we're laughing. Dick looks the same to me now as he did then. Of course, he can't really, but that's the way I see him.

My mind wanders to the present. I can't believe it's the first of October and we're still dealing with house problems.

Dick rolls over, opens his eyes, and smiles. Amazingly, even after all these years, he smiles when he wakes up and sees me.

"Espresso?" he says.

"That would be nice," I say. "I'll wake the birdies and get some biscotti and fruit." I finally got around to making biscotti this past weekend. It's normally part of our breakfast routine. I worried it might turn out differently in the oven here, but then, it turns out a little differently each time I make it.

We settle in the yellow room with the screen door open. I love the view of the pool. It's framed by tall hedges and, at the far end, bordered by geraniums and hibiscus. Two cardinals are playing in the birdbath. I hear the gurgle of the little fountain Dick made, and the coo of doves from somewhere.

"It's sad we can't get these cottage problems taken care of," I say. "Actually, it's ridiculous."

"Bob's message said he's back tomorrow, right?" Dick says. "We'll see if he has a solution." He pauses. "Although maybe he's the problem as well as Benjamin."

"That's what I'm beginning to think," I say.

"This all sounded so easy last August," Dick says. "Maybe we should break the lease, get out of here."

"That's depressing," I say. "A month of trying to get things done, wasted. But, I guess we could be wasting more time if we stay."

Peter Island comes into my mind. A few years after we got married, when Dick's daughter Samantha was safely in college, we quit our jobs, left New York, and took our boat to the Caribbean. We eventually went to Tortola in the British Virgin Islands and tried to see if either of us could find a job. Dick found one at Peter Island Resort, and we ended up selling our boat and living and working there for five years, and became travel writers in the process.

The first year on Peter Island was tremendously stressful. We had traded Manhattan for a seven-mile-long, mountainous island that was deserted except for a forty-room private resort. There were ten full-time residents, all of us either a hotel employee or a spouse. It was a twenty-minute boat ride to the nearest grocery store. For six months, the immigration department kept finding things wrong with my papers.

One of Dick's jobs was resident tennis pro. I had just recently been an executive at a Fortune 500 company and was used to being near the top of the power chain. Suddenly, I was at rock bottom. At the Monday night cocktail parties Dick and I were required to host, I learned no guest wanted to be stuck talking to the tennis pro's wife. I learned a great deal and discovered a lot about myself on Peter Island. So did Dick. It was a wonderful adventure, in the end.

"You know," I say. "We made Peter Island work."

Dick looks at me. "Yeah, we did. But that took a lot of time. I'm too old to do that again."

"Me, too," I say. "So let's hedge our bets, look for another rental. Living in Palm Beach is supposed to be our great adventure."

Dick laughs. "It is. It's an adventure in home repair and managing stress," he says. "We'll look at other rentals."

We spend the day researching rentals online, talk to several real estate agents, and visit several possible cottages. Now it's seven o'clock, and we're both still at our computers, searching.

"I'm done," Dick says. "Let's get out of here, find a saloon."

We change clothes and head out. Not a single car is parked along our block, and we're the only people on the sidewalk. The air is filled with the scent of jasmine. Waves break in the distance. Our house problems slip away.

In a few blocks we come to Amici and go in for a drink. Beth is behind the bar.

"A Miller Lite and a Prosecco?" she asks.

"That would be perfect," Dick says, "but you guys don't carry Miller Lite."

"We do now. Maurizio heard you asking for it the other night," she says.

Just then Maurizio, the restaurant owner, emerges from the kitchen and comes towards us. Medium height. Brown eyes. Five o'clock shadow. Fabulous smile.

"*Buona sera*," he says. "Welcome back to Amici."

Dick thanks him for getting Miller Lite. We stay for a dinner of salad and pasta at a candlelit table on the terrace. The wind picks up a bit, the surf gets a little louder, and distant thunder and lightning again provide a nighttime show. For the rest of the evening, house troubles are forgotten.

Friday, October 2

First thing this morning, my cell rings. It's Bob. He's back. Got my message.

"Look," I say, "Dick and I are through. We're breaking the lease."

Bob says, "Wait, wait, wait. Calm down. I've got a solution."

"Too late."

"No, no," he says. "I was stupid. Benjamin's the son of a friend. I gave the kid too many chances. This is my fault. I've got you a new property manager. His name's Eduardo. He's reliable. He'll be at your place in half an hour. I promise things will get better."

"Okay," I say. "But this is your last chance."

In twenty minutes, Eduardo arrives at the door. Tall. Very thin. Dark-haired. A trim moustache. Notepad in hand, he looks at the leaky toilet, the faulty water heater, the clogged gas jets, and everything else that isn't functioning properly. He writes it all down. "This stuff was patched, not fixed," he says. "It's easy stuff. Just have to do it right."

He makes sure one of us can be here Monday and Tuesday, goes outside to use his cell phone, returns with the news that everything will be fixed by Tuesday afternoon, guaranteed. A gang of workers will start Monday morning.

Eduardo seems knowledgeable and efficient, but I can't help feeling skeptical. This isn't the first time promises have been made.

Saturday, October 3

The weather is still summery. We take the morning papers and Duckie and Blanco in their cage and go out by the pool. So far life in Palm Beach away from the cottage is a pleasure. I'm not sure exactly what Dick and I expected, but it definitely was not the small-town feeling we're experiencing. This is a community where the morning's Shiny Sheet reports, "Police are investigating the theft of a pair of sunglasses."

In New York City, years ago, my car was stolen. I called the police. They told me to come in and fill out some paperwork; I'd never see that car again. Dick and I laugh at the silliness of some of the police reports here, but the truth is, serious crimes are rare in this town. The police force is wonderful, helpful, polite. I feel very safe.

We spend the day outside doing chores. Now the evening sky is a blend of pale blues and pinks, the air is soft and warm, and the family of doves is lined up along the guest cottage roof.

"Dinner at home?" Dick says.

"Sounds great," I say. "Maybe those grilled chicken breasts you make, with ham and Swiss on top?"

"And 'Pam's potatoes'?"

"And an arugula salad?"

"And a bottle of Barolo?"

We go into the kitchen. Dick sets the iPod to Peter Cetera and we get to work. Dick pounds chicken breasts, mashes garlic and mustard for a marinade, and makes a salad. I peel and quarter small potatoes, thinly slice mushrooms and brown them on both sides, then sauté garlic and onions in a cast-iron baking dish. The kitchen fills with the aroma of garlic. I add kalamata olives, then the mushrooms and potatoes, and put the casserole in the oven, covered, to cook for an hour. The potatoes will sponge up the flavors of the other ingredients and become intense.

The space we are working in is tiny compared to our kitchen in New Smyrna, but Dick and I are adapting. It's easier to stay in one place, so there's a lot of "could you hand me" this or that and an occasional "I'm behind you." In a funny way, I find it pleasantly cozy.

Prep work done, we go outside. Dick lights the wood in the fire pit, starts the charcoal, sets the iPod to Elton John. Eventually, the coals are ready, and Dick grills the chicken. I bring out the potatoes and salad. We linger over dinner, watch the fire burn into embers, then walk to the beach.

The ocean is black ink, the night cloudless, the sky glittery with stars. To the north, two stars grow larger, turn into headlights. An airplane is making its way south, following the coastline. It passes us, out over the water and fairly high in the sky, then makes a sweeping curve toward the West Palm Beach International Airport, just ten minutes away by car on the mainland. I have always loved planes, and this beach is a good place to watch them, day and night.

Soon another set of headlights materializes and repeats the sequence. A third set of headlights, these much smaller, comes straight out of the east. A tiny plane appears, probably from somewhere in the Bahamas, seventy or eighty miles away.

Suddenly, Dick says, "What's that? Something's in that first wave."

I peer into the darkness. "I see it," I say. "It's coming onto the beach."

"It's the Loch Ness monster," Dick says.

"Whatever it is, it looks weird."

"Maybe divers?" Dick says.

Now it does look like several people wearing diving equipment, silhouetted against the black sky. They follow the path from the beach, trudge past us, and climb wetly into a parked van.

"We never see anyone at the beach at night," Dick says. "Now people are walking out of the ocean?"

Sunday, October 4

We're sitting on a bench in the gardens at The Society of the Four Arts. Statues and sculptures are set between colorful flower beds and under leafy trees. Brilliant purple and red bougainvillea blossoms hang over wooden trellises. It is an oasis of peacefulness and such a contrast to the cottage.

"Shall we say hello to the statesmen before we head home?" Dick says.

We walk over to admire the almost life-size sculpture of Winston Churchill and FDR sitting on a bench chatting, FDR with his cigarette holder and Mr. Churchill with cigar in hand.

Then we walk out past the two miniature bronze giraffes, zigzag our way south along the empty streets toward the beach, and then on to the cottage.

Back on our block, I check on The Invisible Man's House, so named because we've never see a person there, though we do see a grey Volvo parked in many different positions in the driveway. Sure enough, the Volvo is there this afternoon, but not parked where it was earlier today. So far, the car is the only sign of life at the house.

This evening Dick says, "I was thinking of going to Café L'Europe for dinner."

"Sounds good," I say. I mostly still like to just wander and end up somewhere, but this Sunday Café L'Europe feels like a good choice.

I choose a dress in a blue peacock print, decorated with sparkles. It makes me feel feminine. And blue high-heeled sandals. I have always adored high heels. Dick puts on a navy blue linen suit. He's had it for years, but it's still beautiful.

It's close to nine, and although people are dining, the bar is fairly empty. Dick and I settle into bar stools, order cocktails, and listen to David's piano fill the room. After a quiet dinner, we walk home along the beach. No Loch Ness monsters tonight. Instead, a single spectacular shooting star streaks across the sky.

Monday, October 5

It's eight o'clock in the morning, and I hear a knock at the door (the doorbell still isn't working). Could this be progress?

Tuesday, October 6

Yesterday's eight o'clock knock was just the beginning. By eight thirty, the house was full of people, and by nine it was a real mess, with workers and tools everywhere. It stayed that way until late this afternoon. Even though we put down tarps, the white floors now look like they have chocolate as well as vanilla fudge ice cream smeared all over them.

The good news is that by five o'clock, everything is fixed. Every faulty valve, pipe, knob, and vent. Over five weeks to get a two-day job done. But the cottage is finally functional. Eduardo is a real property manager. Maybe now Dick and I can finally divide our time between getting our work back on schedule and enjoying life in Palm Beach.

We still haven't gotten around to hooking up the television. I think both of us just want to get workmen out of the house and get on with our lives. I'm also interested to see what life is like without that connection.

Thursday, October 8

I'm at my computer, finishing up an assignment. Duckie's on the floor, playing tug-of-war with the rug fringe. Blanco's on my knee, preening.

Dick comes into the office. "We've got a CD at SunTrust Bank that matures today," he says. "I looked in the Yellow Pages. There's a branch across the bridge."

"I think we've walked by a SunTrust," I say. "It's just a few blocks from here."

Dick collects our documents, and we walk to where I remember seeing the SunTrust sign. The sign is actually quite small and there is no obvious entrance. Several paths lead to dead ends. At last I spot a door, and in we go.

"This doesn't look like a bank," Dick says. "There aren't any tellers."

"It looks like a living room," I say, taking in the arrangements of chairs and coffee tables on several large Oriental rugs. I see a woman at an antique-looking desk at the far end of the room. She smiles and waves us over.

"Please, have a seat," she says. "How may I help you on this beautiful morning?"

Dick says, "We have a CD that's matured, but maybe we're in the wrong place."

The woman smiles. "This isn't one of our regular branches," she says. "But I can roll over a CD for you."

"Are you sure?" Dick says. I realize he's slightly embarrassed.

"Yes, yes," the woman says. She reaches for our paperwork, finds us on her computer. We sign papers, she hands us the new CD.

Dick thanks her, and we walk out. "I don't think we're in the right tax bracket for that particular branch," Dick says.

"Sorry I dragged you in there," I say.

Friday, October 9

Now that the cottage problems are behind us, Dick and I are able to really explore the neighborhood, and I have a much better understanding of where we live.

Our cottage is "in town," as the locals say, on the widest part of the island, which stretches about a half mile from the beach and Atlantic Ocean to the Lake Worth Lagoon, an estuary separating Palm Beach from mainland Florida.

The center of our part of Palm Beach is Worth Avenue, which is a few blocks south of our cottage and runs from the ocean beach to the lake.

It's one of the world's most famous shopping streets, wide and lined with palm trees, flower beds, and mostly one- or two-story buildings. Arched walkways, locally called "vias," lead from the avenue to charming courtyard shops and cafes.

In many ways, Worth Avenue resembles an old-fashioned Main Street from the 1950s, except that instead of apothecaries and hardware stores and barber shops, there are luxury boutiques selling designer clothing and linens and handbags and jewelry. And rather than DeSotos, Studebakers, and Packards lining the sidewalk, there are Mercedes and BMWs, and the occasional Rolls-Royce.

The streets just north of Worth are mostly residential, with

OUR PALM BEACH WALKING AREA

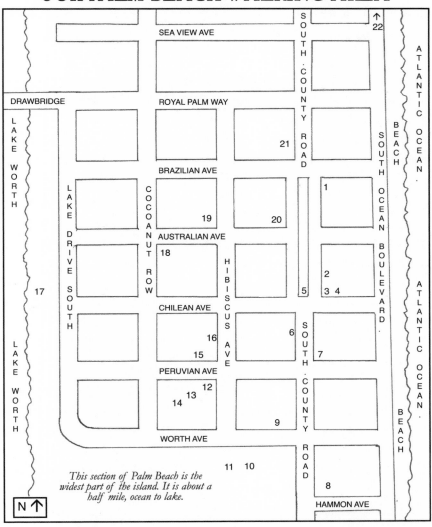

SEA VIEW AVE

ROYAL PALM WAY

DRAWBRIDGE

BRAZILIAN AVE

AUSTRALIAN AVE

CHILEAN AVE

PERUVIAN AVE

WORTH AVE

HAMMON AVE

LAKE WORTH

LAKE DRIVE SOUTH

LAKE WORTH

COCOANUT ROW

HIBISCUS AVE

SOUTH COUNTY ROAD

SOUTH OCEAN BOULEVARD

SOUTH COUNTY ROAD

ATLANTIC OCEAN

BEACH

ATLANTIC OCEAN

BEACH

This section of Palm Beach is the widest part of the island. It is about a half mile, ocean to lake.

N ↑

1. Cafe L'Europe
2. Sandwiches by the Sea
3. Scotti's
4. Palm Beach Fitness
5. Town Hall
6. The Church Mouse
7. Amici
8. Colony & Royal Room

9. Taboo
10. Victor's Cafe
11. Gucci Courtyard
12. Bice
13. Renato's
14. Pizza al Fresco
15. Preservation Society
16. Pan's Garden

17. Town Docks & Park
18. Chesterfield & Leopard Lounge
19. Brazilian Court & Cafe Boulud
20. Gray's Sunoco
21. Classic Bookshop
22. 4 blocks to Breakers

a real estate office or a restaurant or a dry cleaner here and there, plus The Chesterfield Hotel and The Brazilian Court Hotel.

Just south of Worth Avenue is also residential, with the exception of the exclusive Everglades Club and The Colony hotel. Near the center of town, a handful of five- or six-story condominiums border the lake and the ocean, but the rest of the area is made up mostly of one- or two-story houses.

Although our walking routes are random, Dick and I mostly stay within a rectangle that extends from the Breakers resort south to Hammon, and from the ocean beach to the lake.

There are little cottages like ours here and there, but most of the houses range from about 3,000 to 10,000 square feet, though some are much larger, and virtually all the houses facing the lake or the ocean are immense.

Most houses have at least one guesthouse and a pool and are frequently hidden by twenty- or thirty-foot tall hedges. Wrought iron gates open to driveways of coquina or brick.

Many are Spanish Mediterranean in style, with barrel-tile roofs, balconies, and loggias. Others are Italian Renaissance, or Bermuda-style, or even New England clapboard. All are immaculate. Many were created in the 1920s and 1930s by a handful of influential architects, including Addison Mizner and Maurice Fatio. The town has a dizzying set of strictly enforced renovation and new construction rules. No garish McMansions allowed.

To the west, from certain vantage points, skyscrapers are visible in the distance. These are on the far side of the Lake Worth Lagoon, in the city of West Palm Beach.

Saturday, October 10
We take our morning papers over to Victor's Café, in the Gucci courtyard off Worth Avenue. It has a tiny dining room

and alfresco tables set among flowers. As we approach, a delicious aroma mingles with the scent of tropical flowers. Victor stands at the entrance, dressed in his signature Bermuda shorts and golf shirt.

"Victor, what smells so good?" Dick asks.

"Scones," he replies. "Blueberry ones are baking right now." He looks at his watch. "They'll be ready in one minute."

Dick orders one for us to split, plus two espressos, and we settle at an outdoor table. I break open the scone. It's warm, slightly crusty, soft inside, with lots of blueberries. Dick reaches for *The Wall Street Journal* so I take *The New York Times*, but instead of reading, I look around the courtyard.

Brilliant bougainvillea blossoms cover some walls. There's a little sculpture garden with enchanting life-size sculptures of children playing, picking apples, and climbing trees. Several small birds swoop down from a tall, slender cypress tree and land at my feet, hoping for a crumb. Other birds are perched on a tree branch, singing.

It feels far away from our house and our computers and could almost pass for somewhere near the Mediterranean except, of course, we didn't have to go to various airports and stand in lines and take off our shoes and belts and jackets.

Dick looks up from the Shiny Sheet. "It says here, 'A Palm Beach business owner contacted the police to report harassing phone calls he has been receiving for a year.' A year?" he says. "I might have reported this a bit sooner."

Sunday, October 11

Today we discover several blocks not far from us where most of the houses seem to be lived in, apparently by families with school-age children. Although there aren't any people around, simple toys and tricycles and basketballs and even a couple of pogo sticks are on the porches and in the yards. Cars are parked in the driveways. Street signs along these family blocks read, "Children at Play."

This reminds me of the way life was when I was a child, before kids were being snatched right and left, before video games kept children inside all day, before toys became complex and computerized.

These kids can safely walk to school or the beach or the soccer field or the tennis courts. Probably, for these families, Palm Beach is like a small, safe, old-fashioned town. In this day and age, I think, what a privilege to grow up in a place like this.

Monday, October 12

Dick and I have made dinner and set the table, but we feel like having cocktails out. We walk to Taboo, check on the aquarium fish, and settle into seats next to two thirty-something women. Bobby comes over and we order drinks.

The woman sitting next to me reaches into a little shopping bag, takes out a small box, and shows her friend the diamond bracelet she just bought.

"It cost forty thousand dollars," she says. "He'll never know."

I take a discreet peek at the bracelet. It's dazzling.

The woman glances toward Taboo's entrance. "Oh my God, my husband just walked in! I can't let him see this!"

She puts the bracelet back in the box, stuffs the box in the bag, and turns to Bobby.

"Quick, hide this behind the bar!" she says as she hands him a little Tiffany shopping bag.

Forty thousand dollars worth of jewelry, tucked between the olives, the onions, and the Bloody Mary mix.

Tuesday, October 13

Duckie and Blanco need their nails and wings clipped. Naturally there's no place to get this done on the island, so I check the *West Palm Beach Yellow Pages* for pet stores, find Birds off Broadway, and talk to Jay, the owner, who tells me our birds can't be clipped until they've had their annual exam by a veterinarian. Our cockatiels have lived nine years without annual exams.

"Annual exams," I say, "for birds?"

"Before you can bring them here for clipping, they need a physical exam, and they must be tested for ..." and he rattles off a bunch of Latin-sounding words. "Just call this doctor; she'll know what you need," he says, giving me a number. I call and, to my surprise, can make an appointment for this afternoon.

After lunch, Dick and I put Duckie and Blanco in their traveling cage and get in the Audi. The doctor is a good half hour away over unfamiliar roads, but with the help of directions magically beamed to my cell, we get there on time.

I must say, although I have always loved maps and still keep them in the glove compartment, I do enjoy punching an address into my iPhone and having the appropriate route appear on the screen, complete with a little blue pulsating dot that tracks my progress.

Duckie and Blanco pass all the necessary tests, and the doctor hands me a certificate verifying the birds' excellent health. She also takes care of the clipping of wings and nails. Next time I'll take them to the much closer Birds off Broadway, armed with the proper papers.

Thursday, October 15

The weather continues to be warm. Dick reads me disturbing news from the Shiny Sheet: "A thirty-eight-year-old man was

arrested for trying to steal five cases of Bud Light from Publix."
Book him, Danno.

We're interrupted by a singularly Palm Beach-esque courtesy call from a British-accented gentleman who is worried about our staffing needs.

"With the Palm Beach season fast approaching," he explains, "some of our households are finding they might be understaffed. From chefs to chauffeurs, butlers to bodyguards, we offer the finest in insured and bonded household staff."

I assure him our household is quite adequately staffed, thank him for thinking of us, and hang up.

We actually do have a butler, Hank, who has been with us since before we were married. Hank is about four feet tall, made of oak, and holds a tray with just enough room to rest a drink or two. Really all the staff we need, or can afford, or want.

Our life in Palm Beach is developing a routine. On weekdays we work for a few hours, break at midmorning to take a walk, break again for lunch and several games of cribbage, work until the end of the day, then take another walk. Many nights we go out. If we stay home, we usually cook a pasta sauce or grill something by the pool and dine outside.

So far, we have both managed to get our work done while sharing an office, though at times the lack of space and abundance of paper do become tiresome. It helps there are other places to take our work, like out by the pool or in nearby parks.

Both of us like to walk, and so far, it has been our main form of exercise in Palm Beach. I don't think I've walked so much every day since those years we lived on Peter Island, when I followed the island's notoriously steep "Five-Mile Walk" every afternoon just to stay sane.

In New Smyrna we belong to a gym and we'd meant to join

a gym in Palm Beach long before now, but the house problems slowed us down. There's one just a few blocks from the cottage, but I'm somewhat afraid it might be snooty, out of our price range, and as it's "in town," probably way too busy.

However, it makes sense to check there first, so today Dick and I walk over and meet Craig, the owner of Palm Beach Fitness, who's a walking advertisement for the benefits of working out. His rates are surprisingly reasonable, the atmosphere is casual and friendly, and, according to Craig, it's rarely crowded at the times we plan to use it. We happily join.

We leave the gym and take a long walk through the residential part of our neighborhood, never seeing another person and only rarely encountering a moving car. It still surprises me that so many of these beautifully maintained houses are empty. There are no cars parked in the driveways, no signs of activity, no people about.

Many of the houses have definite personalities, like The Invisible Man's House, so we have started giving them names. Piano House features a white grand piano through a picture window. Horse House boasts a full-size, colorfully painted statue of a horse in the front yard.

There's The Ruskies, which for some reason Dick thought was owned by Russians. It's not. Dick talked to the owner, who had flown in for a weekend, and he's as American as Derek Jeter. The name sticks though. We still call it The Ruskies.

Orchid House always has an artful grouping of Phalaenopsis orchids in the living room window. Car House is on the ocean and invariably has five or six expensive automobiles in the driveway. Then there's The Thug's House, so named because the man who lives there looks like Luca Brasi in *The Godfather*. I'm sure there will be many more to come.

Saturday, October 17

We're walking on Worth Avenue. A couple is coming toward us, pushing an old-fashioned pram, its collapsible hood covered with little blue bows. They stop, and soon three women are gathered around looking in, oohing and aahing.

"Must be a tiny baby," I say.

"And they must be grandparents," Dick says. "They're a bit old to have a newborn."

We reach the pram, and I peek in. The baby is an English toy spaniel, dressed in a frilly blue party dress covered in little blue bows.

"That was a first," Dick says.

We turn off Worth and walk toward home.

I've been curious about a store we often walk by called The Church Mouse. Dick and I can't figure out what it is. Today we go in. It turns out to be a resale shop for the Bethesda-by-the-Sea Episcopal Church. Everything in the store has been donated, from clothes and books to furniture and fine china.

Dick sees a cedar chest, the kind that's low to the ground and opens from the top. "This would be perfect to hold towels and blankets and stuff for our guest cottage," Dick says. "It's only fifty-five dollars."

"Sold," I say. I go find a salesman, and we pay for the chest. The salesman says, "It's pretty heavy. If you drive your car over to that side door, we can load it from there."

Dick says, "We don't have a car."

The salesman looks at Dick like he fell off a turnip truck. "Oh," he says. "Well, do you want me to hold the chest for later, when you come back with your car?"

Dick says, "No, I think it's easier if I just run home and get my hand truck."

The salesman looks at Dick as if he's speaking Swedish.

Dick walks to get the hand truck and is back in five minutes. The three of us get the chest onto the cart. It's a bit awkward, but Dick manages to roll the cart along and we make our way home.

Barney, the old fellow with the dyed black hair, spots us and, in a clipped, Long Island Lockjaw, says, "In Palm Beach one walks silly little dogs with berets. One does not walk old sea chests!"

A few seconds later, Craig, the owner of Palm Beach Fitness, passes us.

"What are you guys, hillbillies?" he says. "This is Palm Beach. You can't be rolling furniture around in the streets."

Dick says, "Maybe we are the Clampetts, after all."

Sunday, October 18

Today's my birthday. Dick's birthday is in August, and I'm ten months older than he is, so for two months each year I can tease him we're the same age. Yesterday I was pensive, vaguely wistful, as I usually am the day before my birthday, reflecting on the passage of time, on the fact this was the last day I'd ever be that age.

I've been this way ever since I was little. I may have been happy about turning eleven, but at the same time I was a little wistful about leaving ten. I thought about "don't blink" long before Kenny Chesney wrote the song. I knew I'd blink and be in college, blink and be starting a career, blink and be forty. Now time's going so fast I'm trying not to blink at all.

Dick and I don't give each other birthday presents but we do like to take birthday trips. This year I wanted to stay home, home being Palm Beach. We're already on a trip in a way, a year-long one.

I got a present in the mail yesterday from Sophie, my sister.

She's an artist and lives in Connecticut. We're close and usually e-mail frequently, though weeks can go by without communication. This morning I open the beautifully wrapped package. Inside is a collapsible vase, for use when traveling. Indeed, it's very flat and thin. The note with it reads, "Although it's meant for traveling, I thought this little vase might come in handy in that tiny cottage you're in."

I fill the vase with water and it stands upright. I go outside and pick a geranium and place it in the vase. It looks beautiful. Sophie's right. I don't need to wait until traveling to use it. I begin to wish all sort of things were collapsible—frying pans, stew pots, large platters, colanders, bicycles, even cars. I look around the room. How easy storage would be.

This evening I want to have my birthday dinner at Café L'Europe. We shower, dress, and walk to the restaurant. We both say hello to David, the piano player, and I pat Walker, David's big brown poodle, then Dick and I take a seat at the bar. David takes a break and comes over to join us. He's wearing black pants, a black shirt, a tan sport jacket, and sunglasses. His hair is swept back, and he looks as if he drove to work on a motorcycle. Hopefully, he didn't. David's been blind since birth.

Although Dick and I usually stop and chat with David for a few moments when he's at the piano, this is the first chance we have for real conversation.

"So," Dick says, "I guess you've just started playing the piano?"

David laughs. "Just had my third lesson."

"Seriously," Dick says, "how long have you been playing?"

"Since I was three," David says. And so begins a fascinating fifteen minutes. It turns out that David has performed around the world for many famous people, including President Clinton,

Lady Bird Johnson, Walter Cronkite, James Taylor, Billy Joel, and Rose Kennedy on her 100th birthday. He tells us about a restaurant in Martha's Vineyard, David's Island House, which he owned for twenty years. And we learn that his dog, Walker, was named (by a previous owner) after Johnny Walker Black Label.

David returns to work his magic at the piano, filling the room with music, whimsically switching from Beethoven to Cole Porter to Billy Joel. We linger over dinner, stay until David stops for the evening. We take the long way home and walk along the beach. The night sky is studded with stars. What a lovely birthday.

Monday, October 19

In New Smyrna, Duckie and Blanco lived in my office, but now they live in the room where we are sharing an office. The birds are happy. Cockatiels are social and want people around. They like to have all four of us in the same room.

I'm less happy than the birds with this arrangement. It's actually a big pain. Dick and I each have a triangle-shaped corner desk with a computer on it and not much empty surface. Dick has the ability to just push stray paper out of the way and go on working. I need to know what is where and tend to make piles. Soon I have paper piles lined across the couch and sometimes the floor.

Dick is trying to accommodate my tendency to take over the room, but I can tell he finds it stressful. Somehow we managed to work on a boat, with much less space, but for some reason this office is an unexpectedly big challenge. Each of our offices in New Smyrna, the ones our renters are using, are bigger than the room we are in now, and quite perfect. This present office situation is not.

This morning I'm working to meet a deadline. Dick gets tired of the paper and decides to walk over to the Seaview Tennis Center, the town's public courts. We are tennis players and have wanted to find out where to play ever since we arrived in Palm Beach.

Dick returns, walks into the office.

"The courts are excellent," he says. "There're seven courts, all Har-Tru, with an underground irrigation system and lighted at night. A woman named Mary is in charge; she took me around. And I met a pro, Todd, and set up a weekly hitting schedule with him."

"Did you have to join anything?"

Dick laughs. "We can join or pay as we play. Either way, it's reasonable. There's no country club attached. No social obligations. No politics."

Friday, October 23

"There's an Oktoberfest celebration tonight," Dick says this morning, looking up from the Shiny Sheet.

"Across the lake at Citiplace?" I say.

"No," Dick says, "it's actually in Palm Beach. You'll never guess where."

I'm at a complete loss. A Palm Beach Oktoberfest sounds like an oxymoron.

"Well, it's gotta be outside," I say. "Worth Avenue? No, that wouldn't work. Pan's Garden?"

"No, but close," Dick says. "The Society of the Four Arts, the Sculpture Garden."

"You're kidding. An Oktoberfest there?"

"Hard to imagine," Dick says. "Drunks spilling beer on Churchill and FDR, dropping wursts in the flowerbeds."

"Now I'm curious," I say. "Want to go?"

Dick smiles and says, "Why would I want to do that? There's

going to be lots of beer and food." He calls and makes reservations.

The Oktoberfest begins tonight at five thirty. The weather is cool, the skies clear, there's a soft breeze, and it will be light for another hour. We walk over. I don't know what to expect, but if I'd lived in Palm Beach longer, surely I could have guessed.

There are a fair number of people, but it's not a crowd. No one is rowdy. A beer expert explains the origins and describes the ingredients of various brews. There are several wines and thirty-five different ales, stouts, and lagers. Dick and I stop tasting at twenty-eight. I think.

We walk home, carrying our souvenir glasses.

"What a funny Oktoberfest," I say, "but cool. Let's go again next year."

"Good idea," says Dick. "It'll be a much longer walk, though.

Monday, October 26

October is coming to a close, and the weather is still summer-like. Today's walk takes us through the family blocks. Here and there I see hints of Halloween. A string of tiny, ghost-shaped lanterns wrap around a hibiscus bush. A gauzy witch rides a broom across a front door. Little tarantulas lurk among the leaves of a ficus hedge. Miniature pumpkins, each carved with a fanciful face, line the railing of a front porch.

These decorations are understated. Articles in the Shiny Sheet often refer to Palm Beach's many ordinances. I vaguely wonder if the town has one limiting pumpkin dimensions, another describing the proper size for a ghost, another, the number of tarantulas allowed.

I find this subtlety quite a contrast to the glitzy side of Palm Beach. On one hand, Palm Beach is home to giant mansions, exotic cars, flashy jewelry. On the other, subtle Halloween decor. Sometimes I think there is actually another alternate universe hiding here, and it's a small town from the 1950s.

Wednesday, October 28

Lakeside Park, which is part of our neighborhood, fronts the Lake Worth Lagoon and the town docks. There are clusters of hedges, large lawns, and a handful of old banyan trees with immense canopies of branches. The Lakeside Trail, which runs north along the lake shore begins (or ends) here.

This morning we walk over with our newspapers and take a seat on a bench under one of the banyan trees. Lake Worth is calm, and the office buildings on the mainland reflect the morning sun.

Two men are standing near us, deep in conversation. From their discussion it appears they're real estate agents. One of them says, "So, what's happening with that house on Lake Trail? Weren't you supposed to close weeks ago?"

"You won't believe this," the other says. "The guy put down a million-dollar deposit. Now he's in a messy divorce. So he's just walking."

"Walking on a million?" Pause. "So who gets the money?"

"We're working on that."

Dick says, "Did he say 'a million'?"

"Yeah," I say. We go back to looking at the lake.

The docks extend out into the lake, three long fingers with slips for yachts on both sides. Many of the slips are empty.

Dick says, "These slips aren't your ordinary-size slips. They're huge. It's all so in proportion I never noticed before." He points. "See that first boat, the closest one? See how little it looks? Well, it's got to be sixty feet."

"That boat is bigger than *Maverick*?" I say, referring to the Gulfstar 44 we lived on. "Can't be."

"Yup," Dick says. "I'll show you. Come, let's measure."

I follow him over to the docks, and we walk off the length of the boat Dick is talking about. It's sixty-five feet. We walk off the lengths of some larger yachts. Eighty-five feet. One hundred thirty five feet.

I always thought *Maverick* was a pretty big boat. She'd be a tender to some of these guys here. Recently, from the beach, I've seen several yachts approaching the inlet at the north end of the island. I'm probably seeing some of them again now.

Saturday, October 31

Dick and I wend our way to Victor's for espressos and scones. We enter the courtyard, and I realize this is not just any morning in Via Gucci. Children, dogs, and adults are milling about, many in costume.

"I think we're in the middle of a costume contest," Dick says.

Three costume contests, actually: for children, for dogs, and for dogs and their owners. Sherry, owner of Sherry Frankel's Melangerie and president of the Worth Avenue Association, is the emcee.

"How do you think they tell the dogs from their owners?" Dick says.

"Shhhh," I say.

Dogs are dressed as ballerinas, pirates, and superheroes. There's a dog dressed as Marilyn Monroe, another as Elton John, another as Lady Gaga. One tiny Chihuahua is in an elaborate bride's dress, with a long, sequined trail and a lacy veil.

This Halloween contest makes me wonder if people go trick or treating in Palm Beach, so we take an early evening walk to find out. Most streets are as empty as usual, but on those streets where we saw the decorations a small number of families are out trick or treating.

Adults and children are in costume, and everyone seems to know each other. Some of the front yards now have larger skeletons and ghosts, and some houses have elaborate, scary entryways. Maybe there's a special ordinance permitting larger-sized decor during trick-or-treating hours.

This is a quiet, old-fashioned Halloween. There is no worry of razors in apples here. A memory of a long-ago Halloween floats into my mind. That year my two brothers were too young to trick or treat, but my mother helped my younger sister Sophie and me into our costumes. We were both dressed as fabulous dragons. Because houses were far apart, my father drove us from neighbor to neighbor. I was thrilled that our costumes were so good not a single neighbor recognized us. Lying in bed later that evening, I remembered that all the neighbors had said, "Hi, David," to my father, and realized I hadn't fooled anybody after all. I felt like a dope.

When Dick and I get back home, the message light is blinking on our landline. I push the button.

"Hey, guys," a familiar male voice says. "It's Theo and Deborah. We'll be driving by your house Thursday night. Can we come for a few weeks? Just kidding. But can we spend the night?"

Dick and I look at each. Houseguests. Yikes. We love Theo and Deborah, but there's no bed in the guest cottage yet. There's no place for them to sleep.

six

"I SEE, THAT WOULD MAKE US THE TOWN DOPES."

Monday, November 2

"I just got off the phone with Deborah," Pam says, "and they'll definitely be here Thursday."

"Which means we have to get some kind of bed," I say. "Comfortable, but not too comfortable."

"The place in West Palm where we ordered our bed has futons," Pam says. "A queen futon would work."

I call Bed Man and ask if there is any possible way we can get a queen futon or something like that in a day or two. Bed Man puts me on hold for a minute or so. "I've got a queen-size floor sample in excellent condition that I can deliver Wednesday after six, any color you want, as long as it's beige," he says.

"Beige is my favorite," I say. "See you Wednesday."

It is the beginning of the third month of our adventure in Palm Beach, and we're sort of settled in now. I did think by now there would be at least a trickle of winter people arriving on the island. But this morning, out walking, I discover that White House (it resembles the one in Washington) and Cat House (no, not that kind), with its statues of playful cats on the roof, are both still empty. House after house, the ones that have been empty still are.

And sadly, the crime wave is also continuing. This morning, a woman calling from Greenwich, Connecticut, filed a police report with Palm Beach Police. She seems to be missing a bracelet she remembers having with her on a recent visit to her mother in Palm Beach. How recent? Several months, it seems.

Tuesday, November 3

Pam and I walk to the gym. Signing in, I notice almost all the blanks are filled with names. "Craig," I say, "this list looks pretty full. You cooking the books?"

"Season's coming. They say it starts near Thanksgiving and lasts till Easter, but it's different every year."

Our workouts finished, we walk over to the lake. It's sunny and warm. The impeccably dressed shopkeepers are out cleaning their storefront windows, polishing the brass, and sweeping the sidewalk to prepare for the day. No leaf blowers on Worth Avenue. We get to the lake and sit on one of the benches close to the docks. I'm enjoying the view.

Pam says, "You see that sport fisher over there on the left?"

I say, "Well, yes, what about it? Oh."

"Yes, that's a very healthy naked woman on the aft deck," Pam says.

"I don't think she's naked," I say. "She has on a bikini bottom or thong or something."

"Probably a Palm Beach ordinance," Pam says. "You can only be half naked on your yacht."

"Yes, and it's probably safe for us to start back. There's little danger of her drowning even if she falls overboard. She will definitely float."

Walking back along Peruvian Avenue, I see there are more workers' trucks than usual. I figure everyone's trying to get ready for the season, or maybe Thanksgiving. Whatever is happening, this is as busy as I've seen it.

As we cross South County Road, Barney is standing in his front yard looking like he's just stepped out of the pages of *GQ* in plaid pajamas and a tweed sport coat.

"How are the Walkers today?" he shouts.

"It's the Myers," Pam says, thinking Barney might have finally gone over the edge.

"Nope, you are the Walkers. Everybody around here calls you two the Walkers, even the parking ticket lady," he says.

"So be it, Barney," I say. "We are now officially the Walkers." He laughs. We wave and head back to work.

Wednesday, November 4

This evening, as promised, Bed Man reappears, this time with a futon. Once again he bolts the frame together, lifts the beige mattress, and leaves with a check in his hand. The guest cottage is now ready for guests even if we aren't.

Armed with a couple of glasses of pinot grigio, Pam and I hit the beach. The walk from our desks to the dunes is less than two minutes. We find a bench and settle in to watch the day turn into night, a ritual we have enjoyed together since we were in Manhattan. We stay a little longer than planned, and the stars begin to light the sky.

Walking back home, I notice all the cars and trucks and activities from today have totally disappeared. It's peaceful.

"Hear the train?" Pam says.

"Yes." Ever since we moved to Florida, I've been able to hear the trains, always from a distance. I love the sound, and I love the hazy memories it conjures up. I remember my first train ride. When I was three years old, my grandfather brought my brother and me from Ohio to New York.

"Let's keep walking," Pam says.

We stroll right past the cottage and continue on. "Is that a piano?" I say.

"Sounds like it," Pam says. "Sounds like a cocktail party."

"I don't remember seeing our invitation."

"It's Club Colette," Pam says. "I've seen the sign but I've never seen or heard people there. It sounds festive."

"Well, whoever is here tonight, they're different from the people who were here during the day," I say. "Today there were plumbers' and electricians' and carpenters' trucks, and now there're Bentleys, Rolls-Royces, and Mercedes."

It looks like the winter people are starting to trickle in.

Thursday, November 5

Today our very first houseguests, Theo and Deborah, arrive. I've known Theo since kindergarten, and we've known Deborah for over twenty years. They are both a bit crazy, and we haven't seen them in a while. We're not even fully settled in ourselves, but the futon is in the guest cottage, and we're happy to see these two characters.

They pull into our driveway around five o'clock. After some hugging and unloading of luggage, we all take a walk. In about an hour we end up at the beach. The four of us wander in and out of the surf and chat and continue to catch up on the kids, the news, and who's doing what.

Then it's back to the cottage to prepare for the evening's activities. Pam goes in to feed the birds and change their water.

"Do I need a tie?" Theo says.

"Yes," Deborah says. She turns to me. "What does Pam wear?"

"Theo, you don't need a tie. I usually wear one, but that's me," I say. "Deborah, Pam usually wears a skirt and heels, maybe a jacket. Wear what you want."

After showers, we gather at the pool for cocktails.

Theo says, "My brother told us to have a drink at Bice for him, so I want to do that. The rest of the evening is your choice, and it's on me."

"Theo, I'm thinking if you're picking up the tab maybe the four of us should go to Bermuda for dinner, but how about Bice for a drink, Renato's for dinner, and then maybe a nightcap and dance at The Chesterfield Hotel. And it's on us," I say.

"We'll arm wrestle for the check," Theo says.

"That's what I said. It's on us."

Everyone agrees on the plan, and Deborah says, "We've got your cars blocked in with our car, so Theo'll drive everybody to Bice."

Pam shakes her head, "You don't have to drive."

"It will be easier. We won't have to jockey the cars around," Deborah says.

"No. Theo doesn't have to drive. Dick doesn't have to drive. No one has to drive. We're walking," Pam says.

Theo and Deborah both look at us. Deborah says, "We walked around town with you guys for an hour. I didn't see any restaurants or bars. Just those mansions."

"Deborah, relax. There are a dozen bars and restaurants in a couple of short blocks. They're just in a different direction," I say.

We take the short walk to Bice (much to Deborah's surprise) and have a drink and toast Theo's brother. Halfway through his drink, Theo starts talking wine and speaking Italian to Ronnie and Jose.

"Theo, talking about wine puts people to sleep," I say. "And why are you speaking Italian? Ronnie was born in Sweden, Jose was born in Mexico, and you were born in Bronxville."

We finish our drinks and walk to Renato's. Brad greets us and seats us. "I like restaurants like this," Deborah says, "where the maitre d' wears a suit, the captains wear dinner jackets, and the customers are dressed up."

"It was the same at Bice," Theo says. "We're not in Kansas anymore."

Theo insists on choosing the wine and consults with Luciano, in Italian, of course.

Two hours and two bottles of wine later, we thank Brad and Luciano and we're off to The Chesterfield. After a few dances, the four of us are standing at the bar, and I say, "Theo, remember that chicken step or chicken-walk thing you used to do? The one that got you thrown out of dancing school."

"Remember it? I still do it," he says. He points. "What's with this ceiling?"

Pam laughs and says, "What do you guys think it looks like?"

Deborah looks up and says, "Well, it's definitely R-rated. I see some naked women, some lusty men. Actually, those are satyrs, I think."

"I like it," Theo says. "Everybody should paint their ceilings with stuff like that."

"Right," I say. "Time for one more dance. It's a school night."

Adam starts playing a fast song. "We're doing this one," Deborah says, and leads Theo out on the floor.

Pam and I decide we'll wait for a slower song. Lou comes over and says, "I didn't know you guys had any friends."

"We don't," I say. "We got those two from an escort service."
Lou points and says, "Well, I'd take the guy back."

We turn around. There's Theo doing the chicken-walk thing in the middle of the dance floor. Pam starts laughing. I just shake my head.

Friday, November 6

Over breakfast in the morning, Theo and Deborah cannot stop talking about last night. "We had the most fun we could without getting arrested," Theo says.

"Theo, you should have been arrested. You're way too old for that chicken-walk thing," I say.

Deborah says, "Way too old. But no one minded. Everybody was cool with it. I thought Palm Beach was snooty and stiff and formal, but everybody was so friendly. How come?"

"How come? Honestly, we don't know," Pam says. "Everybody seems nice. It's like a small town."

"What small town do you know where you can walk to restaurants like Bice or Renato's and dance to live music at ten thirty on a Thursday?" Theo says.

"Actually, the walk around town last night was so peaceful it would have been wonderful all by itself," Deborah says.

"I think we'll stay another few nights," Theo says, and pauses. "Just kidding. We're out of here, but we will be back."

I hope so. The late Harry Chapin wrote a song called "Let Time Go Lightly." In it, he sings something about how old friends know who you really are and know where you've been. Theo and I were kids together. We've watched our own kids grow. We've been to each other's weddings and to too many funerals together. We've helped each other for a lifetime. I don't have many friends, but the ones I do have are the best.

Saturday, November 7

This morning is my daughter Samantha's birthday. Amusingly, or perhaps frighteningly, she is about the age I was when I fell in love with Pam. She'll be down in a few weeks for Thanksgiving. I can't wait. We'll call her later with birthday greetings, but first, and for the first time in weeks, Pam and I actually have to get in a car and drive.

A bathroom light fixture has strange bulbs. When the first bulb burned out, we didn't care. When the second one went, we looked for bulbs at Publix. No luck. The third one burned out last night, so this morning I look in the *West Palm Beach Yellow Pages* and find Light Bulbs Unlimited on Okeechobee Boulevard.

Pam drives us over the bridge. "Man, it's a shock to leave the island," she says.

"You mean because first it's tall buildings and then strip malls, car dealerships, and lots of traffic?"

"Yeah, it's just a whole different feeling."

The store has the exact replacement bulbs so we stock up. As we are leaving, I notice a billiards store. I say to Pam, "Look, pool tables. I really miss playing pool with you. Let's just go in for a minute."

Pam says, "Sure."

"Maybe we'll rack 'em up and have a few games of strip pool."

"Perfect," Pam says. "I have on my leopard skin thong today."

Inside there are some impressive pool tables on display. We're walking around looking at them when I see a bumper pool table over in a corner. Pam sees it, too, and laughs.

When we were first together over twenty years ago, we bought a bumper pool table. The two of us had hours and hours of fun playing with friends and with my daughter Samantha and her friends.

A saleslady comes over. "What's the smallest room you can actually play bumper pool in?" I ask her. She looks at me like this is a normal question. Pam looks at me the way she often looks at Barney. I catch the look, and confess, "I was thinking maybe one could fit in the guest cottage."

Pam says, "What about guests?"

"We can just move it. We had hours of fun playing bumper pool, remember? Fun is good, and it's Samantha's birthday."

"Fun is good," Pam says, "but do you think you can fool a Corleone into thinking Samantha's birthday has anything to do with this?"

"I guess the birthday idea was a bit of a stretch." The saleslady is back with a copy of the dimensions needed to play bumper pool. When we get home, I measure, and there is enough room.

"Let's do it. It'll be our Christmas present to each other," Pam says.

"I'll call and order it right now," I say. "Merry Christmas."

Monday, November 9

Tonight as we're walking to The Chesterfield, Pam says, "Are those Xs chalk?" She's pointing at two big Xs scrawled across two squares of the sidewalk.

"I don't think so. Maybe kids playing with spray paint."

As we continue walking, I notice more whites Xs drawn across some of the squares, four or five on several different streets. It looks like too many to be just some kids playing with chalk or paint.

We get to The Chesterfield. It should be a fairly quiet night with Bill on the guitar. We'll hear a couple of jokes from Lou or John, have a few dances, and head home. As we walk through The Chesterfield's courtyard, however, the place seems noisier and more crowded than usual. Just inside the door of the Leopard Lounge, a lady is sitting at a table, collecting money.

"Has to be some kind of private party or special function," Pam says.

"I think so," I say. "Want to try Café Boulud or just head home?" We turn around and start back out. Candy, tan and perfectly coiffed, is bartending tonight. She spots us and waves us in.

"We're open, you two," she says.

"Not a private party?" I point to the woman at the table.

"No, no, no," she shakes her head and laughs. "This is just the Millionaires Club."

Pam and I look at each other. "Candy, if this is the Millionaires Club," I say, "we are definitely in the wrong saloon."

Mark, the Restaurant Manager, comes over and says "No, no, no. Come on in. Everybody's welcome. There's room at the bar."

Lou brings us a drink. "So this guy comes into the bar. I look at his pants and say, 'Is that a steering wheel in your pants?' He says, 'Yes, and it's driving me nuts.'"

I ask Lou and Candy about the Millionaires Club. The best anyone can determine, it is an eclectic assemblage of singles who have get-togethers at local bars, organized by the club's founders, allegedly two of the early Doublemint Twins. These ladies have the table set up at The Chesterfield tonight, and they collect ten dollars from each of their members who come into the bar.

I say, "Lou, members have to pay ten dollars to get in here and non members like us get in for free? Does that make any sense?"

Lou wrinkles his forehead. "It doesn't make a lick of sense

to me, but it's making the twins ten bucks a head."

On the walk home, we pass Club Colette. Eight or nine Bentleys are parked in front. I'm thinking maybe it should be called Club Bentley instead of Club Colette.

Wednesday November 11

This morning I awaken with what is known in our family as "Dick's wing-thing." This is a partially frozen and painful shoulder blade condition that I have somehow acquired while sleeping. I used to be a decorated student athlete, a man of steel. Now I can injure myself when I'm asleep. Sleep-related injuries?

Sometimes I can work it out with heat and ice or by lying on a golf ball. If not, it takes a few visits to the chiropractor. Today, no luck with home remedies, so this evening I say, "Pam, you think Bobby would know a chiropractor?"

"Let's walk to Taboo," Pam says, "perhaps have a cocktail and ask him."

There is room at the bar. Bobby greets us and brings us a drink. When he has a free moment, I say, "Bobby, I've got a question for you tonight."

Pam says, "Actually, I've got one, too. We'll pay the usual fee."

He laughs. "You said two questions. I'll have to double the fee. But I guess two times zero is still zero."

"Okay, first, do you know of a good chiropractor in town?" I ask.

"A great one," he says, "but he's not in town. He's in Lake Worth. Dr. Keith. He's helped me. He's helped Cindy. Heck, he's helped most of the people who work here. He's the chiropractor for the U.S. Olympic and National Triathlon teams. He's really good."

"Sold," I say. "How far away from here?"

"About twelve or fifteen minutes," he says.

Pam says, "Okay, we have a chiropractor. Now do you know where can we find a fresh fruits and vegetable stand, fresh produce?"

He smiles and nods his head. "Don Victorio's Market is right on the way to or from Dr. Keith's. Really fresh produce at great prices," he says.

We finish our drinks, thank Bobby, and start home for dinner with all the pertinent information safely recorded on a bar napkin.

On our walk home it is a little cool and just misting a bit. Fall must be on its way. We both notice more and more sidewalk squares with large white Xs drawn across them.

Pam says, "These Xs are not from kids, and they're not chalk, they're paint."

"Are you ready for this? They seem to be only on the cracked squares of sidewalk," I say.

"You mean you think the town's actually going to replace all these squares?"

"Looks like it to me," I say, "but who knows. We'll see."

Thursday, November 12

My wing-thing is better this morning, so I put off making an appointment with Dr. Keith. Almost pain-free, I'm enjoying an espresso.

Pam says, "The Shiny Sheet has a calendar of the season's upcoming events. It looks like there's something every day, balls, luncheons, you name it. Do you think the town will be different with all these events happening?"

"I don't know. Maybe there'll be more traffic. We'll wait and see," I say.

On an afternoon walk, we come upon two men with a jack-hammer and a wheelbarrow, breaking up the X-marks-the-spot sidewalk squares.

Pam says, "Amazing."

Later, we see two guys with rolling cement mixers pouring, spreading, and smoothing the new portions of sidewalk. The ones not being replaced are being pressure washed.

I tell Pam that I'm walking to Scotti's to pick up some beer. On the way, I pick up a stick and etch a heart with an arrow through it and the initials "P" and "D" into one of the damp squares. I drop the stick, pick up my beer, and go back home.

Friday, November 13

Pam and I are watching a Knicks game at Bice. We still haven't done anything about hooking up our TV. A small entourage of thirty-something "area people" is finishing up their drinks and discussing where to go next. The apparent leader of the crowd exclaims, "Okay, okay, come on, we're going to go to the Zebra Lounge at The Colony. We can dance there."

Well, yes and no. There is no Zebra Lounge at The Colony or anywhere on the island. There is the Leopard Lounge at The Chesterfield, and the Polo Lounge at The Colony. No Zebra Lounge. But since it is a weekend night and there is dancing at both The Colony and The Chesterfield, they'll be able to dance wherever they end up.

The Knicks are depressing me, so I suggest we walk over to Amici. As we approach the restaurant, I stop next to a certain section of sidewalk.

"What are you doing?" Pam says.

I sort of nod my head towards the sidewalk.

"Dick, why are you stopping?"

"Look down."

She looks down and sees the heart with our initials. She laughs and puts her arms around me. "When did you do that?" she says. I just smile.

We walk on to Amici and take a seat at the bar. Two men next to us cash out and leave. As they hit the sidewalk, Beth, the bartender, comes over with her wonderful smile. "Do you guys know who you were sitting next to?" We look at each other. "That was Jimmy Buffett," she says.

Pam says, "We had no clue. None. And actually Dick and I are big fans of Mr. Buffet and his music."

His songs were the sound track for our escape from Manhattan to the Caribbean several decades ago. I can still see Pam dancing crazily by herself to "Cheeseburger in Paradise" on the aft deck of *Maverick,* the boat we were living on then.

"Well, it could have been Warren Buffet next to us for all I knew," I say. "Jimmy got by us this time. Won't happen again."

Tuesday, November 17

This morning the Shiny Sheet informs me that a lady in Palm Beach has notified the police that her flatware is missing. She last saw it in May. What's with these people?

Our cottage problems are a thing of the past. I'm even adjusting to the Lilliputian doors and ceilings. But the longer we live here, the more the lack of storage space becomes an issue. My clothes closet is packed so tight I can't even get a jacket off the rack. The cabinet under the sink is so full it takes me five minutes to find the Windex.

I'm in the kitchen, thinking, why don't we just turn this little room and tiny bathroom off the kitchen into a closet? Get a clothes rack, a few shelves, whatever will make it work. There are two other bathrooms in the house and one in the guest cottage.

I tell my plan to Pamela, and after work we head out for supplies. By the end of the evening, Pam and I have put shelves in the shower, a rolling clothes rack in the utility room, file holders on the walls.

"Seems like a great solution," I say

"At least for a while," Pam says.

Thursday November 19

We walk over to the tennis courts. It is now mid-November, and trucks fill every available parking space: air conditioning repairers, security system installers, plumbers, painters, electricians, and wallpaper hangers. People are actually going to be coming to Palm Beach. It looks like all the houses will soon be full.

Pam and I have hit tennis balls for almost an hour and are now sitting by the courts, sharing a bottle of water. A woman who seems about our age (which means she is ten to fifteen years younger) is on a rapid and direct approach to where we are sitting.

"Rehydrating?" she asks. We look at each other, our water, back at her. "Mary said you're the one who wrote this book," she says. She has apparently just bought *Tennis for Humans* in the pro shop.

I nod and say, "Yes."

"Mary says you'll sign it for me," she says.

"I don't have to do what Mary says, you know."

She looks a little puzzled.

"I'm just kidding," I say. "I'd be happy to sign your book." She says her name is Melissa, so I sign her book: "For Melissa, good luck on and off the tennis court."

We start talking with Melissa, who is actually very nice. "I'm just down from New York to help the housekeeper open our house for Thanksgiving. My husband Mark and our three sons are still up north," she says.

"When are they going to join you at the house?" Pam asks.

"Well, I'm not really staying at the house yet. I'm at The Brazilian Court," she says. "I'm flying home in two days, and then we'll all fly down for Thanksgiving next Wednesday. Then home again for Christmas, and then Mark and I are here for January and February. Mark is a good player, Dick, maybe you two could play some tennis then."

I say, "If I'm still breathing, I'd love to hit with Mark. Have him call me."

We wish Melissa a happy Thanksgiving, walk home, and open our house, with no help from our housekeeper, in four or five seconds.

Saturday, November 21

Pam and I are sitting on a bench under the giant canopy of a banyan tree at the town docks. I say, "The twin forty-fours on that sport fisher are missing today."

As usual, there is little activity and few people are around. In all the times we have visited these slips in the last two and a half months, I've rarely seen a boat arrive or leave. Yet there are many more yachts here today than usual. "Boats must be sneaking in at night," Pam says. "I think the docks are more full than empty for the first time."

"Nobody's ever around here but us," I say. "We should have some official monitoring position with the town." I think for a moment. "The Docks Official Protectors, Examiners, and Supervisors."

Pam looks at me. "I see. That would make us the town DOPES."

Returning from our dock duties, we see a large truck parked in front of a house on Australian. A moving van? Well, sort of. Two men are carefully unloading a spotless Bentley that is going into the garage of that house. The people aren't quite here yet but their toys, the boats and cars, are arriving.

Around seven o'clock, Pam says, "I think we need pizza tonight."

"That we do," I say. "I have a doctor's prescription for one pizza, two salads, and a bottle of wine."

"Let's go to Pizza al Fresco," Pam says.

At the restaurant, a young lady greets us and takes us to a table in the courtyard. "The prescription is for salads and splitting a pizza?" Pam says.

"Yes, and a bottle of Italian red. Your choice."

"How about two Caesars, a pizza with Italian sausage and mushrooms, and a bottle of Chianti Classico?"

The setting is a small, romantically lighted courtyard with bougainvillea growing up the sides of the walls. I can't help but picture the dozens of dinners Pam and I have had in similar settings on St. Barts or St. Martin or even Virgin Gorda. For some reason, tonight is reminding me specifically of a dinner we had on our honeymoon at a little outdoor restaurant in Antigua. That night we shared a cardboard box of wine, a first.

Pam says, "Sitting here, I feel as if we have come a lot farther than five minutes from our house. Remember that box of wine we had at that place in Antigua?"

I laugh. "Exactly what I was thinking," I say

Monday, November 23
Perhaps I should have made an appointment with Dr. Keith the other day because it took me ten minutes to get out of bed

this morning. When I sneezed, it felt like my shoulder blade was exploding. Pam calls and Dr. Keith's office promises to fit me in. Pam drives me to Lake Worth. With some adjustment, some ultrasound, and some magic, Dr. Keith has me feeling almost human. I make a follow-up appointment and we're gone.

Driving back, we pass Don Victorio's, the market Bobby suggested, on Dixie Highway in West Palm Beach. Pam decides it is time for a visit and circles around the block. As we pull in the parking lot, I say, "Man, this looks like a parking lot in the islands. Cars are parked every which way."

"Yeah, I'm going to park all the way in the back. You and your shoulder stay in the car. I'm just going to check it out," she says.

About four songs later, she emerges and I start laughing. She looks like a New York bag lady. She's carrying so many bags I can barely see her. I reach over and pop the trunk and she unloads her haul.

She gets in the driver's side, smiling, and says, "Well I guess I did a bit more than check it out, but you should have seen it. There were bins of fresh fruit and vegetables everywhere. I got grapefruits and oranges and tomatoes, bunches of carrots and beets with the greens still attached, lettuces of all kinds, a pineapple, bananas, and apples."

"A little more than just checking it out," I say.

"It is just like the farm store I went to as a kid," she says, "and all this stuff cost less than twenty dollars."

Tuesday, November 24

It is now two days before Thanksgiving, and the Shiny Sheet informs me the police were called to a north end home because of a dispute about ficus trimmings being left in a yard. A ficus trimmings dispute? I'm wondering if it could be gang-related.

Our morning walk is to Worth Avenue, which is completely closed to cars today. Workmen are repainting all the curbs and parking space lines. We weave our way through, wander about for a while, and head toward home. Turning onto our street, we almost run into a man squatting at the curb next to a bucket of bright yellow paint. He is hand-painting the no-parking curbs along our street. His companion has a bucket of white paint and is hand-painting the parking-allowed curbs. Another man on a ladder is coating the lampposts with glossy black paint.

"Pretty soon there won't be a cracked sidewalk or a faded street line or street curb in all of Palm Beach," I say.

"It reminds me of getting a house ready to put on the market," Pam says.

"They'd better not be selling it," I say. "We just got here."

Wednesday, November 25

The alarm gets us up before dawn. We dress, fill a thermos with breakfast tea, grab our beach chairs, and we're off to watch the sunrise. The street is peacefully empty. We set up the chairs at the ocean's edge. It is a bit early for animated conversation or probably any conversation at all, so we just sip our tea and be.

In the few months we have been in Palm Beach, we have seen more sunrises and moonrises and spent more time stargazing than we have in many years. I feel it's giving us a better perspective on what's important. Whatever it's doing, I like it.

The show begins. Slowly, the sun rises out of the Atlantic. Slowly, the night becomes a new day. Slowly, the sun warms the sand. We sit for a few minutes enjoying the new morning, then pick up and head home.

When lunchtime rolls around, I suggest Victor's. Walking

out, Pam says, "The street is still quiet. There are no trucks today, there's no commotion. Strange."

As we approach South County, we hear cars and even a honking horn. "I can't remember hearing a car honk in Palm Beach," I say. "Wow, South County is crazy. Look at this traffic."

We continue on to Worth Avenue, and Pam says, "Look at this."

"What the hell happened to our quiet hometown street?" I say. There are people everywhere, people and dogs. People driving with dogs in their laps. People walking with dogs on leashes. People carrying dogs.

The scene could not be more different from yesterday or any day so far. It's like a B movie. I live in a quiet, empty little town, and suddenly the entire population of Greenwich, Connecticut has somehow dropped in overnight. I've sort of been waiting for this, but I'm not sure I'm going to like it.

"Victor's? Lunch? Not today," I say.

Returning home on South County, I see Amici is busy inside and out. Maurizio is nodding his head and smiling. He gives us two thumbs up and laughs.

Thursday, November 26

Pam and I are excited. My daughter Samantha is flying down from New York for the Thanksgiving weekend. She arrives today. Her mother lives across the bridge in West Palm Beach, and her grandmother lives in Palm Beach Gardens, about twenty minutes north of us. The logistics of the weekend should work out beautifully for everyone, which has not always been the case.

Pam and I get one night and a day. And I'm hoping very much it will all be easy and hassle-free for Samantha. Well, that's what I'm hoping.

Samantha is having Thanksgiving dinner with her mother and grandmother tonight. We have a quiet cookout by our outdoor fire pit with a soft-mix playlist, walk to the beach for some stargazing, and then home for more stargazing from our front yard.

Friday, November 27

Because it is the Friday after Thanksgiving and because Samantha is here, I want everything to be absolutely perfect, so I make a dinner reservation. A first for us in Palm Beach. I pick her up at her mother's condo across the bridge and come back to the cottage.

The three of us have a glass of champagne, and Samantha wants a tour of the cottage. She seems to approve, but I can tell she thinks it's a little strange. She's okay with it, I think, because she sees we're happy. The three of us walk to the restaurant. It is packed, but our table is ready. We talk and laugh and catch up on each other's lives a bit. Samantha is getting very tired of her job and thinking about packing it in. She's been there over a decade. (How is that possible?) I sense there is a gentleman in her life, but she is a bit vague on this subject.

Meanwhile, the restaurant, or rather the diners, are getting louder. The many large tables of ten and twelve are raising the decibel level. None of this bothers Samantha, but it does bother me. I suggest dessert and coffee at our cottage.

The three of us walk over to the beach and back towards home. "I'm sorry it was so crowded and noisy tonight. It's usually much more civilized," I say.

"Dad, I live in Manhattan," Samantha says. "Trust me, that was not crowded and noisy. It was quite civilized."

Pam laughs and says, "You're right, Sam. I think your dad

and I are getting spoiled. Until the day before yesterday, we sort of had the town to ourselves."

Samantha looks around. "Well, we seem to have this part of town to ourselves right now. I haven't seen anyone else since we left the restaurant," she says. "If you're used to New York like I am, this is a little spooky."

At home, the three of us sit by the pool, sip espressos, and talk quietly for over an hour until it is time for bed. I drive Samantha back to her mother's for the night. Driving back over to the island, I'm thinking to myself, what could be better than spending an evening sitting and talking with the two women I love?

Saturday, November 28

This morning, I pick up Samantha again, and she, Pam, and I walk to Worth Avenue for some shopping. After lunch, Samantha and I hit some tennis balls. I love hitting with her. When she was two or three, I'd bounce balls to her, and she'd swing her sawed-off racquet and blast them all over the court. Now she's hitting the balls beautifully, and I seem to be blasting them all over the court.

Dinner for her is with Granna tonight, so I take her back and drop her at her mother's building and say goodbye.

Sunday, November 29

Pam and I venture out to Amici. The Thanksgiving crowds, people and dogs, are gone. It is quiet there, and so are we. I'm always quiet after Samantha's visits. As an every-other-weekend father for much of Samantha's teenage life, I felt like she was always leaving. Whether Pam, Samantha, and I had a great weekend or a disaster, and we had our share of both, I was always sad when Samantha left. I still am.

Maurizio comes over to the table. Pam says, "We walked by here a few times. You were really slammed."

"Thank God," Maurizio says, "but it will be quiet again until Christmas."

"You mean that's it?" I say. "The people were here and now they're gone again?"

"Gone for now," Maurizio says, "but over Christmas it is just really insane."

Monday, November 30

For reasons I cannot even begin to understand, I want to go to see the Christmas tree lighting ceremony at Bradley Park this evening. It's near Publix on Royal Poinciana Way. Pam does, too. Something seems to be happening to us. We've never been to a tree lighting together before, ever.

We drive the mile north and park. It's dusk. To make the tree lighting more dramatic, the town streetlights are turned off. A policeman stops traffic so people can cross the street to the park. Some parents with young children are standing in the grass. It's a small crowd in a large park.

After ten minutes, the dusk has turned to dark, and a brilliant full moon glows above us. Building lights across Lake Worth shimmer in the distance. A small choir of children sings Christmas carols, and then everyone joins in a simple countdown— five, four, three, two, one—and the Christmas tree lights up. A big red fire engine, blowing horns and flashing lights, arrives to drop off Santa and Mrs. Claus. All the children run toward them.

On the short ride home, Pam leans her head on my shoulder. "That got to me," she says. "I don't know why, but it got to me."

"You, too?" I say.

She sits up and turns to look at me. "This is weird, isn't it."

seven

"WHAT'S THAT?
WE MUST BE UNDER ATTACK."

Tuesday, December 1

At eight this morning, the temperature is already seventy-two, which is pretty warm for December, even in south Florida. Dick brews two cups of espresso, and we take these and the morning papers to a bench overlooking the beach. The sun is bright and the ocean is flat, deep blue in the distance, a pale turquoise close to shore.

Dick is reading the Shiny Sheet. "There's another tree lighting tonight." He pauses. "Actually, it looks like there're two."

"Two?" I say. "Where?"

"One's in that park across from Café L'Europe. The other's on Worth. Want to go?"

"Sure," I say.

We go back to our papers. But I can't concentrate. I'm trying to figure out why I want to go to more tree lightings. All the years Dick and I've been together, we've skipped this type of gathering. We avoid crowds unless it involves a basketball or baseball game. We don't do festivals. But last night's event was simple and quaint, and quite a contrast to the sophisticated restaurants and fancy Worth Avenue shops. It's like there's an old-fashioned small town here we never knew about, a Palm Beach secret. To my surprise, this old-fashionedness appeals to me.

I look up at Dick. "This is a little weird, isn't it? Going to three tree lightings?"

"I think last night's lighting tapped into something, for both of us," Dick says. "Might as well follow it, see where it goes."

We work all day. At five o'clock, we make the short walk to tonight's first tree lighting. It's even smaller than the one at Bradley Park. Again, a choir sings, and Santa and his wife arrive in a fire engine.

We take a seat on a bench in the little park. "This feels like Christmastime in the nineteen fifties," Dick says.

"Yeah," I say. "No crowds, no noisy kids, no gaudy decorations, no canned Christmas carols."

I think over Christmases I've had as an adult. Dick and I have basically skipped Christmas unless Samantha was involved. Before I met Dick, I had a job that involved lots of travel, and sometimes I even traveled on Christmas Day. One Christmas, because of delayed flights, I ended up having five Christmas dinners on planes. I was so busy back then, fast-tracking up the career ladder. Now that feels like foreign times.

On both sides of us, couples and families are walking south along the sidewalks. The crowd grows thicker. "Think they're going to the Worth Avenue lighting?" I ask.

"Yeah," Dick says. "Looks like it's bigger than the other two. We'd better get going."

We join the parade. The sidewalks are full.

"I've never seen this many people in Palm Beach," I say.

"Me, either," Dick says.

The streets are far more crowded than they were at Thanksgiving. All the parking spaces are taken, even on the side streets, and drivers are searching for empty spots. By the time we get to Worth Avenue, it's closed to cars and holds a sea of people.

Shopkeepers offer glasses of wine and plates of hors d'oeuvres. The crowd is polite and festive. Although this tree lighting clearly draws people from across the bridge and from towns south and north, it feels like a local event. People know each other and I hear lots of "catching up on the news" conversations.

We follow the throng west toward the Christmas tree and find a space to stand. The tree is probably thirty feet high, at least twice as big as the previous two. Soon, I'm surrounded by taller people and can only see the top of the tree. I grab Dick's hand. The sound of bagpipes rises above the noise of the crowd.

"Can you see what's happening?" I say. Dick's almost a foot taller than I am.

"The naked lady from the sport fisher is leading a parade of naked bagpipers," he says. "Just kidding." He pauses. "Santa and Mrs. Claus are behind the bagpipers. They're close now. No fire engine this time. They're in the back of a Mercedes convertible."

Everyone joins in the countdown chorus, and tiny white lights on the tree sparkle to life. We learn through the grapevine the fire engine Santa was supposed to arrive in had to go to a real fire.

"So," Dick says, "three tree lightings in two days. Are we nuts?"

"I don't know," I say. "But let's get out of here and go find a saloon."

People are everywhere. We can't get near Bice or Taboo or Renato's or Pizza al Fresco.

"Let's try The Chesterfield," Dick says.

We thread our way through the crowd and eventually get to

the Leopard Lounge. The bar is already pretty full of the tree-lighting crowd, but we find two seats.

Lou comes over, bringing us a beer and a glass of champagne. The place is so busy there's no time for a joke.

Dick looks at me and says. "So, you and I don't like crowds, skip parades, don't do holiday events."

"And we just went to three tree lightings, including one that was crowded, and wouldn't mind going to another one?" I say.

"What's going on?" Dick says.

"I don't know," I say. "Something to do with the past. Simpler times, maybe."

I wonder if this move to Palm Beach for a year will be more significant than I imagined.

Wednesday, December 2

It's another sunny, balmy morning. We're sitting by the pool reading the morning papers. I love being out here, looking at the tall seagrape trees and the thick border of ficus hedges. Duckie and Blanco are nearby in their outdoor cage, peering up at the family of doves perched along the roof of the guest cottage. Do our birds wish they could fly up and join the doves, I wonder.

The Shiny Sheet reports that a homeowner on Seaview told police his lawn was "damaged by a delivery truck." Interpol may have to be notified.

We walk over to Worth Avenue around noon and see only the occasional pedestrian. I guess the craziness of Thanksgiving was just a blip. Maurizio warned us the other night that we had-n't seen anything yet, that Palm Beach would be much busier over the Christmas holidays. It's hard to believe today.

The workers are back in force. The residential streets are full of laborers painting and sawing and hammering and hedging. It's quite noisy. Trucks and vans are in all the parking spaces. The preparations and repairs for the winter residents continue. I'm curious about when they will actually arrive and stay.

This evening we walk to The Chesterfield for an early dance. There's little traffic. The restaurants that were slammed over Thanksgiving are not even close to full now. We take seats at the bar.

Two forty-something men in suits next to us are engaged in a heated discussion. One says, "Well, he doesn't live in Palm Beach year round. It's not his primary home."

His friend says, "I know that. I'm not saying any of these team owners lives here all year. I'm just saying they own homes here. They have a Palm Beach presence."

"Okay, okay, now which team owners are these again?"

His friend takes out a scrap of paper and says, "Listen, the owners of the Steelers, the Giants, the Tampa Bay Bucs, the Packers, the Magic, the Patriots, the Browns, the Mets, the Islanders, the Red Sox, the Eagles, the Flyers, the Phillies, and the Sixers are all Palm Beachers."

"Whoa, that is unbelievable."

Dick looks at me. "I didn't know all those team owners had houses here."

"Me, either," I say.

Adam is entertaining tonight, and Dick and I dance to some slow songs, including "Lady in Red" and "Come Monday." Then Adam switches to "Rolling on a River" and several other rock and roll songs, and Dick indulges me and we dance fast.

Back at the bar, Dick says, "Pasta at Amici tonight?"

"Sounds great."

We walk in that direction. It begins to drizzle. We pick up our pace, but so does the drizzle. We run. As we reach Amici, a man who is leaving holds the door open for us.

We take a seat at the bar. Beth stands there, smiling.

"So?" she says.

Dick and I look at each other. "So," Dick says, "what?"

"So, did you recognize your doorman tonight?" she asks.

"That guy who held the door? No, but it was nice of him, considering the rain," Dick says.

Beth laughs. "That was Jimmy Buffett again."

Are we idiots? Perhaps we need new prescriptions, more antioxidants, oat bran. I don't know.

Saturday, December 5

This morning, in the bedroom, I try to get a pair of jeans from a high shelf in the closet, and a pile of clothes falls down on me. I let out a few swear words, and Dick appears. He looks at the clothes lying on the floor.

"What happened?" he says.

"I was trying to get a pair of jeans, and everything came tumbling down."

He picks up a pair of pants and says, "Here, I'll help you put it all back."

I look down at the stuff around me. "No," I say. "I'm not sure it all should go back. I'm going to just look through this stuff."

"Okay, let me know if I can help," Dick says.

I'm confused. Our house in New Smyrna has a space for everything. Here, in Palm Beach, we're living with much less, but there isn't room for what we have.

I think back to New York. Dick and I lived in several apartments much smaller than this cottage and it didn't fuss us. Of course, we were younger then, and had much less. I do remember being delighted, the first time we moved into a house, that we had a closet just for coats.

I pick up each piece of clothing, one by one. Some I fold and put back. Whatever I don't really need or wear, I put in several large shopping bags for The Church Mouse, the secondhand store where we bought the chest. The closet shelves look much more accessible now.

I ask Dick if he can help me carry the bags to The Church Mouse, and we walk over and make our donation. I make a brief pass through the women's section. Many items were bought just two blocks away, on fancy Worth Avenue. A year out of fashion, perhaps, but a tenth of the original price. I pick up a lovely teapot, put it back. We came here to get rid of stuff, not acquire it.

"Looks like this shop takes just about every kind of donation," Dick says, looking around at the tables and chairs, china, linens, and paintings. "Maybe we'll just donate everything in our cottage. That'll solve the space problem."

He's close to being right, I think. He often is when he makes these wisecracks.

Dick suggests we walk over to the town docks. "After all," he says, "it's our job as DOPES." We take a seat on a bench and check on the yachts. Only a few slips are empty, and it looks as if they might be all filled before Christmas. For the first time we see a mega yacht tied up at the end of a pier. It's too big even for the regular oversize slips.

"Did I tell you what happened at the gas station?" I say. "Yesterday, the attendant asked me if I knew how to pop the gas tank."

"You mean because he thought you were a dumb blonde?"

"No. Be serious. He said many people who get gas there have no idea how to open their tank, so the attendants do it for them."

Dick says, "I'm not sure those people should be driving."

We sit for a while longer. There are actually people on some of the boats. I see a man hosing off a deck, another sanding a railing.

Two women walk by, and we catch a bit of conversation. One says, "No, no, no, you don't have to go to two doctors. My dentist gives me my Botox injections. I get my teeth cleaned and my smile fixed up at the same time."

Dick looks at me. "Only in Palm Beach," he says.

Tuesday, December 8

I've begun to notice holiday decorations on houses and in front yards. They're understated, just like the Halloween ones. Simple wreaths hang on front doors. Tiny white lights embrace hibiscus bushes, thread through ficus hedges, encircle trunks of trees. I catch glimpses of indoor Christmas trees, decorated with colorful lights and glass balls. We haven't put up a tree or holiday decorations in years. Now I'm trying to remember why.

Late this afternoon, on our way over to the tennis courts, Dick and I see two men wrapping strings of holiday lights around palm trees in a front yard. The printing on the side of the van parked in the driveway says the company buys, puts up, takes down, and stores holiday decorations. Dick looks at me and says, "That's a job our parents never told us about."

We play tennis, finish up about six o'clock. As we walk off the court, two men dressed in tennis clothes are walking onto the next court. The first man says, "Yeah, I'd be happy to hit with you, but tell me, why the hell are you playing here instead of your own court?"

"Good question," the other replies. "I was hitting at home on the ball machine late this afternoon, and Janie gets a call from our neighbor citing a Town of Palm Beach ordinance. You won't believe this, but in this town you can't use a ball machine after five o'clock."

Dick looks at me. "This town must have tons of ordinances," he says.

Thursday, December 10

All the windows along Worth Avenue are decorated for the holidays. We stop in front of William Eubanks, an expensive antique shop. A Christmas tree is in the window, decorated with beautiful white birds that look like Blanco.

"Let's go in," I say.

Dick looks at me oddly. This is a shop where a lamp could cost $9,500, a pair of dining room chairs $15,500, a chest $51,000. "Sure," he says.

We go in. I go look at the birds and see there are also grey birds that look like Duckie.

A woman appears. "May I help?"

"Well, yes," I say. "Do you know how much these birds are?"

"I think they're seven-fifty," she says, "I'll check." Off she goes. I don't know where to put the decimal point. I can't imagine anything in this store costing only seven dollars and fifty cents, but seven hundred and fifty dollars seems a little steep. Maybe these birds are rare antiques. I take a careful look at one of the white birds. Now I'm afraid to touch it.

She comes back. "Yep, they're seven-fifty each," she says. "So, that'd be fifteen dollars for both birds."

I look at the tree. A quick count shows there to be about twenty birds. I consider buying them all, then remember we're trying to get rid of stuff, not accumulate it.

"I'll take these two," I say and point to a white and a grey bird.

Dick smiles. "Christmas tree decorations?" he says.

"No, no, no," I say. "I'll just put them around the orchids in the yellow room."

Friday, December 11

Santa's supposed to deliver the bumper pool table between nine and noon. I'm excited. I don't know why. It's just a bumper pool table. We graduated to billiards a long time ago. But I remember how much fun we had with that little bumper pool table in our early days.

At eleven the doorbell rings. The driver gets the crated bumper pool table off the truck and into the guest cottage and leaves. It's our job to uncrate it and put it together.

We get to work. As usual, opening the packaging turns out to be the hardest part. Assembly is relatively easy: just four thick legs bolted to the top. After half an hour and a few mild expletives, the table is ready. It fits in the cottage. Playing on one side could be a little dicey, even with these short cues, but it looks like there's just enough room.

However, there's no time to try. Deadlines are looming. Dick gets us a sandwich from Sandwiches by the Sea. We eat at our desks, work the rest of the day.

By six the office is a mess, with paper everywhere, but the projects are finished and ready to go. Dick carries the packages over to the Fed Ex drop box while I put the office back in shape.

"A game?" I say to Dick when he returns.

"Fifty bucks I beat you," Dick says.

"Make it a hundred," I say, "and you're on."

We go out to the cottage, set up the balls, start playing. Or not. Billiards has been our game for many years, and it's played on a table over twice the size of this one. We hit the balls too hard. We're terrible.

"What's happening?" I say. "How can we be so bad? We used to play this game."

Dick, the resident game guru, starts laughing. "That was a long time ago. We gotta slow down. Forget the bet. Forget the bumpers. Try the angles."

We try to play, fumble everything.

"Did we make a mistake to buy this?" I say.

Dick laughs. "We'll be okay. It's just going to take a while."

Saturday, December 12

The outdoor thermometer is hovering around eighty. The sky is cloudless. I'm behind the guest cottage at my gardening table, potting some geraniums. Dick comes around the corner.

"Feels like summer," he says. "Burgers and dogs tonight? Potato salad?"

"Great idea," I say.

"I'm off to Publix," he says. "We need charcoal and rolls."

"I'm about finished here," I say. "Okay if I come?"

Dick drives us north to the store. Christmas trees are stacked along the front of the building, wrapped in twine and arranged by size. The air smells like pine trees.

Dick says, "Wow, doesn't that aroma take you back?"

"Ummm," I say.

Not many people are inside and we're home in no time. I go to the kitchen and start boiling potatoes for the potato salad. The door to the living room is open, and I see Dick standing there, looking up. He reaches as high as he can with his right hand.

"What're you doing?" I say.

"Measuring," he says.

"Measuring?" I say. "Measuring what?" His hand isn't touching anything. Then I say, "You mean, for a tree? Are you thinking of getting a tree?"

"Well, I was just wondering how tall a tree we'd need if we got one."

"Which would be?"

"Eight or nine feet," he says.

"We gotta go," I say. "There weren't many big ones left." I turn off the potatoes. "But how'll we get it home? It's not like we have one of those giant SUVs."

"We'll tie it to the top of the Audi. Not a problem," Dick says.

I grab a ball of twine and some scissors, and we're off.

Dick goes to find the man in charge of trees, and I choose one. I pull out my tree-tying supplies. The man laughs and says, "Boy, you guys come prepared. Most of these people in Palm Beach, they expect a miracle. They drive up in their Mercedes two-seater and expect to just drive off with a ten-foot tree."

He gets the tree onto the top of the Audi and expertly ties it down. We cautiously drive home, branches brushing the windshield. Dick takes the tree to the side of the house. It won't be going inside until tomorrow. There's some furniture rearranging to be done.

Sunday, December 13

After lunch, we clear a space in the living room for the tree. Yesterday when we got the tree, we both forgot all about things like tree holders and decorations and lights, so we go over the bridge, find everything plus four poinsettias for outside the front door, and get to work. Dick puts the tree into the holder, and we arrange the lights and hang up the little glass balls. Dick places the two birds up high. The tree looks festive.

We are going to have a civilized Sunday at Café L'Europe, but first Dick and I have our third try at the bumper pool table. We're getting better. Even the annoying bumpers are occasionally becoming useful. And old memories are coming back.

"Remember when we got that first bumper pool table?" Dick says. "We had it in the end of that little living room in that funny house we rented."

"Yeah," I say. "I had no idea how to play. But then we started playing with Rick and Betsy."

Dick says, "Remember how that first year the four of us played almost every other Saturday, sometimes until three or four in the morning?"

"Remember when Samantha was little, and you and she were playing, and she had your Dad's hat on, and maybe his coat? She looked like Minnesota Fats," I say. "And remember when Lee and Ann visited, and you beat Lee badly. So the next morning we get wakened before dawn by the clacking of pool balls. We go downstairs, and there's Lee, furiously practicing his shots."

"I still miss Lee," Dick says.

"I miss him, too."

I think of Lee, and remember how much fun he was. He was Dick's dearest friend since seventh grade. He died when he was forty.

Monday, December 14

Both birds need their wings and nails clipped again. Luckily, they now have their papers in order. I call Jay at Birds off Broadway, who tells me the woman who clips will be in this Saturday. He signs us up for eleven o'clock.

Somehow, in the middle of December, hibiscus, impatiens,

ixora, and vinca are flowering all at once. Everywhere, bushes and hedges and flowerbeds are covered with blossoms. Everywhere, that is, except around our pool. Today, walking home from the dry cleaner, I see a landscaper working at the edge of the sidewalk.

"Hi," I say. "Do you have any idea why the plants all over town are blooming at the same time?"

He laughs. "The winter people want flowers when they arrive, so we give them flowers," he says. "This time of year we fertilize like crazy, make the plants bloom."

Blossoms on demand. It seems nobody has time to wait for anything to grow in Palm Beach. I've seen entire yards ripped out —trees, bushes, everything, right down to bare dirt.

Then gardeners arrive with truckloads of replacements, and plant mature trees twenty or thirty feet tall, ten foot-high trellises of blooming bougainvillea, hibiscus bushes covered with blossoms, beds of colorful flowers, lush green lawns. Within a few days, the grounds look completely different, and as if they've been there forever.

Friday, December 18

A mixed salad is on the table, next to a covered plate of marinating chicken breasts, pounded with garlic. The Beatles are playing on the iPod. Dick lights the charcoal in the grill, and we sit by the pool, sipping pinot grigio and waiting for the coals. Dick bought more poinsettias this week and arranged them around our table. It amuses me we have a Christmas tree and red poinsettias for the holidays.

I start thinking about Aunt Jane, who passed away this year. We spent the last ten Christmases with her. She was in a nursing home a mile from our house. Dick or I stopped by every day un-

less we were traveling, and often the three of us would have afternoon coffee.

But Christmas Day was always special. She would wear one
of her nicest dresses, and we would come over, bringing fresh
coffee and cookies. We'd go down to the library, joining other
residents and their families. I'm going to miss celebrating the holiday with her.

"It's going to be strange to spend Christmas Day without
Aunt Jane," Dick says. "I miss her."

"Are you reading my mind?" I say. "I was just thinking that
same thing."

"Oh sure, copying me again," Dick says.

"And it's going to be weird not to spend Christmas night with
Henry and Michele," I say. "We must have spent the last five
Christmas nights with them."

"Maybe they could come down," Dick says.

"I miss them," I say. We haven't seen them since the move.
Their restaurant has kept them too busy to leave town. "If they
left New Smyrna by five or five thirty on Christmas, they'd be
here by eight thirty. That's the same time they used to arrive at our
house. Let's call. They could leave here as late as two the next day
and still get back in time to open the restaurant."

"Might work," Dick says. He gets up to examine the charcoal. "These coals need some more time. I'll go call."

In a few minutes, Dick returns.

"Nobody there, of course," he says. "It's Friday. They're both
at the restaurant. I left a message."

Dick puts the chicken on the grill and we spend a quiet
evening outside at home, with a half moon peeking through the
trees, and the sound of waves breaking in the distance, and the
occasional distant noise of a train.

Saturday, December 19

I get the birds' traveling cage out, and Dick and I take Duckie and Blanco to their clipping appointment at Birds off Broadway. It's across the bridge, in a part of town we haven't been to, but conveniently just ten minutes away. Rita and the birds get along famously, and we make another appointment for two months from now.

As Dick is driving us home, my cell rings. It's Henry.

"Henry," I say. "You guys coming?"

"We can't," he says. "Christmas Day is a mess this year. And we've got to be at the restaurant early the day after. We'll miss you. But we'll get down there after the first. Promise."

We chat for few minutes, then say goodbye.

"So," I say to Dick, "It's you, me, and the birdies."

In recent years, Aunt Jane has been the only family member I have seen on Christmas. My sister and two brothers live in New England and like to stay there for Christmas. My father died over a decade ago. My mom is healthy and energetic, likes to travel, and spends Christmas on cruises where the weather is warm.

Dick's only family is Samantha and me. Samantha spends Christmas with her mom. Dick's mom died three months after we were married, his father two years after that. Dick's brother, Cam, was killed in a car accident when he was twenty. Dick was sixteen.

"Here's looking at you, kid," Dick says. "It'll be fun with just the four of us. I hope it gets cold. We'll have a fire in the fireplace on Christmas morning."

"We'll have to get stockings for the birdies," I say. Dick gives me a look.

We're driving over the bridge, back to the island. There is almost no traffic.

Dick says, "When do you think the winter people actually come here? It's the week before Christmas and Palm Beach is still pretty quiet."

"I was wondering that myself," I say.

Dick pulls the car into the driveway and gets the birdcage out of the back seat, and we walk toward the house. "Look in the window. Doesn't the tree look nice?" he says.

"Yeah," I say. "Now that we have a tree, and poinsettias by the door, don't you think we need a wreath?"

Dick rolls his eyes. We take the birds inside, drive to Publix. No wreaths. We go over the bridge to various stores, and all the wreaths are gone. Maybe next year we'll try earlier, I think.

Next year? Try earlier? What am I thinking? It occurs to me a florist might have a wreath. I call Flowers of Worth Avenue. No problem. One will be ready Tuesday.

Monday, December 21

It's eleven o'clock in the morning. Dick comes back from a trip to the post office. "You won't believe what's going on outside," he says. "It's just like Thanksgiving. People are everywhere. South County's full of traffic. Cars are honking again."

"So people are finally here," I say. "I want to see."

We go over to Worth Avenue. People are walking in twos and threes and fours. Tiny dogs peek out from carriages and purses. Palm Beach is bustling. How did all these people get here overnight again? It's a little unnerving.

Dick and I hop in the car to get supplies from Publix before it's too late. It's already too late. The parking lot, valet parking, and all the spaces on the nearby streets are full. I tell Dick I'll try again early in the morning.

Now I worry about being able to get a haircut. Lena's the

one person who understands my hair and she could be fully booked. Back home, I call Hair Classics. Adriana, Lena's daughter, answers the phone. "It's a good thing you called now," she says. "I just got a cancellation for this afternoon. Otherwise, Lena's booked solid until the first week in January."

Tuesday, December 22

"Listen to this," Dick says. He looks up from the Shiny Sheet. "Twice last night, at two different restaurants, a valet parker brought the wrong car to a customer, and the man drove off, not noticing it wasn't his car. What's the guy thinking? Gee, I thought I drove my Bentley here, but I must have driven the Aston Martin instead?"

The phone rings. Dick answers. "Yeah, yeah," he says. "Great. Terrific." He hangs up. "Henry and Michele are coming for Christmas," he says. "They'll get here around six that night."

The phone rings again. The wreath is ready. We walk to pick it up. It's decorated with holly and small gold balls and a red and gold ribbon. It looks festive on our front door.

Wednesday, December 23

Tonight we walk around town to see if there's any possibility of having dinner out. Taboo, Amici, Renato's, and Bice are completely full. Café L'Europe is three deep at the bar, and tables are jammed with large groups of people. We stop anyway and have a drink, standing among the festive crowd.

David is playing a Christmas medley. It's from his Christmas CD, and Dick buys a copy. For a couple that doesn't do Christmas, we're acting pretty strangely, I think. We now have a tree, a wreath, ornaments, and holiday music. We walk home. After seeing all the crowds, pasta and an outdoor fire are looking good.

Thursday, December 24

All our favorite restaurants are open on Christmas Eve, but Dick and I plan to avoid the crowds, stay home, and dine in front of our tree. In the early afternoon, we stop at a French bakery for a baguette to go with dinner.

A basket of crepe paper surprise balls is on the counter. As a kid, I loved unwrapping these. On impulse, I pick up two. A tag on the basket says nineteen dollars each. I put them back.

Curiosity overweighs common sense. "Okay if I buy one?" I ask Dick.

"Sure," he says. "You'd be a fool not to."

We buy a surprise ball and a baguette, leave the store, and walk to the lake.

At the end of the day, Dick says, "I thought we might go out tonight, instead of staying home. Walk around, see what's going on. I know it'll be way too crowded to eat, but maybe we could stop for a drink."

I'm a bit startled, but actually it sounds like fun.

"Great idea," I say. "It'll be fun to see the town all festive on Christmas Eve."

"And then I was thinking of going to church," Dick says.

"Church," I say. I am completely nonplussed. "Church?"

"There's an eleven o'clock service tonight at Bethesda-by-the-Sea. We can walk there," Dick says.

"Church," I say again. "Tree lightings, putting up a Christmas tree, church on Christmas Eve. Henry and Michele won't know who we are." I laugh. "Anyway, that sounds fine," I say. "Should we make something to eat for dinner, you know, for after we walk to a bunch of restaurants we can't actually get into, and before we go off to church?"

"I was thinking of one of our antipastos," Dick says.

We get to work to the sounds of Peter Cetera. I boil shrimp and make cocktail sauce, cut red and yellow peppers and carrots to dip in salsa. Dick puts Dijon mustard between thin slices of ham and Swiss cheese, rolls them up, and cuts them into bite-size pieces, then makes deviled eggs, and puts a bottle of pinot grigio in the icebox.

We stop by every bar and restaurant in the neighborhood, say Merry Christmas to the people we know who are working tonight, and have a drink at the bar when there is room. The restaurants are jammed. It's fun to be part of the festivity, and nice to have the antipasto and Christmas music waiting at home.

Now the birds are in bed, the antipasto is finished, most of the pinot grigio is in the icebox for another time. We dress for church and walk toward Bethesda-by-the-Sea. The weather is warm, the ocean is calm, and the stars are out. As we approach the church, I realize just about everyone has decided on church tonight. Cars are parked in every possible space.

"Looks like we may not be able to get in," Dick says.

"That's okay. We'll walk over to the nativity scene," I say.

As we get closer, I see people standing in groups on the lawn, some around the nativity scene. Seems quite a few other residents couldn't get in the church tonight. Rod Stewart and his wife and young son are standing by the manger as well.

Friday, December 25

"Think we can have a fire?" Dick says. "The temperature's already up to sixty."

"Well, it's a pretty chilly sixty. How about a little one?" I say. "I'll open some more windows. Want me to turn on the AC?"

It's Christmas morning. Dick builds a small fire and turns the tree lights on. We gather the birds and settle into the couch. Dick and I give presents to others at Christmas, but not to each other. This seems to be the only tradition we're sticking to this year.

We open boxes from Samantha and other family and friends. Finally, the only thing left under the tree is the surprise ball. Dick hands it to me, and I start unwinding the crepe paper. How much I loved these balls as a child. However, maybe I've glorified the experience. This expensive ball is a bust. Tied for best prize are a tiny cube of Bazooka bubble gum and a Santa tattoo. Well, not a complete bust. Duckie and Blanco have fun turning the paper into confetti.

We make lunch, dine with the birdies, and go for an afternoon walk to get a snapshot of the town on Christmas Day. The weather is sunny and warm. There's very little traffic, but couples and families are walking along the sidewalks. A lot of people are at the beach.

Now it's almost six o'clock. Dick and I are working in the kitchen. The doorbell rings, and in walk Henry and Michele, both carrying cardboard boxes. They head straight to the kitchen and put the boxes down. We all hug, everybody talking at once.

"We brought flatbread from the restaurant. For appetizers," Michele says.

"And vast quantities of wine," Henry says.

"How's my kegerator doing?" Dick says.

"Your kegerator?" Henry says. "It's my kegerator now." He grins. "It's gotten used to Heineken. Doesn't ever want Miller Lite again."

We all go into the living room. Michele looks around. "What's with the tree? You guys never had a tree before. And am I hearing Christmas music?" she says. David's CD is playing.

I start to explain when Henry says, "Quick, guys, where's the TV?" He looks at his watch. "We missed Boston and Orlando but the Lakers are on now. And then Phoenix."

"We don't have a TV," Dick says.

"Yeah, right," says Henry. "Come on, where is it? We gotta catch these games."

"We really don't have a TV," Dick says.

Michele looks at me questioningly. I smile. "It's true," I say.

"Henry," Dick says, "we can get the scores on the computer. Let's open some wine. And then we have a surprise." We take them to the guest cottage and show them the bumper pool table.

"It's not quite a pool table," I say. "But we can sort of have our traditional Christmas tournament."

We settle in chairs around the pool. Henry opens a bottle of red and pours us each a glass. "Sim Sala Bim," we say in unison, holding our glasses aloft.

We sit around the pool and talk, play bumper pool, eat the flatbread, walk to the beach, enjoy our traditional Christmas dinner of penne rigate with a vegetarian sauce, linguine with pork ragu, and a huge arugula salad. We drink superb wines, compliments of our guests.

We play more bumper pool. Henry and I, and Dick and Michele, have our classic dispute about which team is the reigning champion. Finally, quite late, we move the bumper pool table to the corner of the room, unfold the futon, and say good night.

Saturday, December 26

Everybody is moving slowly this morning, kind of like the day we moved. At least this time we could all sleep in. We go out for brunch at Taboo and then say goodbye. There are hugs all around, then Dick and I watch Henry and Michele drive away.

"That went way too quickly," I say. "I'm glad they came."

"Me, too," Dick says. "I miss seeing them."

Tuesday, December 29

I'm reading the Shiny Sheet. There's the usual article about not drinking and driving on New Year's Eve. But then I start reading out loud to Dick. "Police remind residents that officers will provide a safe ride home for those too impaired to drive. Police will help make other arrangements for those living outside of town limits."

Dick says, "In most towns, when the police offer you a ride, it's not to your home. Here they hand out business cards, drive you home. Palm Beach is some kind of alternate universe."

Thursday, December 31

Between Christmas and New Year's, we take time off from work and from the town. This is no time to go to restaurants or try to shop. Maurizio was right; people are everywhere. We stop in a bar once or twice, have some dances at the Leopard Lounge, but mainly stay around the house.

Now it's the last day of December. Dick and I usually avoid the crowds and stay home on New Year's Eve.

"What do you want for dinner?" Dick says. "I was thinking of making a pasta sauce with your braised pork. Maybe adding some mushrooms and cipollini onions."

"Sounds delicious. I'll be your sous-chef," I say. I've gotten many good ideas from Mark Bittman's cooking column in *The New York Times* and one of the best is braised pork. I cut the pork into small pieces, brown it (even though he says you don't have to), then cook it for a long time with onions, garlic, and red wine. The pork shreds, becomes exceptionally tender. I freeze this in batches, and we use it as a base for quick stews or pasta sauces, adding tomatoes or mushrooms or carrots or potatoes or cannellini beans or whatever else grabs our fancy.

"Thought we'd dine outside in front of a fire, with a bottle of Barolo," Dick says.

"Magnificent," I say.

Tonight, New Year's Eve, it's about seventy-five degrees. The sky is clear. We spend much of the evening outside, dining by the pool, listening to playlists Dick has made, and, between bumper pool contests, walk back and forth to the beach to moon-gaze.

It's just about midnight. We are sitting in lounge chairs, enjoying the last of the Barolo. Suddenly, there's the sound of explosions and the flicker of lights through the trees to the northwest.

"What's that?" I say.

"We must be under attack," Dick says.

The flickering lights grow bigger, and the explosions get louder.

"Must be fireworks," I say.

"Let's walk out on the road, see if we can get a better view," Dick says. We walk to the end of the block. Dazzling fireworks streak across the sky. The displays are huge and feel as if they are coming right at us. Fantastic colored bars of light explode out of balls of colors. Shapes drop out of shapes. As one display fades, out pops something even more spectacular, filling the entire sky.

"Do you remember seeing anything about fireworks in the paper?" Dick says.

"No," I say. "From the direction, it could be the City of West Palm Beach, but you'd think someone would have mentioned them."

"These can't be ordinary fireworks," Dick says. "Can they?"

"No way. I've been watching fireworks all my life and I've never seen anything like these. They're extraordinary."

The show goes on for thirty minutes. It's spectacular.

We watch the smoke from the last display fizzle across the sky and then head home to bed.

It feels good to be starting the new year here in Palm Beach. Despite the rough beginning, the decision to come here for a year has been the right one, at least so far.

eight

"I FEEL LIKE TONY SOPRANO WHEN THE DUCKS LEFT."

Friday, January 1

"New Year's Day," Pam says, "and we're reading the papers with our feet in the pool. It must be almost eighty degrees."

"A nice way to start the year," I say. "Those fireworks last night, the Shiny Sheet says, were donated by some guy for a party at the Flagler Museum. And by the way, they were designed by Grucci, the people who do presidential inaugurations and Olympic ceremonies. It also says the total cost for last night's show was in the neighborhood of two hundred thousand dollars. That's some neighborhood."

I'm surprised at how fast our year in Palm Beach is going. It has already been four months. First there were the several months of the island's emptiness. Then the sudden influx at Thanksgiving, followed by another lull, and then the festive buildup to the holidays. Now Christmas and New Year's Eve have already come and gone.

Meanwhile, the crime wave is continuing. "There has been another arrest at Publix," I tell Pam.

"That guy stealing beer again?" she says.

"Nope, this time the police arrested another guy after Publix employees saw him stuff a sandwich down his pants," I say.

Pam smiles. "You men."

Pam and I are now in the living room, again surrounded by boxes. The birds are helping us take down our Christmas tree. Well, actually Duckie is overseeing our work, and Blanco is wrestling with a piece of string on the coffee table. Pam's putting ornaments in cartons, and I'm grappling with lights.

"I want to have a tree again next year," Pam says.

"Then you shall."

Having a tree this year and taking it down today are stirring memories I had almost forgotten: images of taking down Christmas trees with my brother and parents and later with Samantha and her mother. I remember Pamela's and my first Christmas tree in New York. It was about four feet high and had almost no decorations. I think it cost six dollars, and when Christmas was over we didn't really have to take it down. It was more like just pick it up and throw it away.

Monday, January 4

I'm trying to put a book away. Every bookcase in the cottage is stuffed. There are stacks of books on the floor by the bookcases. Books are piled on window sills.

"If we fill these two cartons with hard covers that we're never going to read again, we can take the books to the Four Arts library and donate them," I say to Pam.

"Good idea," Pam says. "It'll give us a little space, at least get them off the floor."

"We're both book people, but why on earth did we bring all these down here?"

"I guess so we could donate them to the library," Pam says.

In about four minutes, we have two cartons filled. I dump them in the car and head to the library. The librarians seem happy with our donation, and I'm quite happy to have made another small step toward getting rid of stuff we don't need.

Driving home, I flash back to when Pam and I first dated. I'd just gotten divorced and had been living in my office for almost a year. All I owned was a couple of suits, a sport jacket or two, some slacks, and a bunch of tennis clothes. She lived in a tiny Manhattan apartment and didn't own much more. Neither of us owned a car.

Now we have two houses full of stuff. Just how does this happen?

Tuesday, January 5

The temperatures have suddenly dropped since yesterday, and even colder weather is coming soon. I need to find some socks and maybe a sweater.

I'm walking back from tennis today, and as I turn onto Hibiscus I see, about a block away, a tall guy dressed in a dark pinstripe suit and a fedora. He is holding one end of a leash.

As he gets closer, I see that on the other end of the leash there is a rather large pig. The pig is decorated with a little pink bow on its tail and tiny blue bows on its ears. As they pass, the man raises his hat and says, "Good afternoon." A moment later, I watch them both get in the driver's side of a Lexus. I find this scene a bit strange, but what do I know? The pig probably finds me strange. Actually, the guy walking the pig is probably the strangest of the group. Maybe it's the year of the pig.

Later, I tell Pam about the pig. Around six-thirty she says, "I've been thinking about that pig. Let's go to Renato's and get some pork chops tonight."

"That's a little strange," I say.

"I know. I was kidding, but let's go anyway," she says.

The town is suddenly quiet again. Not quiet like October, but certainly quieter than it was over the holidays. Renato's courtyard has several empty tables, but it seems a bit chilly so we decide to sit inside. Brad seats us, and Luciano arrives with a Peroni and a champagne.

As Luciano finishes telling us the specials, four people next to us get up to leave. One of the men looks familiar, but I can't figure out why. Suddenly, Brad materializes, the way he does, and says, "We hope you had the time of your life here tonight. Always a pleasure to see you again, Mr. Cunningham."

"Of course," I say to Pam, "that's Billy Cunningham."

"Billy who?"

"Right, sorry. Back in the day, Billy Cunningham played high school basketball in Brooklyn, then went on to North Carolina, and then the NBA. He is one of the NBA's fifty greatest players, a class act."

Pam smiles. "I knew all that."

Monday, January 11

This morning the temperature has dropped down to the forties. Pam and I take a quick walk over to the docks to catch up on our DOPES duties. The yachts now fill every slip, and it is apparently too cold for our sunbather.

Heading home along Brazilian, we see two men in the distance walking towards us. Four people walking on the same side of a residential street is a crowd in Palm Beach. The first man is walking with two of those small, silly-looking Chihuahuas with bows and ribbons and jewelry. He smiles and says, "Happy New Year," and we respond in kind.

The second man, who is still about thirty yards away, is fairly tall and has his sweatshirt wrapped around his waist like a kid walking home from the playground. Even from this distance, the walk is unmistakable. His fellow senators might remember the walk from the Senate floor. I remember it from a rather different floor, the floor of Madison Square Garden.

"You know who this guy is coming towards us?"

Pam looks ahead. "Should I?"

"It's Bill Bradley," I say.

"The guy who used to play basketball for the Knicks and then was a senator?" Pam says.

"The same," I say.

As he is about to pass us, I say, "Happy New Year, Mr. President."

He smiles, nods his head, and says, "And Happy New Year to you both."

After he goes by, Pam says, "He was a senator. Why'd you call him Mr. President?"

"Because," I say, "back in the early seventies, when number twenty-four Bill Bradley was helping the Knicks win two championships, his teammates nicknamed him Mr. President. I just wanted him to know people remember those times. I guess I was trying to thank him."

"I knew that," Pam says.

Tuesday, January 12

Tonight there has been a shift from the hall of fame to the hall of shame. Pam and I are sitting at the end of the very busy bar at Bice. The town is filling up again.

Next to me a young lady, cute as a button, starts talking to us. "You guys look cold. Isn't this weather freaky? I'm originally from

Connecticut, but this is really cold for down here. My condo doesn't have any heat. I used to have one on Worth. It had heat. You guys live here all the time?"

She's reminding me of those early FedEx commercials where the guy talked so fast. I'm starting to get a headache. Actually my teeth are starting to hurt. Thankfully, she wanders to the other end of the bar. Philippe comes over to us, grinning, and says, "She's some piece of work, huh?"

I look at him. Philippe smiles. "Don't you guys know who you've been talking to?" He says her name.

"Who?"

He says her name again and explains, "She's one of Tiger Woods's friends."

"Well, I've never heard of her, but I'm happy she's moved along," Pam says. "She could certainly talk."

Talk? I felt like I was being beaten up. "Let's get out of here and have a quiet dinner at home by the fire, just the two of us."

We walk home briskly along Peruvian, passing Club Collette. The Club Colette Bentley Barometer is hovering around ten.

Wednesday, January 13

Overnight, Mother Nature sends south Florida record-breaking cold, news which the media pounce on like snow leopards. The frigid weather makes newspaper, radio, and internet headlines (and, we assume, TV). Reports tell of snow in Florida, freezing temperatures, orange crops being destroyed, farmed fish freezing to death, frozen iguanas falling out of trees. Frozen iguanas falling out of trees?

"I don't need this media blitz to tell me it's cold," Pam says.

"You mean because the fireplace is roaring, the heat is set at eighty degrees, the electric fireplace is blasting in the bedroom, and it is still freezing in here?"

"Our blood is way too thin for this."

To my horror, I realize our outdoor plants must be hosed down and the more fragile ones, like the orange tree and the lemon bush, covered, to prevent damage from the possible freeze.

"I'm going out to hose down the plants outside. Maybe move and cover a few."

"I'll help," Pam says. "We'll only be out half as long."

So, looking quite ridiculous, suited up with layers of clothing, various scarves, and some mismatched gardening gloves, Pam and I uncoil two hoses and begin our mission to save the planet, or rather our planting. Pam works her way up the west side of the pool. I work my way up the east. We meet at the north end. There, on the ground next to a fishtail palm, looking very much like it has just fallen out of the tree, is an iguana. It is not a big one. Maybe two feet from tip to tail.

"Is it dead?" Pam asks.

"Can't tell." I pick it up carefully by the tail and carry it to a sunny area of the pool deck to warm up. Pam leaves a hibiscus flower for food and a little saucer of water within reach. "Let's see if the sun warms him up."

"I'll come out later to move him to keep him in the sun," Pam says, "if he's still here."

Pam has moved our visitor twice to make sure he stays in the sun, but now the sun is setting. We go out to see how the iguana is doing. "He's moved a little. He must be alive," I say, "but he won't make it through the night out here."

"No, he won't. It's supposed to get much colder. Let's move him into the guest house," Pam says.

I move the iguana, and Pam moves the water and hibiscus

into our tiny guesthouse. "We'll sacrifice our bumper pool games for a night or two to see if we can save this guy," I say, "although I'm not sure if we're Dr. Kildare or Dr. Kevorkian."

Thursday, January 14

Early this morning, Pam and I check on our guest. I think we're both expecting to attend an iguana memorial service sometime later in the day. The water and the hibiscus are right where Pam left them. The iguana, however, is nowhere to be seen. This is a very small guesthouse, with really no place to hide.

"He's got to be under the futon," Pam says.

I get down on the floor and look. "Nope. And he's not under the bumper pool table. Or the bureau. Or the bookcase."

"This is really weird," Pam says.

I move the futon away from the wall. Nope. Yep. "Here he is. He's not under the futon, he's clinging to the back. Got to be alive to do that," I say.

I carry him back to his untouched water and hibiscus. Our new friend's eyes are open and he's somewhat more responsive.

Pam checks on him several times throughout the day. His eyes open and close a couple of times. He moves a little bit. That's it. This is going to be his second night in a heated environment. I think if he doesn't get better by tomorrow, he's done.

Friday, January 15

Pam makes some tea, and the two of us walk out to see about the patient. Déjà vu. The water and hibiscus are there but the iguana is nowhere in sight. "Can't fool us," I say and walk right to the back of the futon. "Nope, he's not here," I say.

Pam starts laughing. We start a search. "This is unbelievable. There is no place for this iguana to hide in here," she says.

We finally discover our friend clinging to the inside of a cloth draped over a table. He doesn't seem to want to let go, so I leave him there. He is definitely alive.

The weather warms up considerably during the morning. A noontime check reveals that the patient has left the tablecloth and moved to the floor. He's quite still at the moment, but he's been moving around more so he must be doing better. It's time to put him back outside in the sun and whatever will happen, will happen.

I move him to a warm area by the pool. Pam and I both go out to check on him after lunch. Our iguana is gone. We check the nearby bushes and trees, but he is nowhere to be seen.

"I feel a little like Tony Soprano when the ducks left," I say.

"He's happily back home with his family now," Pam assures me, "and the weather is supposed to warm up. He'll be just fine."

Sunday, January 17

Pam and I are in The Society of the Four Arts Chinese Garden. A quiet pond forms the centerpiece. Water lilies are in full bloom, and a school of koi are chasing each other around the water lilies. The garden is filled with papyrus, bamboo, and flowering jasmine.

Pam goes over to read a plaque on the wall and says, "Dick, you've got to read this."

I walk over, put my arm around her, and read over her shoulder. When we're both finished, the Master of Understatement observes, "I guess gardens are important to the Chinese."

"I guess," Pam says. "They feel a person cannot even 'grasp the reason for existence' without gardens."

"I'm not sure about that," I say, "but I like the part about having a 'quiet space free of tension ... an aid to contemplation.'"

We sit on one of the benches. We're quiet. Pam and I have spent more time in parks and gardens down here than anywhere else we've lived. But then, the whole island is a garden. We're always surrounded by beauty here. I think we're both happier, more relaxed.

I feel that tonight, to relieve my separation anxiety from the iguana, Pam and I should visit Taboo. Hugh and Bobby are behind the bar. Two women are admiring the koi's cousins swimming around in Taboo's large tank. Hugh points out a new arrival, a tiny puffer fish. One of the women asks Hugh if he has to take care of the fish and clean the tank.

"Are you kidding?" he says. "Those fish would be dead in two days if I were in charge. Tanks A Lot comes and does everything."

Two seats away, a third woman chimes in. "Oh, aren't those people wonderful? They designed a floor-to-ceiling custom tank for me right in the middle of the wall-to-wall bookcase in my library, filled it with all kinds of fish and plants, and now they take care of it. I don't have to do a thing! They even rake the sand at the bottom of the tank."

Raking the sand on the bottom of a fish tank is a job I never thought about.

Wednesday, January 20

This morning's Shiny Sheet reports, "Police were called to a condominium after the manager discovered there had been rummaging through a doorman's desk." Rummaging? Was this first- or second-degree rummaging, I wonder?

We had a day or two of milder weather, but it's gotten cold again, so before we go out tonight, I check the pool deck to see if our iguana is back. He is not. Maybe Pam was right and he is happily back home with his family. We bundle up and run the several blocks to Taboo for dinner. Luck is with us, and Kevin says someone can seat us right next to the fireplace. Michael, super server and *Godfather* scholar, takes us to the table.

As we're sitting down, Pam says, "Aren't you freezing?"

"Warm as toast," I lie. "Look at these people coming into the restaurant. They're not cold. They're not even wearing coats. You're wrapped up like Nanook of the North and you're cold? You're a wuss."

"Whatever. I am freezing," she says.

"Pam, I'm goofing," I say. "No one else in Palm Beach walked here tonight. They leave their properly heated house, get into a warm car, get out of the car three feet away from the front door, then walk into the restaurant while somebody else parks their car. We walked three blocks in an icy wind. You're not a wuss and, trust me, I'm not warm as toast. I'm freezing, too."

"You're a wuss," she says.

Dinner is over. Pam and I are both finally warm, so of course it is time to go outside again. Parked in front of the restaurant are three Ferraris in a row—an old red 308 GTS, a red F430, and a magnificent dark blue Scaglietti with tan hides, a valet parker's dream come true.

I actually had an old 308 GTS, and, no, it wasn't expensive. A new Miata would have cost more. I bought it from a neighbor, and Pam and I had a great deal of fun with it. From long Sunday drives to overnight trips to out-of-the-way inns, I put the Ferrari through its paces.

After two years, I sold it back to the same neighbor for about the same price. I loved looking at it, listening to it, driving it, even washing it. In those two years, Pam and I both became big Ferrari fans.

We walk to South County and see two more Ferraris parked right in front of Amici, a yellow F355 Spider and another red 308. We already have a Bentley Barometer. Maybe we'll have to institute a Ferrari Factor as well.

Friday, January 22

Pam looks up from this morning's Shiny Sheet and says, "John Pizzarelli is at The Colony Royal Room. I'd like to go see him."

"Me, too."

We haven't seen him since The Carlyle in New York several years ago, and we haven't been to the Royal Room since we moved. What is the matter with us? Roger Everingham and Rob Russell have created one of the best cabarets on the planet, and we haven't been in four months? I call and book for two.

At the end of the day, we turn off our computers, shower and dress, and then walk several blocks to see Mr. Pizzarelli. The Royal Room is intimate, a perfect cabaret setting. There are only about eighty seats. Tonight, dinner guests are taking most of the space. A few other show-only people are just arriving, and the hostess escorts us to a table near the stage. I order us a bottle of champagne.

The quartet consists of John on guitar and vocal, his brother Martin on bass, Larry Fuller on piano, and Tony Tedesco on drums. I feel like a guest at a private concert. I can actually watch Mr. Pizzarelli's hands zipping along his guitar. From Gershwin to James Taylor, Broadway to the Beatles, the evening is a potpourri of selections. Between songs, in typical cabaret style, Mr. Pizzarelli tells stories about the music and chats with the audience like we just dropped into his living room.

Walking back from the show, we see Maurizio in front of

Amici.

"*Buona sera*, Maurizio. What is with all the Ferraris in town all of a sudden?" I ask.

"This is Ferrari week," he says. "It happens every January."

"I thought that was at The Breakers."

"Yes, yes, the Cavallino Classic is at The Breakers," he says, "but the best show is here. Sunday night, all these amazing cars will be heading home and driving right by Amici."

As if we needed an excuse to return to Amici. I tell him we'll be back for the show.

Saturday, January 23

More than a dozen major art galleries are located along Worth Avenue and in its connecting courtyards. Openings are held throughout the year, but there are more of them in January and February.

Tonight we have been invited to a Hunt Slonem opening at the DTR Modern Gallery. His oil paintings of birds, row after row of them, are favorites of Pam's. I have no idea why we were invited, but Pam is thrilled, and I'm interested in how gallery openings in Palm Beach will compare to those in, say, New York and San Francisco.

The gallery is crowded. Guests have dressed for the occasion. Both men and women are in one-of-a-kind outfits. One woman is dressed completely in silver, from her stiletto heels and sequined dress to her purse the size of Montana and the sparkly eyeglasses she must have stolen from Elton John.

A tall, exceedingly slender man is wearing a black suit made out of some kind of animal, a long white silk scarf, black sunglasses, and a fedora. I start looking around for the guy with the pig on a leash. This feels like his kind of crowd.

Almost no one is looking at the art. Everyone's busy drinking champagne and schmoozing and posing for photographs. Pam leans around a gentleman large enough to be a planet and mouths, "Too many people." I nod. She squeezes by Jupiter and we're out.

Walking home on Peruvian, we notice that the Club Colette Bentley Barometer is holding steady at an even dozen.

Sunday, January 24

Pam and I are at a table on the outdoor terrace at Amici, facing South County Road. They have the outdoor heaters working tonight. Along with some Cerignola olives, a bottle of Allegrini Palazzo della Torre, a plate of linguini with shrimp, and a plate of spaghetti Bolognese, Pam and I are enjoying the sounds and sights of exotic Italian cars.

We can hear the Ferraris' exhaust notes from blocks away. If the light is green, they speed right past us. But if they catch a red light at Peruvian or Worth, we can admire them for a minute and then watch and listen as they accelerate through the gears and head out of town. Yet another dinner and floor show at Amici. No cover.

Monday, January 25

Melissa, whom we first met when she was down to open her house before Thanksgiving, is back in Palm Beach with her husband Mark for January and February. We have seen them several times at the tennis courts, and Mark and I have hit together a couple of times.

Today, as Pam and I are walking off the court, they wave us over. Mark says, "Our boat got here yesterday. We'd love it if you would come aboard and have a drink with us this evening."

Pam says, "That's very nice. We'd love to. What can we bring?"

"Bring yourselves. Any time around six is fine. It's the blue hull at the Peruvian docks, but I'll see you coming."

Walking home, I say, "If it took her three days and the help of a housekeeper to open the house, how long do you think it took them to open the boat?"

Pam says. "Stop. It'll be fun to see their boat, and they seem nice. They like each other."

After work we dress, and I grab a bottle of Montrachet as a gift. As we get to the docks, Mark is walking towards us. I guess he did spot us. He welcomes us and leads us down the dock to a beautiful blue hull Cape Horn trawler that's got to be eighty feet long. Melissa is on the aft deck with drinks and hors d'oeuvres. The four of us talk tennis and boats and Palm Beach. After a few minutes, Mark says, "You guys want a tour of this tub?"

"If this is a tub, the boat we lived on was a sink," I say. "We'd love a tour."

Mark and Melissa lead us through sliding glass doors to the main salon, which has several seating areas and a built-in fifty-inch television. The television is tuned in to some game show, and there are two monkeys, live monkeys, sitting on one of the couches, watching.

"The crew?" Pam asks. That actually should have been my line.

"No, no," Mark says, "that's Roberta and Hal. They live aboard. Wherever this boat is, in Palm Beach or Newport or the Caribbean, you'll find these two. They might as well be crew."

Our host and hostess continue the tour down a wooden spiral staircase that leads to the master stateroom with a king-size bed, plush carpeting, and another huge television. While the tour is continuing, I'm thinking Roberta is probably the monkey in the yellow dress, which means Hal is the monkey wearing what looks like a diaper. What the hell are they doing here, and why doesn't Hal know he should dress for company?

We're finishing up the tour in the U-shaped galley that makes the kitchen in our cottage look like a can of Sterno and an ice bucket. I say, "Melissa, this is a magnificent yacht, but I've got to confess I'm a bit curious about Roberta and Hal. There has to be a story there."

Melissa says, "Mark likes to say we bought the two most expensive monkeys in the world, and they just happened to come with a yacht. The truth is, the monkeys belonged to the previous owner of the boat, and when we bought it last year, they were just part of the deal. They came with the boat."

Our final stop is the fly bridge. Drinks in hand, the four of us settle into the cushioned seats and talk and admire the glittering nighttime lights across the lake in West Palm Beach. The whole time, I'm wondering if the monkeys are actually watching that game show or if they've changed to the Nature Channel or maybe slipped in a *Planet of the Apes* DVD.

Tuesday, January 26

It is now late afternoon and we're out walking. There's a chill and the faint smell of seaweed in the air. The residential block we are on is long and empty. Parking is allowed on both sides of this street, but there isn't a car parked anywhere. However, two guys are getting ready to valet for a private party. They are setting up their chairs and a board full of hooks for car keys.

We walk past and on toward the lake. Next to one of the mansions on the water, there are dozens of trucks and even more people. Three gigantic tents are being put up, and two portable generators hum in the service road.

"This has got to be some over-the-top Palm Beach wedding," Pam guesses.

I walk over and ask three guys unloading flat screen TVs who is getting married. No one. It turns out all this excess is being unleashed for an upcoming Super Bowl party. Of course.

Pam and I head back along the same road. As we get close to where we saw the valet parkers, we see the first car arriving. One after another, people pull up to the valet station and stop. Soon there is a line of cars, all waiting to be valeted.

Pam says, "There are twenty empty spaces on this street alone. Nobody parks their own car?"

"Probably a Palm Beach ordinance against it," I say.

Thursday, January 28
The town is again as full as it was over the holidays. During the day, people busy themselves shopping on Worth Avenue. Everyone, it seems, is carrying shopping bags from Ferragamo and Cartier and Gucci and Valentino and Giorgio Armani.

We're strolling along Worth and it is crowded, but a crowded sidewalk here looks quite a bit emptier than a crowded sidewalk in New York.

As we're approaching Via DeMario, a woman says, "Oh, look, Via DeMario. That's Palm Beach's best Italian restaurant! William and I had the most romantic dinner there."

I think not. This Via DeMario isn't a restaurant. It's simply the name of the Via.

Sunday, January 31
It's late for us. There are only about fifteen minutes left in the month. Pam and I are walking home from The Chesterfield after

an evening of dancing. We're a block and a half from The Chesterfield when Pam says, "Wait a minute, stop please."

I stop and turn.

"My knee really hurts," she says. "I don't know if I can make it home."

"Are you kidding?" I say.

Her look explains that she is not.

I say, "Take off your heels and see if that's any better."

She does and it's no better. "I'm really sorry," she says.

"Don't be stupid," I say. "You don't have to be sorry. Give me your shoes and put your arm around me. We'll do a slow three-legged-race thing. No hurry. If it hurts too much, tell me."

We are making awkward but (Pam assures me) fairly painless progress towards home. She starts laughing and says, "We're going to be arrested. This is so stupid. I'm so sorry."

I say, "Pam, relax. If we're not arrested for public awkwardness, we'll be home in five or six minutes and we'll ice your knee."

It turns out to be probably ten minutes, but soon we are home and Pam is resting in bed with ice on her knee. We'll see where, or if, we stand in the morning.

nine

"THEY'VE ORDERED PIGGY PIE FRECKLES TO LEAVE."

Monday, February 1

I open my eyes. Morning light is filtering through the gauzy bedroom curtains. My bedside clock reads seven thirty. Dick's side of the bed is cool, so I know he's been up for a while. I stay under the covers, hoping last night's knee incident was just a dream.

Finally, cautiously, I bend my right leg. It feels okay. I get out of bed and start to walk. Not good. I limp for a few steps, thinking maybe I can stretch it out, but the pain gets worse. I make my way into the living room.

"Doesn't look good," Dick says.

"No, it doesn't," I say. "I'll call Dr. Keith's office as soon as they open."

I call and they fit me in at eleven. Dick drives me. Dr. Keith examines my knee, sends me across the hall for a laser treatment, tapes my knee, smiles. "Nothing serious," he says. "Just ice that knee twice a day, stop the gym and the daily walking, don't do anything that makes it hurt, come in for tape and laser treatments twice a week, and you should be walking normally in maybe six or eight weeks."

I pretend this is fine. I know I'm fortunate, the injury is temporary, and surgery won't be necessary. Secretly, I'm stunned. Walking is a major part of our life this year in Palm Beach. So is dancing. In the car going home, I silently start crying and turn my face to the window.

"You okay?" Dick says.

"I'm okay."

He looks over. Very softly, he says, "Hey, look at me. Are you crying?"

"I'm being a baby," I say. "I mean, I know I'm lucky it's not serious." I wipe tears away but they keep coming. "But this is our one year in Palm Beach. We walk everywhere here. Walking is what we do here."

"So, we haven't driven much. We like our cars. Now we have an excuse to drive," Dick says. "And we can stay home more. It'll be fine."

"I'll miss dancing," I say.

"So we'll dance at home. I'll just hold you, and we won't really move."

We're both quiet for a while.

"I'm really sorry to wreck our year like this," I say.

"Don't be silly. You're not wrecking anything," Dick says.

I know on the one hand he's right. This isn't a big deal. But on the other hand it's not just me who's suffering here. I may have to deal with the pain, but Dick's temporarily losing a walking and a dancing partner.

Also, walking is when we talk, when we hash out ideas, smooth out our misunderstandings, come up with revelations. Walking has always been a vehicle for managing our life together. We've figured out a lot as we walk along. For the next six or eight weeks, walking won't be a big part of our life.

Saturday, February 6

Our life is different now. Although Dick still takes walks and plays tennis and goes to the gym, I do none of that. Instead, I hobble around the house, ice my knee twice a day, and mostly try to stay off my feet, determined to heal my knee as fast as possible. Not walking and not exercising gives me lots of extra time to work, and I'm way ahead on several projects, but I miss my regular life.

Although we both like to cook we're not used to doing it nightly, and this evening, our sixth night in a row at home, I browse through last Wednesday's *The New York Times* dining section, looking for inspiration from Mark Bittman.

"Listen to this," I say to Dick, "Bittman's got a pasta that drinks."

"Well, anything that drinks sounds good to me."

"He says to put dry pasta right in the sauce, short pasta like ziti works best," I say. "Think the pasta would really cook enough?"

"Probably," says Dick. "But you might need extra stock or wine."

I look back at the article. "That's what he says. Make the sauce first, add dry pasta, stir it off and on, add broth or wine when you need to. Want to try it?"

"Sure," Dick says. "Do we have any short pasta?"

I go in the kitchen to look. "No ziti," I say. "But we have penne rigate."

"That'll work."

Dick comes into the kitchen carrying the Nano and its little speaker stand and turns on Peter Cetera. He opens a bottle of Amarone and pours us each a glass. I make a salad. Dick sautés garlic and onions, scrambles some Italian sausage, adds some chopped red peppers, cannellini beans, a little arugula, some vegetable broth, and some Chianti we use for cooking.

I have gotten used to the smallness of this kitchen and quite enjoy cooking here with Dick. I wish I could adapt so easily to the rest of the cottage. After all these months, I'm still bruising my elbows in doorways.

"This stuff needs to simmer," Dick says. "Shall I light a fire?"

We go into the living room, Dick lights a fire, and we sit and talk for an hour or so. Dick periodically goes into the kitchen to stir.

Eventually, the mixture turns into a sauce, we both go into the kitchen, and Dick dumps in the pasta. "This could take a while," he says, and pours us each more wine, adds more Chianti to the sauce. For the next twenty minutes we sip Amarone and the penne drink Chianti. Dick keeps stirring, adding wine and broth. The aroma is intense. The penne turn reddish brown.

We move a table in front of the fireplace, Dick puts another log on the fire, sets the Nano to random, and we dine. I have always liked the ceremony of sitting down and enjoying a meal, the formality of a tablecloth and napkins, lighted candles, sparkling wine glasses.

The music tonight is eclectic. First the Gipsy Kings, then Carly Simon, Bankie Banx, Michael Bublé, Survivor, Aaron Neville.

"This Bittman stuff is great," Dick says.

"Yeah," I say. I wiggle a piece of penne onto my fork and taste it. "The pasta is intense. The sauce gets totally into it."

"Makes boiled pasta seem bland," Dick says. "But we might get a bit crazy eating this. I added an awful lot of wine."

We finish our dinner and watch the fire turn into glowing embers.

"Think if we bundled up we could sit outside for a few minutes, look for shooting stars?"

"I'm game," Dick says.

We put on heavy sweaters, get a blanket, go to the two chairs in our front yard. It's a dark, moonless night, still and cold. The air is rich with the aroma of our wood fire. The night sky glitters with stars. In the distance, waves break.

"I'm sorry about my knee," I say.

"Don't be a dope," Dick says. "It's a reminder. We're alive. We're basically healthy. We need to use our time well, good knee or bad knee."

"Thanks." I think about time, how fast it goes now. Too many people have already died. Yet, despite making so many resolutions to use time better, I am still capable of wasting it, occasionally in huge quantities. And I still spend too much time doing things I don't want to do. Will I ever learn, I wonder?

Sunday, February 7

I've had two laser sessions with Dr. Keith, and today my knee feels slightly better. I hobble out to the garden to water and clip. Keeling is impossible, but it feels wonderful to be back outside. I miss the gym.

The other day, a brochure from the Armory Art Center came in the mail, and this afternoon I idly browse through it. I learn the center is just across the bridge and hosts art exhibits and classes. I read the course descriptions.

When Theo and Deborah were here last fall, Deborah, who teaches art, set her easel up outside. She asked me if I wanted to paint with her. I told her I didn't know how, but I'd try. She gave me a small canvas and helped me paint a hibiscus. It was fun, and the painting looked kind of nice, and she and Dick both said I should take lessons.

I didn't pay much attention to them. I'm not really a hobby person. And I haven't been in a classroom in years. But now the idea intrigues me. Why not spend time taking art lessons? Maybe it would be fun.

"I'm thinking of signing up for an art class," I tell Dick.

He looks at me and smiles. "It's about time."

"What do you mean?"

"You're talented," he says, "but that doesn't matter. You'll like the class. You'll have fun. That does matter."

I sign up. My first class is in less than three weeks. I feel excited and somewhat anxious. Like our impulsive move here, little do I know how important these classes will become to me.

Monday, February 8

The weather continues to be unseasonably chilly, and this morning we read the papers in front of a fire in the living room. Dick is skimming an article about the Knicks in *The New York Times*, Duckie on his shoulder. Blanco is on my forearm, shredding the outside edge of the Shiny Sheet as I try to read it. An ice pack drips from my knee.

"Munchkin Manners Dinner Socials," I report. "They're formal dinners for kids in first to fourth grade. The next one's at Café L'Europe. Boys have to wear jackets and ties, girls, white gloves and party dresses. Where do you think one buys white gloves in this day and age?"

Dick says, "Aren't first graders like, five or six? How do you think they keep the kids at the table?"

"There's more," I say. "Chaperones teach the kids 'table manners, party manners, standing and sitting postures, tips on making introductions, friendship etiquette, and the fine points of receiving and giving gifts.'"

"Maybe I should sign up," Dick says. "My party manners need help, and I like getting gifts."

The town hall clock chimes ten. The windows are closed against the cold, and the sound is muted. The clock only chimes during the day. There must be a town ordinance against chimes when people might be sleeping. I love telling time by that clock. It makes our clocks seem unnecessary, at least during daylight hours. Another possession we don't need.

Homemade biscotti is part of our breakfast ritual. We ate our last two pieces this morning, so I go into the kitchen to make a batch. I turn the knob to preheat the electric oven. Bang. There's a huge noise, and the inside of the oven bursts into flames.

"Dick," I yell.

He comes running. The flames disappear.

"What happened?"

"I just turned the knob and, whoosh, the oven was full of flames."

Dick crouches to look through the oven window and then cautiously pulls open the door. The bottom heating element is in charred bits and pieces and is lying on the oven floor.

"Time to bother Eduardo," Dick says.

"I hope he remembers who we are," I say. We haven't needed him since he did his magic last October.

"We'll see," Dick says, and goes off to make a call. He reappears. "Eduardo knew exactly who we are. A stove guy's coming this afternoon."

The stove guy miraculously appears when he says he will and inspects the oven.

"You just need a new element," he says.

"Those flames didn't damage the inside?" I say. "There was a real fire in there."

"It's okay," he says. "I've seen that happen. It looks scary, but that's just how they burn out sometimes. I'll order you a new one. Should be here in a few days. You won't have an oven, but the burners still work." He turns one on to show me.

Later, Dick comes into the office. "You know, that wine dinner at Amici is tonight. Can you walk that far?"

"Yes, yes, yes," I say. "Plus, I'd love to get out of the house."

At the end of the day I shower and start to dress. Normally, I wear high heels and a skirt or a dress when we go out. But my knee is a big mess of tape going this way and that, and pants seem a better option. I don't have many pairs of pants but I find some that work. I slip into high heels and my knee rejects them. I go searching for a pair of flats.

We walk slowly to Amici, with me holding on to Dick's arm and limping slightly. The wine dinner is in Amici's private room and hosted by Bob and Gudrun, owners of the Livernano and Casalvento wineries in Tuscany. Gudrun introduces the wines offered with each course, and Bob and the dozen or so of us at the table enjoy drinking them.

After dinner, we stop at the bar for a nightcap. Maurizio, Amici's owner, is near us at the bar going through little envelopes.

"*Buona sera,*" I say. "What are you doing?"

"*Buona sera.* These are heirloom tomato seeds my mother sent me from Italy, from the little town where I was born. I'm going to plant them tomorrow."

"I love fresh tomatoes," I say. "I eat them right off the vine, whole, with salt."

"Me, too," he says. "Hey, do you want some seeds? Can I give you some?"

"I'd love to grow tomatoes down here," I say.

"Excellent." He disappears into the kitchen with the envelopes and reappears with several tiny containers of tomato seeds, each one labeled. "Now you will have Italian tomatoes in Palm Beach. Excellent."

Wednesday, February 10

This winter is colder than normal for this part of Florida and much colder than either of us expected. It still hits the forties some days, but predictions are for warm weather soon.

On Groundhog Day, I wasn't out but Dick said he didn't see a groundhog. I don't think Palm Beach actually allows groundhogs. According to an ongoing story we have been following in the Shiny Sheet, the town does not allow pigs to live here, either. The one parading around on Hibiscus last month must have been a tourist.

There has been a problem with a potbelly pig, one Piggy Pie Freckles, living in an apartment in town. Some neighbors objected, and the Code Enforcement Board ordered Piggy Pie Freckles to leave. But apparently the pig and the pig's owner did not get the message.

However, according to today's Shiny Sheet, after a bit of intrigue, some definite pig sightings, and the threat of a one hundred and twenty-five dollar per day penalty, Palm Beach is once again pig-free. Cats, iguanas, doves, and even renters can live here. No pigs.

It's lunchtime, and I'm getting cabin fever from being home so much. I say to Dick, "My knee's better. What about a short walk, and maybe even lunch out somewhere?"

"Your call. I can always get the car if you can't walk back."

We start inching our way toward Taboo. We come up to a

corner, and a woman in a Bentley breezes right through a stop sign, giving a slight honk on her horn and holding up a hand to alert everyone she is not going to stop.

"Did you see that?" I say.

Dick looks at me. "Because of your knee, you haven't been out walking since the February people arrived. This stuff is normal. The Bentley Bunch apparently answer to different traffic rules than the rest of us."

"I guess we'd better walk carefully," I say. "Not just because of my knee."

We walk by Amici, and it's full of people.

"We may not get into Taboo," I say. "Look how crowded Amici is."

"The town really changed once February started," Dick says. "It's more crowded than over Christmas." He looks at his watch. "But it's two o'clock. Taboo might have room."

We get to Taboo. It's slammed.

"Trevini?" Dick says. "That's pretty close."

We walk there. The restaurant is quite full, but Gianni finds us a table. Next to us sit two men, both probably in their early fifties. One says to the other, "So what's going on with them? Why all the problems?"

His companion replies, matter-of-factly, "I just think he spoiled her. You know, buying her all those Ferraris."

Dick looks at me. "Only in Palm Beach," he whispers.

When we leave Trevini, we follow an older couple out of the restaurant. They were sitting near us, and the woman had a blue, basket-style handbag on her lap, which I admired. When we get outside, the woman reaches into the purse, lifts out a tiny dog, snaps a leash onto his collar, and gently sets him down. Off the threesome goes, past Trevini and on into Saks.

"So that dog was inside the restaurant the whole time, on that woman's lap," Dick says.

"And now they're all going into Saks. I still can't get used to seeing all these dogs inside stores."

Dick says, "Dog, dogs, dogs. I can't get used to seeing so many dogs everywhere, and so many tiny dogs."

My knee is holding up nicely, and we make our way home, slowly. Now that I'm out I see what Dick is talking about. There are people everywhere, and tons of traffic. The town feels fuller than ever before.

"It's funny," I say, "to have the town change so fast. This traffic is amazing."

"Yes, the February people are here," Dick says. "But not around us. Our little cottage still has empty houses on three sides."

Friday, February 12

Now that I have signed up for an art class, the Armory Art Center has started sending me e-mails about upcoming events. The current exhibit, I discover, is a retrospective of the work of Muriel Kaplan, a local portrait artist. I ask Dick if he wants to go and he does, so we get in the Corvette and he drives us across the bridge to West Palm Beach. It turns out the Armory is less than ten minutes away. Because of my knee, Dick lets me off and finds a parking space, and then we walk in. The show is called "Face of Humanity."

Impressive sculptures are arranged in a spacious exhibit hall. Most are on pedestals, and some are of family members and friends of the artist. Paintings, drawings, and mixed-media pieces hang on the walls, often accompanied by written observations from the artist. Occasionally, a handwritten message is scrawled in large letters right across the canvas. One says, "Our pursuit of youth blinds us to the possibilities of age."

"That should be on billboards all over Palm Beach," Dick says.

"The town would never allow billboards," I say. "But it's a great message. Too bad it's not the American way."

Dick gets the car. The day has turned summery, and he's put the top down. He picks me up and drives back toward Palm Beach. As we approach the bridge, I think how driving back onto the island now feels like coming home. Just then I hear a throaty "zoom" coming from behind us.

"Ferrari?" I say.

"Nope, a black Lamborghini," Dick says. "Look to the right. It's about to pass."

The car roars by with its top down. Up ahead the drawbridge light goes red. We come to a stop alongside the Lamborghini, and I can see the whole gorgeous car: the giant wheels, the blackness, the singular shape and design.

As the bridge comes down and the gate goes up, Dick gives the Corvette's engine a provocative little rev. Next to us, tires squeal and the engine screams. The Lamborghini bolts ahead of us like an Air Force F-22.

"These kids today," Dick says.

Saturday, February 13

Tonight is the first in quite a while it's warm enough to eat outside. It's a lovely evening, dark now. Our backyard family of doves is asleep. Earlier, we saw them head to their sleeping place in the giant seagrape tree when we went to play bumper pool.

During the fall months, they would line up along the cottage roof in the evening and stare down at us. It took us a while to realize this staring contest meant they were waiting for us to leave the area so they could go to bed. One night, they got tired of their vigil and flew into the boughs of the seagrape while we were watching, revealing where they slept. They're used to us now.

We're outside by the pool, sipping glasses of Barbaresco and admiring the wood fire Dick built in the fire pit. The playlist selection for tonight includes Peter Cincotti, Matt Dusk, Steve Tyrell, and Tony DeSare.

Dick gets up and checks on the charcoal in his Weber Smokey Joe. "Still a little too hot," he says. "Maybe another couple of minutes." He comes back and sits down. We're waiting for the coals to calm down so we can grill onion and red pepper kebabs and skewers of marinated shrimp.

"Looks like something's going on over there through the trees," I say. "See that red light in the distance?"

"Yeah," Dick says. "There are lots of red lights. Looks like a fire engine."

I hear the rough noise of diesel engines. "Sounds like a fire engine," I say. "It's going quite slowly, like it's looking for something."

A searchlight scrapes across the sky. Another points along the tree line. Soon there are many searchlights. Clearly, people are looking for something in the yard north of us. I hear voices.

"What could be going on?" I say. "Think they're after someone?"

We both stand up to get a better view. The lights are moving much too slowly for a chase, but they are definitely getting closer. We walk toward the far end of the pool and look through the branches above the fence bordering our property.

I see maybe seven or eight firemen, in full gear, milling about. They're holding monster flashlights, obviously looking for something, and getting closer and closer.

One of them shines his light over the fence onto our pool area. He waves the light about, zeros in on our fire pit, and yells, "I have the source!"

"Oh, my God," I say. "It's us."

The firemen gather on the far side of the fence. One of them keeps a light focused on our fire pit. Another finds us with his flashlight and tells us to stay put, they'll drive the truck around to our street.

"Do you think we're in trouble?" I say.

"I don't know," Dick says. "A fine for an illegal fire? Maybe jail time for endangering the neighborhood? Deportation?"

The fire engine stops in front of our house, red lights revolving, and the firemen file along the side of our house to the scene of the fire. They seem relieved. We, on the other hand, are both rattled.

Dick says, "We are very, very, sorry. We've been having fires like this since September. We didn't know it was a problem."

"It's not a problem," says the head guy. "We just got a call from a woman who smelled burning wood so we followed up on the call. It's what we do."

Two of them walk over to the fire pit. "It can't get much safer than this," one says. "Maybe you could move it a little bit away from the planting, but it's fine."

"We just need some information to fill out our report," another says, "and then we'll leave you alone." He asks some routine questions, then apologizes for bothering us.

Dick says, "Well, as long as you're here, why don't you all stay for dinner?"

The head guy eyes the Smokey Joe and says, "I don't think you could grill enough on that thing for all of us."

"Okay, you're right," Dick says, "but we have lots of beer."

The firemen give us some scattered applause, say maybe another time, and head back to the station.

Dick pokes what's left of the coals, adds more charcoal. "This is going to take a while," he says.

"That's okay," I say. "I need time to recover."

Dick pours us another glass of wine. We both start laughing. "Wonder if we'll be in the Shiny Sheet Police Report," Dick says.

Sunday, February 14

The weather continues to be warm, and I'm admiring the view from the yellow room. The hibiscus plants somehow survived the severe cold, and now there are pink and red and orange flowers. Blanco's on my knee, enjoying a neck massage. Duckie's on the floor playing her favorite game, rug-fringe tug-of-war.

"Want to hear something crazy?" Dick says. "The police report that a man was cited for leaving the scene of an accident. He crashed his car through trees, a wall, and onto someone's yard. Then he used his cell to call a cab to take him home. Left the car right where it was."

I start to answer but am interrupted by a loud, throaty engine noise. It's very close, sounds like it's next door. Definitely a Ferrari. Dick and I get up and go toward the kitchen window to take a look. A second Ferrari starts up. Out the window and through the hedge, I see two Ferraris, a blue 360 and a red 430, parked next door. The two cars muscle their way out of the driveway and roar down the street.

"Guess we finally have neighbors," Dick says.

We tend to stay close to home on Valentine's night to avoid the crowds. We have made an avocado and Bibb lettuce salad and boeuf bourguignon and set a romantic table out by the pool, complete with candles.

"Think it's okay to have a fire," I ask Dick, "after our event last night?"

"Of course," he says, and sets up some wood in the fire pit.

I set the table while he lights the fire and we dine under the stars to a late-fifties playlist: Elvis, The Platters, Mickey & Sylvia, and Buddy Holly. I notice Dick has built a particularly small fire tonight.

After dinner, we walk to the beach. The sea air is almost balmy, and I can tell spring is on its way. The ocean is flat; moonlit clouds are drifting slowly westward. Apart from the occasional Loch Ness monster, we almost never see other people here late at night, but tonight there's someone in the distance moving towards us along the water's edge.

"Look at that," Dick says. "It's a couple."

Sure enough, a rather formally dressed couple is dancing slowly along the beach. She has on a long white dress and he is wearing a suit, but they both are barefoot. They look to be in their early twenties and are performing a classic waltz in time to the breaking waves. I look around for a camera crew, thinking this might be staged, but it's just the two of them, together on the beach, lost in love.

Wednesday, February 17

I read in the Shiny Sheet this morning that a homeowner has reported to the police that his house has been battered by at least eight eggs. These February people.

Over the weekend, I drove to the mainland to get seedling containers and a soil mix, and this morning I plant the tomato seeds Maurizio gave me. The weather forecast calls for another bout of cold, so to be safe I keep them inside, lined up on a table in front of the living room windows. I won't leave them there for long. The cottage is far too small to be used as a greenhouse.

My knee is improving. Dick and I now take several short walks each day, timing them carefully so I can get back home before I start to feel sore. I am also learning where every available bench or ledge is, where I can sit and rest. Dick is patient with my slow pace and frequent stops.

I do feel old when I have to stop so often, and I get glimpses of how daily life might be when I am older. I'm grateful this limping is supposed to be temporary, although I know sometimes these things don't go completely away. I still have periodic back pain from a diving accident when I was a teenager, and a shoulder injury when I was forty continues to haunt me.

Tonight we snail our way over to Renato's. For the second time since we moved here, because the town is so full and Renato's is a long walk, Dick has made a reservation. Brad asks us where we have been, and I give a quick explanation about my knee. Then I hobble after him as he escorts us to a table.

We enjoy a quiet dinner. As we are paying the check, Brad comes over and says, quite formally, "Mr. and Mrs. Myers, your car will be here in just a minute."

"Would that be the Bugatti or the Lamborghini?" Dick asks. Brad knows we always walk to Renato's.

"No, I'm serious," Brad says. He turns to me. "Mrs. Myers, I watched you limp in here. It would be my great pleasure to drive you home. I'm leaving now, anyway, so I'll go get my car and meet you at the entrance."

I feel embarrassed and try to talk Brad out of it, but he insists. "Renato's is, after all, a full-service establishment," he says.

Brad goes to get his car. Dick and I walk out to the sidewalk, and Brad pulls up at the curb. I get into the passenger seat, Dick gets into the back. As he pulls the car away from the curb, Brad turns to us and grins. "Of course, now that I have your complete attention, I can give you a taste of why I rarely miss a Grateful Dead concert," he says, popping in a CD.

Our cottage is close, so all we get to hear is "Jack Straw." As Brad pulls away, "Friend of the Devil" begins. We don't do concerts but do like the Grateful Dead.

Saturday, February 20

In late January, Dick and I tried to make reservations at The Colony's Royal Room for another cabaret night, only to discover that just about every performance for several months was sold out. We found one opening, for Johnny Rodgers and his band. We'd never heard of him but read that he's won numerous awards, including the Great American Song Contest. We made reservations and tonight's the night.

All eighty-two seats in the intimate room are taken. Johnny Rodgers and his band members Mud Man, Mad Dog, and Cotton Eye Joe entertain with *Great American Songbook* standards, Elvis and Billy Joel hits, and some of Johnny's outstanding originals, including "Mary Jean," "The Best of You in Me," and "One More Moment." Dick will no doubt download these from iTunes as soon as we get home.

When the show ends, Rob Russell, the Royal Room's entertainment director, stands up and says, "Everyone's invited to a cast party, just through those doors, in the Polo Lounge. Come dance to the Switzer Trio."

"What's that about?" I say.

"I don't know, but if we can eat there this late, let's go," Dick says. "I'm starving."

The Polo Lounge has a bar, a dining area, and a small dancing area. The kitchen is still open, and we are taken to a table near the dance floor. Fast dancing is still out of the question because of my knee, but Dick and I dance slowly several times while we wait for our food.

Johnny Rodgers and his band have settled in at a nearby table. When they are finished with dinner, to our surprise, Johnny gets up, walks to the front of the room, takes the mike, and sings a few songs. The setting is casual and even more personal than the Royal Room. Our waiter explains that the cast party happens every Saturday, and the Royal Room headliner always makes an appearance and performs a few numbers.

"I guess we never came to a show on a Saturday," Dick says.

"It's funny the things we still don't know," I say, "after being in this town for almost six months."

Sunday, February 21

Dick and I emerge from Taboo after a leisurely brunch and walk along Worth Avenue. All the parking spaces are filled.

"There are even more exotic cars than usual," Dick says.

"And I don't see any non-fancy cars," I say. "Two Ferraris, no, make that three, a Lamborghini, two Maybachs, plus a whole bunch of Rolls-Royces and Bentleys."

"You missed the two Maseratis," Dick says. "And there's a Lotus and an Aston Martin."

"Every single one of these cars is showroom-clean," I say.

"Well, that Ferrari has some dirt on its right front wheel."

Almost all the cars I am looking at can go about 200 miles an hour. They do zero to sixty in three or four seconds. Just what one needs on an island where the top speed limit is thirty miles an hour. Whenever I read about a brand-new model of an expensive or exotic car, I invariably spot one soon after on the streets of Palm Beach. No wonder there are so many exotic car dealerships just across the bridge.

"Your knee okay to walk over to the lake?" Dick says.

"It seems fine," I say, and we continue on to the lake.

"Let's find a bench," he says. "We've been remiss in our duties as DOPES."

We settle onto a bench under one of the banyan trees. The town docks are as full as can be, with mega yacht after mega yacht.

As I gaze out at the bridge to the mainland, which is just north of the docks, the bells sound and the drawbridge goes up.

I flash back to all the times we drove over that bridge for our Palm Beach escapes. The feeling of getting off I-95 and then getting onto the bridge was something. I could feel the real world slip from my shoulders and get left behind on the mainland.

But I knew it was always a brief escape, could never be where we really lived. In fact, I was sure we would never even want to be here for more than a few days. Sometimes we know so little about ourselves, I think. I'm glad we still have more than six months ahead of us here.

Tuesday, February 23

February is supposed to be the busiest month of the year in Palm Beach, and so far this holds true. The stores, streets, and restaurants are full and the town feels crowded to me, which is bizarre.

When we lived in New York, crowded meant twenty women in line for a dressing room at Bloomingdale's, or a movie queue snaking around the corner and up the next block. Going to a Knicks game involved jostling with thousands of people fighting for space on the escalators in Madison Square Garden. Somehow I've gotten so re-adjusted that if four other women are in the shoe department at Saks, it feels busy to me.

The restaurants are so full this time of year it's impossible to get in without a reservation on weekends. We've learned that Monday and Tuesday after nine are the best nights to be spontaneous. Tonight we stop by Café L'Europe late, and they have a table for us.

"Lots and lots of people, night after night," Dick says.

"I know the restaurants need the business, but I'd sort of like these crowds to go away," I say.

"It's funny," Dick says. "It wasn't long ago we were looking forward to the season. Now we want it to be over."

"You know what's even funnier?" I say. "You and I were here before these people arrived and we'll be here after they leave. We've already been here almost six months. Many of the seasonal people only see Palm Beach for six or seven weeks, or maybe even less. It's starting to feel like the on-season people are the visitors, not us."

We finish dinner close to eleven and walk the block to the beach. The evening's so beautiful we walk along the ocean for several blocks and turn east onto Worth Avenue. My knee is getting better and I walk more, but still slowly. As we pass Saks, the door opens and Terri, who works there, walks out.

Dick says, "Terri, you lose your watch? Saks closes at six."

"Not tonight," she says. "Not for me, anyway. I just spent two hours with a private shopper whose name you would certainly know if I could mention it. I can't."

"So Saks opens the entire store just for this one shopper?"

"Exactly. And it is well worth it for the store. And for me." She smiles.

Thursday, February 25

I drive to my first art class today, where I hope to learn how to paint with acrylics. The instructor e-mailed his students a list of necessary supplies, and I have everything with me, I hope. I haven't been to a class of any kind in many years and feel excited and a little scared.

The classroom is big and high-ceilinged and full of paint-splattered easels. I love how it looks. The teacher is a young guy. There are seven other students besides me, all adults and all different ages. He asks us to introduce ourselves, and I learn there are several other true beginners like me.

The teacher talks to us about types of brushes, shows us how to mix primary paints to make a whole range of colors, then suggests we try to paint a still life he has set up. The class is three hours long but goes by quickly.

"So, how was it?" Dick says when I walk in the door.

"I really liked it," I say.

Dick smiles. "I knew you would."

Tonight Dick and I are walking slowly toward The Chesterfield. I'm encouraged by the progress of my knee, but life is still not quite normal for us.

We hope to dance tonight, but it won't be to "Hungry Like the Wolf" or "Shout," one of my all-time favorite dancing songs. It'll be more like "Lady in Red" and "Second Time Around." As we pass The Invisible Man's House, I see the telltale glow of a television.

"Dick," I say. "Look in that upstairs window. He could be in there watching TV."

We walk a little further, and I hear a cacophony of squawking. It's above me somewhere, coming closer.

"What's that noise?" I say.

"I have no idea," Dick says.

Dozens and dozens of bright green birds appear overhead. They land on the phone wires and on the palm fronds directly above us.

"Those look like parrots," I say. "But they can't be. Isn't it way too cold here for parrots? Don't they live in South America or something?"

There must be at least sixty birds now perched above us. They are beautiful. We watch them for a while, then walk on to The Chesterfield, take a seat at the bar. Michelle, John, and Lou are working this evening.

"Michelle," I say, "Dick and I just saw a flock of birds that look like parrots. They landed on the telephone wires. Have you ever seen them?"

She laughs. "Yeah, I've seen them. Aren't they noisy? They're parrots, green-cheeked Amazon parrots, to be exact. I think it began with pet parrots that escaped, but now there's a huge colony of them."

John, who is listening, adds, "They're protected. The entire island of Palm Beach is a designated bird sanctuary. And some people say a designated nut sanctuary, as well."

Adam plays a slow song, and we dance. After a minute or so, another couple gets up to dance. They are doing a *Dancing with the Stars* thing, with kicks, and twists, and spins, and dips. They look like professionals.

The music stops and we go back to our stools. Lou, John, and Michelle are standing there, expressionless.

"No jokes tonight?" Dick says.

"No jokes," Lou says, "but some of us here do have a serious question: Were you two dancing to the same music as that other couple?"

Sunday, February 28

The tomato plants are sprouting, but it is annoying to have them cluttering up our living room. This morning the weather is warm enough that I take them outside, repot them, and line the little plants alongside our pool.

Now Dick and I are curled up on the couch with books. Dick is reading *Gone Tomorrow*, a Jack Reacher I just finished. I'm reading *Lifeguard* by James Patterson. Part of the book takes place in Palm Beach, and some of the characters are actually our favorite Taboo bartenders.

"Dick," I say, "I'm reading about people at the Taboo bar. Cindy and Bobby. And those two guys who used to work there, Andy and Michael." I hand Dick the book, open to the page. "See, they've been written into the story."

"Nice," Dick says. "So we'll go ask Bobby about it tomorrow night."

ten

"I'M LOOKING AROUND FOR A WOOD CHIPPER."

Monday, March 1

"So you were a star in one of James Patterson's novels," Pam says as we take a seat at Taboo's bar.

Bobby laughs. "Yeah, that's when Michael and Andy were still here. You saw he mentions those two as well as Cindy and me. He has lunch here a lot."

"How did you find out you were in it?" I ask.

"He just came in one day with four signed copies of the book, one for each of us. He's a really nice guy," Bobby says.

"Well, if we decide to do a book about Palm Beach, you'll be in it," Pam says.

Bobby laughs. "Okay, just be sure you spell my name right."

Tuesday, March 2

Spring has definitely sprung. Daytime temperatures for the next several days are forecast to reach the high seventies. It is hard for me to believe we had all those second thoughts about moving down here. I love living here. I read in the Shiny Sheet the police have cited a man in town for "illegal spearfishing." Illegal spearfishing two blocks from Neiman Marcus and Saks.

Well, the town is still jumping even if some of the fish apparently are not. When Pam and I are on our walks, Worth Avenue is still crowded and restaurants are full. There are plenty of February people still in town. Don't they know it's March?

This morning, the Shiny Sheet has even more photographs of people than usual at balls and parties and various charity events.

I'm looking at all these people and I say to Pam, "This is scary. I've seen some of these faces so many times, I'm beginning to recognize them."

"I think that may be the point," Pam says.

I'm so obtuse. Of course that's what these people are doing. It's a different kind of Facebook. And along with the Shiny Sheet, you can see these same faces in *Palm Beach Today*, *Palm Beach Illustrated*, *Palm Beach Life*, *Palm Beach*, *Palm Beach Society*, *Palm Beach Young Society*, and, although it may be hard to believe, *Palm Beach Pet Society*.

It's funny, if we didn't get the Shiny Sheet or pick up one of these magazines, we would never know any of these faces or that these events had even taken place. I don't think I've seen any of these faces other than on the printed page.

Wednesday, March 3

We're surviving quite well without television. In fact, we are outside more at night, we read more, talk more, and probably think more. We caught some World Series games at Bice and Taboo last fall. Otherwise, Pam and I have been TV-free.

But this month may pose a problem. "March Madness," the NCAA basketball tournament, is coming up. Tonight I want to try and catch the second half of an ACC Tournament game at

Taboo or Bice. Pam says she's going to check the score on her computer before we head over.

A minute or so later, she comes out and says, "The game's on in the office."

"What game is on in the office?" I say.

"The Duke game."

"What are you talking? The game is on what?"

"My computer," Pam says.

I follow her into the office. I have no idea what she is talking about. The game is on her computer live and in color with announcers and everything. I can't believe it. "How is this happening?" I ask.

"I'm not sure, but we can watch the game here if you want."

"If this magic can work on my laptop, we can watch it out by the pool," I say.

So, we take my laptop out by the pool and watch the second half. Who needs TV?

Thursday, March 4

I start to take an espresso outside by the pool but stop at the screen door because there is an animal on the guesthouse roof. This animal does not look friendly or familiar to me. I close the door rather quickly. I'm standing safely inside looking out when Carmen, the lady who helps us tame the chaos in the cottage each week, comes over and says matter-of-factly, "It's just a fox."

Of course, a fox, why didn't I expect that? Iguanas, pigs, foxes. Palm Beach the wildlife sanctuary.

It's now lunchtime and I'm at Sandwiches by the Sea picking up some soup and a sub for our lunch. Maybe a chef salad for the fox. A man and a woman come in. They are discussing what to order when the woman sees my soup on the counter. She turns to me and asks, "Is the soup any good here?"

"The soups are homemade and all very, very good here," I say.

She looks at me for a second and says, "You mean for a place like this, in Florida."

I look at her for several seconds. "No, ma'am, that is not what I mean." Goat Breath. "What I mean is the soups here are very, very good. Period." Have a nice day.

As it happens, about a week ago, I almost bumped into America's Mayor, Rudy Giuliani, as he was coming out of Sandwiches by the Sea with a couple of bags of subs. You know if a New Yorker like Rudy gets his lunch there, the place has to be good.

Friday, March 5

As lunchtime approaches, Pam says, "You want to take a ride in the car? My knee's been keeping us inside too much, and it's a beautiful day."

"The car? Do we still have a car?"

"Yes, let's play hooky for a few hours, drive to Delray," Pam says. "We'll have lunch. And I can pick up some art supplies I need at Hand's."

I like the part about lunch.

I drop the top of the Corvette, and we head south on A1A. It is a lovely, leisurely drive. The speed limit is thirty-five miles an hour. Not exactly a workout for the Corvette, but a fine speed for us to be able to talk with the top down and enjoy the scenery. The drive runs south with the ocean on one side and beautifully landscaped mansions on the other. Occasionally, we cruise under canopies of trees or through a public park. No one takes this route if they're in a hurry.

After about thirty minutes, I turn onto Atlantic Avenue, Delray's main drag. "Quite a change from Worth," Pam says.

"A lot more casual and a lot more crowded, you mean."

"But plenty of restaurants. Your choice."

I pull in and park in the lot behind Hand's. "Let's do Cubano," I say. "Nothing like that in Palm Beach." We walk over and ask the hostess for a booth inside, away from the crowds. Pam orders portobello and shitake mushrooms drenched in garlic sauce with warm pressed Cuban bread, and I pick the picadillo, a Cuban stew of ground beef, tomatoes, peppers, olives, and lots of garlic. We will have no problems with vampires today.

Finished with our lunch, we make our way through the crowds to Hand's, an art and office supply store that's been in business since the 1930s. It's one of our favorite places to shop. The people who work there are always happy and helpful.

Pam picks up things she needs for her art class. She's started a painting of a bird. It's realistic and quite good. I purchase a one-million-dollar bill that looks quite authentic. Always good to have an extra million in your wallet, especially in Palm Beach.

I'm now driving north again with the top down in cool, sunny weather. What a simple, wonderful pleasure this is, driving around with the person I love. I don't want to go back to work yet. Directly across from the Ritz Carlton, I make a hard left into a small shopping area.

"What's the matter?" Pam says.

"Nothing."

"Why are we stopping?"

I nod towards the shop directly in front of our car, the Ice Cream Club.

"Ice cream? You want to get ice cream?"

"Why not?" I say. "When was the last time we had an ice

cream cone? Ten years ago?"

"It was in Blowing Rock," Pam says. "That time we couldn't stop laughing."

"Right," I say. "And neither of us can ever remember what we were laughing about."

I get a strawberry cone. Pam gets a chocolate chip mint, and we sit on a bench and eat our ice cream like little kids.

Saturday, March 6

We're working on the plants around the pool and talking.

Pam says, "You know, we've tried to take advantage of everything the town has to offer, the parks, dining, dancing, cabaret, museums—"

"—galleries, exhibits, tennis, the ocean, the lake," I say. "But we've still missed stuff."

Even in Palm Beach, you can't have everything. I missed the Bob Newhart and Tony Bennett shows. I know Pam wanted to see the Moscow Ballet, though I'm okay with missing that one.

My thoughts are interrupted by the sound of the phone.

I walk inside and pick up.

"Dad, it's Samantha."

"Who?" I say. I love the sound of her voice.

"Dad, stop. Quick question. If I come down to Palm Beach in a couple of weeks, are you and Pam going to be there?"

"Of course. If you're coming down, we'll be here no matter what. Is this a vacation?"

"I wish, but no. It would be for just two or three days, and it's not definite."

"Whatever it is, we're here," I say.

We talk for a few minutes, and she has to run and promises to keep us posted.

Monday, March 8

The morning is drawing to a close. "Are you ahead of schedule or behind?" I ask Pam.

"Actually, ahead a bit," she says.

"Remember last March when we met Samantha in Tampa for the Yankee spring training games?"

"Yes, of course," she says.

"Remember last week when we drove to Delray and had ice cream?"

"Yes, I do. Where is this going?"

"Well, it's another beautiful day, and there's a spring training game starting in about an hour at Donald Ross Stadium. Looks like an easy forty-minute drive north."

Pam says, "Give me fifteen minutes to finish up here and let's go."

I've seen dozens, maybe hundreds, of baseball games. My first game in Yankee Stadium, I was four and my brother Cam was eight. My father took the two of us, just the men. I didn't know what was going on, but I got hot dogs and Cracker Jack and orange soda. It seemed like a good deal.

We're here. I pull in and park on the grass, and we walk to the ticket window. Lots of good seats are still available. I buy a couple of tickets, and we're in. Easy.

The Marlins and the Twins are playing today, and our seats turn out to be right in the middle of dozens of Minnesotans. None of them seem to have any interest in the baseball game. These people are nonstop talkers, and their accents are straight out of Fargo.

One woman is loudly explaining that she doesn't know the name of the town she has been staying in all week, but that it's easy to find. I'm looking around for a wood chipper when Pam nods to an empty section, lots of empty seats. We slide out and walk up the steps.

"We're higher up, but the game's easier to see," Pam says.

"And it's quiet," I say. "I was not suffering those fools gladly."

Pam and I each get a hotdog and a beer. It's the law.

We know nothing about either team, but the boys of spring are hitting and catching and running. As always, I think back over a lifetime of baseball games. What a relaxing, enjoyable way to spend a spring afternoon. The Marlins win the slug fest and we make our way to the car. No crowds. No hassles.

Driving home, Pam says, "I like going to spring training games better than going to games at Yankee Stadium or even Giant games in San Francisco."

"Me, too, but you've to go to Yankee Stadium at least once a summer. Like hot dogs and beer, it's the law."

"I know, but today's game seemed so simple, so uncrowded. More like just a game."

Tuesday, March 9

Pam and I are walking over to Café Boulud for a special wine tasting event: Italian reds. It is never hard to get me to go out, but when Italian reds are in play, it is hard to get me to stay in. It's a beautiful evening, almost balmy. As we're walking by a tall ficus hedge, I hear a man's voice say, "Honey, you're not washing the car with bottled water, are you?"

I don't hear the reply.

I look at Pam. "Either a very big bottle or a very small car," Pam says.

"What do you think it would cost to wash one of those giant SUVs with Pellegrino?" I ask.

"I don't know. That he even asked the question is very

strange, even in Palm Beach," Pam says.

Pam and I cut through the courtyard and into the lounge at Café Boulud. The tasting has not quite started, so we're just standing by the bar when I hear a man sitting behind me say, "This baby cost more than my Ferrari."

I turn to see what this guy has with him that could possibly cost more than a Ferrari. He's pointing to his watch, and then adds, "It's waterproof to thirty meters."

"Waterproof?" I whisper to Pam. "Are you kidding? Who's going snorkeling or taking a dip in the pool with a quarter of a million dollars strapped to his wrist?"

Thursday, March 11

The tomatoes are now living outside. I've been out by the pool working on them, trying to keep them staked up. As I'm coming in for an espresso refill, Pam is hanging up the phone. "Who was that?" I say.

Pam is smiling. "That, Mr. Myers, was your daughter."

"And?"

"And she's coming down for a visit in about two weeks."

Pam is still wearing a wide smile, so I say, "And?"

"And she's bringing Jason, a 'gentleman caller,' as she put it, whom she wants us to meet."

"Oh my. A guy she wants us to meet? Oh my."

"Serious, maybe. Interesting, definitely," Pam says.

I head out to hit some balls with Todd. Pam's knee is still a little fragile so almost all of my tennis is with Todd, and he's beating me up. Palm Beach drivers are still making my walks to tennis an adventure. It's a volatile combination of the winter people driving way too fast and looking at nothing, the locals driving normally, and the tourists driving way too slow and looking at everything. But I make it to tennis unscathed, and Todd runs me around for an hour or so.

I thank him for the abuse and drag myself over to the Gatorade machine. I'm rehydrating and watching some guy out on the soccer field taking shots on goal. He shoots, his friend in the goal rolls the ball back to him, and he shoots again. All I can see is his back, but whoever this guy is, he has a very good right foot. The shots are not wrist-breakers, but they have some pace, and he's putting the ball right in the corners.

Carrying what's left of my Gatorade, I start the walk home. Passing the soccer field toward Royal Palm Way, I catch sight of the soccer player from the front. It's Rod Stewart. That makes it two for two on Rod Stewart sightings, but still zero for two on Jimmy Buffett sightings.

Saturday, March 13

Pam is supposed to walk a little more each day. She's still getting treatments twice a week and has made definite progress. We're out and about today, just north of the bridge, at The Society of the Four Arts grounds. Pam points to people milling around in the grass in front of the library. "What do you think this is?" she says.

"Some kind of fair or something?" I say.

We walk over. Homemade canopies and card tables are placed all along the edge of the lawn just west of the King Library, and all the booths and signs are homemade. "All of these things are for sale," Pam says. "The orchids, hand-painted tablecloths and napkins, pottery. This is cool."

The scene is decidedly low-tech and very old-fashioned, so we fit right in. Two different booths are selling only ladies' hats.

"I'll buy you a hat," I say.

"A hat?"

"Yes. I want to buy you a hat."

Pam starts sorting through the dozens of different hats, trying one on now and then to show me. She is being silly. I love it. A floppy light blue cotton hat with a wide brim is her final selection. It really looks nice on her and quite springlike and makes us both laugh.

We spend time browsing and people-watching and enjoying the spring weather.

"We've talked about it before. There is something nostalgic, something simple, almost quaint, about life in Palm Beach," Pam says.

She is absolutely right, although before we moved here I don't think either of us would have put "quaint" and "Palm Beach" in the same sentence. But living here we have discovered a parallel, low-profile universe that is the opposite of the high-profile ritz-and-glitz that we expected to find. We've not only discovered it, we're somehow connecting with it.

Tonight I want to go to Amici. Maurizio makes me laugh and (what's new?) I'm hungry and thirsty. The restaurant and the town are still quite crowded, but tonight Pam and I actually recognize Jimmy Buffett finishing dinner at one of the bar tables.

Beth, behind the bar, is laughing because she sees we finally recognize Mr. Buffett. He comes to the bar.

"Dick and Pam are big fans of yours," Beth says, "and this is the third time they've been here when you were here."

"The last time it was raining and you held the door for us," I say rather stupidly.

Jimmy laughs. He says something like "I was holding the door for her" and gestures toward Pam.

"They write books on the Caribbean," Beth says.

This last statement opens the show. Yes, we all knew Bankie Banx on Anguilla and Foxy and Ivan on Jost Van Dyke. Somebody mentions Bomba's Shack, and Pam tells of her first visit years ago to Bomba's for a *Travel + Leisure* article. She admits she was a little surprised that the restaurant's primary decorating theme consisted of bras dangling from the ceiling.

We all swap stories and outrageous memories of the Willie T, a floating saloon off Norman Island in the British Virgin Islands. Pam, Jimmy and I are all laughing like a bunch of expats at some island beach bar. Except we're this sort of square old couple, and Jimmy Buffett is, well, Jimmy Buffett.

Sunday, March 14

This morning I was up early and set all the clocks to spring forward. I'm scanning the Shiny Sheet's special advertising section on "Health and Beauty Solutions." I've noticed this section from time to time but have never really looked at it. I say to Pam, "Have you seen this beauty section?"

"The one with ads for liposuction and body sculpting and boob jobs?"

"That's the one," I say. "But I was reading somewhere else the other day about adjustable breast implants."

"Adjustable?" Pam says. "You mean you can adjust the size of your boobs to fit your mood?"

"I guess. And they also had six-pack ab implants, male pectoral implants, calf implants, dimple creation, nipple enlargement, and, my favorite, the Brazilian butt lift."

"Instead of getting your butt lifted today," Pam says, "why don't we go see the inside of one of those houses we walk by all the time?" She shows me a picture of the house in an ad. "There's an open house here today."

"That isn't a house, it's a mansion," I say. "Do you think it's okay just to go and look?"

"Why not? The real estate agent has to be there anyway, and how many people that go into these open houses actually end up buying them do you think?"

"Probably none," I say, "and it'd be fun to see the inside. I'll have my butt lifted another day."

A little after noon, we're walking up the impressive driveway to an expansive two-story white stucco house. At the entrance, double doors, arched and ornately carved, open into a two-story round foyer with marble floors.

Inside, the real estate agent, Stephen, greets us, and we sign in. He ushers us into a living room with a twenty-foot ceiling and more marble floors. "This, as you can see, is a serious house," he says. "Notice the two fireplaces, one at each end of the living room."

"Notice them?" I say. "You could fit a Volkswagen in each of them."

"And you could easily have a cocktail party for a hundred in this room," Pam says.

"Yes, it is a gracious house for entertaining," Stephen assures us.

Across the room, two-story wall-to-wall windows and several sets of French doors look out to a flagstone patio, a pool with an elaborate fountain at one end, and manicured flower beds.

The rest of the house is just plain huge. A wide stairway out of *Gone with the Wind* rises to the second floor, but there is also an elevator, not a little elevator, a hotel-sized elevator. Upstairs are two guest bedrooms, each with its own elaborate bathroom.

Then we come to the master suite, which actually makes me laugh, it is so ornate and over decorated.

"Quite roomy, and nicely decorated," I say to Stephen.

"Oh my, yes. Notice the his and hers bathrooms."

Notice? His bathroom is black and gold, and there is a shower with eight showerheads. Hers is decorated in gold and blue and silver and white. A raised soaking tub sits in an alcove. There is a makeup table with more jars, tubes, and brushes than I have ever seen.

The master suite also has a kitchenette with a built-in espresso-maker, microwave, sink, and icebox. The owners would, I believe, call it a mini-fridge.

The his and hers closets are enormous. Each is the size of a large bedroom in a normal house. The closets are organized and extremely neat, with clothing either on handsome hangers or perfectly folded, doubtless by someone other than him or her. In the woman's closet, at least two hundred pairs of high-heeled shoes are lined up next to each other, shelf after shelf, arranged by color.

We go back to the first floor by a different set of stairs and make our way to the billiards room with mahogany paneling, leather easy chairs and sofas, three giant TV screens, and two full-size pool tables with black felt. Yes, there is a temperature-controlled wine room at the south end. "This is where the men play," Stephen says.

"And apparently where the men pee, as well," I say. I've just opened the door to a black marble bathroom with gold fixtured showers, a sauna and steam room, two massage tables, and three urinals.

Next we check out the kitchen, which is, of course, outfitted with top-of-the-line equipment. There's a double-door refrigerator. Another separate freezer. Several Sub-Zero refrigerator drawers, two commercial dishwashers, three sinks, two islands, and a

Wolf six-burner gas range. Henry and Michele would love to have a kitchen this size in their restaurant.

We move on to the formal dining room. The walls are covered in red silk and sport gilt sconces. Two glittery chandeliers hang above a polished mahogany table, which is surrounded by twenty upholstered chairs.

"You must come see the guest house. It's quite special," Stephen assures us.

"Thanks, Stephen. I'm sure it is, but this is far too important a house for us," I say.

"I can appreciate that," he says. "You know who owns it?" He says the name, which is a name we recognize. Surprisingly, it is not Imelda Marcos.

"And," Stephen adds, "George Hamilton's brother owns a house just a few doors away."

With that tidbit of information, we head out the door. As we are leaving, a woman who has apparently been viewing the guest house with Stephen's partner is also leaving. "There is another open house just down this street," she says, and we all introduce ourselves. Her name is Katie.

"A nice little place," I say nodding towards the palace we have all just left.

Pam says, "Did you see that billiards room? Two billiards tables, three TVs, and the walk-in wine cellar at one end? That was something."

Katie says, "Actually, that's what I do for a living. That's why I'm in Palm Beach this weekend."

"You play pool for a living?" I say.

Katie laughs and says, "No, I'm down here taking care of a wine cellar for a gentleman over on South Ocean."

"Taking care of?" Pam says.

"Yes, my job is to replenish the collection, add some new selections, and generally make sure the cellar is in tip-top condition. I fly down from Chicago at least once a month," Katie tells us.

"I hope you get to drink some of this wine as well," I say. "This is really your job?"

"It really is. I have clients all over the country and two in Mexico."

Two clients in Mexico. I think of the song by Fountains of Wayne, about changing, but instead they have another glass of Mexican wine or something. Oh, well.

"They keep me busy," Katie continues, "probably too busy, but I love it."

Pam and I decide to skip the next open house, say goodbye to Katie, and wish her well. Walking back, Pam says, "Another job our parents never told us about."

When we get home, Pam looks at the clock and says, "Were we really gone that long? It's already five thirty?"

I look at my watch. "You didn't by any chance turn the clocks ahead, did you?"

"Yes, of course. I always do," she says.

"So did I. It's only four thirty."

Saturday, March 20
The Shiny Sheet reports one hundred fish are missing from a pond on a site where a house is being built. First, illegal spearfishing, now fish rustling. Hmm.

We're both in the office, buried under paper. I'm looking around, and there are piles of folders and books and pamphlets spread on every available surface, including the floor. It is impossible to find anything. I feel like drenching everything with gasoline, grabbing Pamela and the birds, and tossing a match in as we walk out the door. I say to Pam, "Remember the line in *The Magnificent Seven* when Steve McQueen says, 'We deal in lead?'"

"Why," Pam says. "Are you going to start shooting people?"

"No, but it seems for you and me, it's 'We deal in paper.' And too much paper. There's paper everywhere in here. You can't even walk across the room."

Pam looks around and starts laughing. "If we get any more files or piles or stacks of paper in here we might not be able to get out."

"Well, I'm getting out right now and taking a bunch of this paper with me," I say.

"I'll miss you." Pam says. "Can you leave the keys to the Corvette?"

"Everybody's a comedian," I say. "I'm taking my laptop and this entire project out to the big table in the yellow room. I know we said work stays in the office, but this has to be an exception."

Pam bends her arm, points her index finger, moves her arm back and forth, and says "This one time, Kay. This one time."

"If that was supposed to be Michael Corleone," I say, "it's the worst imitation I've ever seen."

She just smiles and says, "Take your stuff out there. Leave the cannoli."

Sunday, March 21

Pam loves her art classes and is painting another bird. She also made a drawing of Duckie and captured exactly how Duckie stands and holds her head. Today a French artist, Duaiv, is giving a demonstration in a gallery on Worth Avenue, and she definitely wants to go. We choose the beach route to Worth. As we're walking toward the beach, I say to Pam, "Remember that naked woman on the sport fisher at the docks?"

Pam looks up ahead, sees what I'm seeing, and laughs. "This one's not naked, she's wearing the bird."

This young lady is not, in fact, naked. She is wearing the absolute tiniest bikini I have ever seen and a large white cockatoo on her shoulder. I say, "Good afternoon." Both woman and bird answer, "Good afternoon."

We cross South Ocean and I cannot believe the scene. The beach is totally covered with kids and volleyball nets, Frisbees, and coolers. "What happened?" I say.

"Spring break has arrived," Pam says.

"I guess."

We continue on to the demonstration at the Phillips Galleries. Rows of folding chairs are set up, but all the seats are taken, so we find a space against the wall.

Monsieur Duaiv is standing before a canvas, rapidly creating a painting of a harbor. He uses several palette knives at once, scooping globs of pastel-shaded paint out of an assortment of cans next to him. In moments, the bare canvas becomes a scene of colorful sailboats at anchor in front of a quaint village.

He does this again and again—sailboats, harbors, flowers, villages, and more. Now, I am a cultural infidel, but even I find this amazing. Pam is mesmerized. We watch for about a half hour, but there are people waiting to come in, so we leave to make space for them.

"Don't try that at home," I say to Pam.

She smiles. "You know I'm going to try it, but I don't think I'll have the same results. The stuff I do is pretty realistic."

Wednesday, March 24
This afternoon Samantha and her gentleman caller Jason are

flying down from Manhattan. I've been looking forward to this day for weeks. I'm picking them up at the airport this evening. This explains why, when I go out at four o'clock in the afternoon to shuffle the cars in the driveway, the Audi's right rear tire is flat. The Audi dealer put these tires on the car only two weeks ago. I'm crazed.

I call the Sunoco station around the corner and explain my problem to the guy who picks up. He apologizes and says they are quite busy and no one can get to our house for fifteen or twenty minutes. Ten minutes later, two men arrive, fill the tire, and drive the car back to the station for further inspection. They call me about fifteen minutes later with the problem (a faulty valve) solved. I pick up the car and explain how tremendously happy I am that they fixed it so fast. I get to the airport but the plane is late. Samantha and Jason are behind schedule so there's not much time and I drop them at The Chesterfield.

Thursday, March 25

Jason and Samantha are in town on a three-night whirlwind tour. Samantha wants to introduce Jason to us, her mother, and her grandmother. This leads me to believe the relationship is serious. This also leads me to believe that if Jason can make it through these three days, he should receive a Purple Heart or Medal of Honor or something.

Last evening they had dinner with Samantha's mother in West Palm. Today and tonight we have the pleasure, and tomorrow they're with Samantha's grandmother in Palm Beach Gardens. So far, they have had a walking tour of the island, a driving tour of the island, and a jog along the beach.

They are staying at The Chesterfield, and the plan is for them to come here at eleven and we'll play it by ear. I'm very interested in talking to Jason and, of course, I want to see Samantha. I'm pacing around the house. They arrive at our cottage about eleven. We all sit around the pool and talk.

Jason, it turns out, played soccer in college and is still playing in a men's league. I played soccer, too, a hundred years ago, so the two of us talk soccer for a while. The conversation switches to talk of work, and spring training, and March Madness.

A little after noon I say, "All right, we can get subs, soups, and salads right around the corner and bring them back here. Or we can walk over to Pizza al Fresco, great pizza."

"Pizza always sounds good to Jason," Samantha says. "Do they have salads and lighter stuff, too?"

"Great salads," Pam says. "And maybe we could do a little shopping off Worth. There are some neat shops."

The four of us are ambling down Worth towards lunch. As we pass by the Polo store, we can't help but hear a guy in front who's practically shouting into his cell phone. "No, no, NO! I said meet me at the Polo store in Palm Beach. NO. Palm Beach Gardens is not Palm Beach. Palm Beach Lakes, Palm Beach Shores, North Palm Beach, South Palm Beach, Royal Palm Beach, West Palm Beach have nothing to do with Palm Beach. There is only one frickin' Palm Beach," he barks, and snaps his phone shut.

After we've passed this guy, Samantha says, "He seemed a little intense."

I laugh and say, "For sure. I think he told someone to meet him in front of the Polo store in Palm Beach and, whoever it was is now in front of the Polo store in Palm Beach Gardens up where Granna lives."

The four of us walk across to Via Mizner and get a table in the courtyard. Pam orders the lobster salad, Samantha a chicken

Caesar, I order an antipasto misto, and Jason orders a Hawaiian pizza.

I check the menu and say, "Jason, ham and pineapple? Real men don't eat ham and pineapple on their pizzas. They eat stuff like pepperoni or sausage."

Samantha rolls her eyes and says, "Dad."

"You wait and see," Jason says. "I'll give you one piece and you'll be begging for more."

Pam is discussing some post-lunch shopping possibilities with Samantha, and Jason and I are talking basketball as our food arrives.

True to his word, Jason separates a piece of his pizza, hands it to me, and says, "Here, the first piece of your newest favorite pizza."

I thank him and take a bite. The table is awaiting my reaction. I think about spitting it out and making a scene, but it's quite good. "Not bad," I say.

Jason turns his head and gives me a look. "Okay, it's actually very good," I say, "In fact, it's great."

After lunch, Pam suggests a couple of stores Samantha might like, and we cut them loose for the afternoon, a few hours to themselves. Pam goes off to her art class.

They meet us at Bice for dinner. When Samantha walks in decked out in a new dress she bought at Biba, I am speechless. This cannot be the little girl who played second base on an otherwise all-boy little league team, or the munchkin who used to shoot baskets sitting on my shoulders. She can't even be that beautiful Tulane graduate smiling in her cap and gown.

The four of us have dinner and laugh and talk easily. Pam and I walk them back to The Chesterfield for a nightcap. To-morrow they'll have a day to themselves and then dinner with

Samantha's grandmother. Saturday we will take them back to the airport. Tires permitting.

Saturday, March 27

This morning, we pick up Samantha and Jason at the Chesterfield and make the short drive to the airport. We say goodbye and drop them off.

I have the usual sort of sad feeling in my stomach, but somehow it's different this time. Maybe because Samantha seems so happy, maybe because she's not going home alone.

The sky is a brilliant blue, and the temperature is in the high seventies. Driving back with Pam, I say, "I like Jason."

"So do I," Pam says, "and so does Samantha. Did you see them together?"

"I did. It makes me very happy."

"How about dropping the car off," Pam says, "and having a quiet espresso and maybe a scone at Victors?"

"Sounds good."

I drop the car at home, and Pam and I walk over to Victor's. As we enter the courtyard, it's filled with people and dogs in costume, again. Pam starts laughing. "So much for a quiet espresso."

"Help me here," I say. "Isn't it March? It can't be Halloween. What's going on?"

What is going on is the annual Worth Avenue Pet Parade and Contest. Sherry, President of the Worth Avenue Association, is again the emcee.

Once again, we see dogs in pink tutus and in blue sequin dresses and dogs with nail polish to match the color of their outfits. One dog is dressed as Michael Jackson, another as the White Rabbit in *Alice in Wonderland*. The courtyard is overflowing with people and pets in costume.

"I think once a year is enough," I say. "Actually, once a year is more than enough."

"I agree," Pam says. "Let's go home for an espresso."

Wednesday, March 31

March is almost over, the winter people are mostly gone, and the spring breakers are back in class. The island has gone quiet again. We are sitting at the edge of our pool, dangling our feet in the water and talking.

Dinner tonight is a simple cookout by the pool with Kenny Chesney. Afterwards, dishes in the sink, we sit in our front yard, looking at the night sky. No one is around, just the stars and clouds and the distant sound of the waves and, occasionally, a passing train.

"I think Samantha and Jason are in love," Pam says.

"So do I."

"You and I are still in love," Pam says.

"Yes we are. It's amazing," I say. "Just the two of us here, two old lovebirds sitting together in the yard."

"Yes, this is wonderful," Pam says. "But don't forget we have houseguests coming tomorrow."

"That's tomorrow," I say. "Tonight we have us."

Pam and I have written books on Florida's many romantic escapes. We've stayed at dozens and dozens of supremely romantic resorts and inns all over the world. Tonight, I can't imagine a more romantic escape anywhere than the front yard of our little cottage in Palm Beach.

eleven

"MAYBE IT'S TIME TO START THROWING PAINT AROUND."

Thursday, April 1

I rush home from my art class. I'm working on two paintings, a bird and some flowers. Tony and Karen, friends from Connecticut, are arriving this afternoon. Dick has known them most of his adult life. I met them soon after I met Dick. They've spent the last three days and nights wining and dining clients at the Four Seasons and warned us they do not want to see a restaurant or any people other than us before heading back north tomorrow.

A taxi arrives at our house in the late afternoon, and Tony and Karen roll out looking exhausted. Dick and I take them and their luggage to the guest cottage.

"Laze around the pool or go for a walk?" Dick says.

"A walk sounds wonderful," Karen says. The four of us head west along residential streets, catching up on news of kids and families and friends. My appointments with Dr. Keith are over, although I still have some pain and wear a brace for long walks.

"That's Cat House over there," I say.

"What?" Karen says.

I point. "See those cats on the roof? We named it Cat House.

We've named lots of houses."

"Names? You've named the houses? Why on earth would you do that?" Karen says.

"I don't know. We just have," I say.

Tony seems distracted and I wonder if he's worrying about work. Suddenly he says, "These parking signs are absurd. For the last three blocks, the rules change every couple of spaces."

He points to the sign we are passing. "See, 'No parking nine a.m. to six p.m. except weekends.' That next one," he points, "just one space away, says, 'No parking without a permit.' The one over there says, 'No parking nine a.m. to midnight except Sundays.'"

Karen picks up the thread as we keep walking. "This one says, 'No parking without a permit eight a.m. to five p.m.,'" she says. "That one, 'No parking without a permit except Saturdays, Sundays, and holidays.' Parking poetry."

"Palm Beach haiku," I say.

We follow a beach path down to the sand and walk south. The waves are gentle today, but the weather is cool and the beach almost deserted. Our guests roll up their pants and test the water, saying that they never got anywhere near the ocean during the business part of the trip.

By the time the four of us get back to the cottage, Tony and Karen look a little more relaxed. We have champagne and chilled shrimp by the pool. The doves sit in a row on the cottage roof, observing us.

"Karen, what music do you want with dinner?" Dick says.

"Well, Enya would be nice."

Dick sets up the iPod and lights the grill. I bring out a salad, a dish of roasted vegetables, and marinated filets and chicken breasts. Dick opens a bottle of Chianti Classico Riserva, and the four of us spend the evening dining under the stars. It gets a bit smoky, so Dick relates the tale of the visit by the fire department. I see Karen eyeing the smoke and worrying about a return visit, but the smoke goes away, and we're safe for tonight.

"Bumper pool, anyone?" Dick says.

"And maybe an Irish Coffee," Tony says.

"Of course," Dick says. "The only beverage with the four essential food groups: alcohol, caffeine, sugar, and fat."

After a heated match, we take a last walk to the beach, and then agree it's time to call it a night.

Friday, April 2

As I come back inside with the morning papers, I hear Dick making espresso. I go get Duckie and Blanco and the four of us settle in the living room. Tony and Karen are still among the missing. Duck seems quiet and is moving slowly. I study her for a few minutes.

"Think Duck's okay?" I ask Dick.

Dick watches her.

"She seems okay," Dick says. "Maybe the Duck and Tony stayed up for a few after the rest of us went to bed."

Tony and Karen walk into the living room.

"You guys sleep okay?" Dick says.

"Yes," says Karen. "The futon was a surprise. It's quite comfortable. But, you know, the water pressure in that cottage is not good."

"I'm sorry," I say.

Dick says, "We'll have a plumber install an auxiliary pump before your next visit."

I say, "How about a walk to breakfast?" I put the birds back in the cage, and we walk toward Victor's. As we turn onto Worth, Karen says, "Saks Fifth Avenue and Ferragamo? Yesterday, we were on quiet streets and the beach. I would never have believed town was so close."

As we approach Victor's, Karen looks at me skeptically. "This is the restaurant? It doesn't look like much. It's really okay?"

I look at her and nod my head. "Trust me."

As everyone is finishing up omelets and fresh fruit and espressos, Karen says, "Sorry I questioned this place. Best breakfast we've had since we got to Florida." She looks around the courtyard. "And what a setting. That wall of purple bougainvillea is dazzling. Tony and I also have to apologize for thinking you guys were crazy to move here for a year. I mean what couple could be less Palm Beachy? But we get it now."

"No apology necessary," Dick says.

Tony looks at his watch. "We'd better go," he says.

Karen looks at me. "Is there an Armani store here?" she says.

"Yes, it's very close," I say. Tony frowns.

We walk to the Armani store, and Karen finds a black silk T-shirt she wants.

The salesman asks if she would mind coming back in fifteen or twenty minutes. Karen looks around the store, sees no other customers, says, "Why?"

"A gentleman just called and ordered seventy-five shirts," the salesman says, "twenty-five for each of his three houses, and we've already started ringing up the sale. It's going to be a little while before the computer's free."

"Karen, I don't want you guys to miss your plane. I'll come back later, send it up to you," I say.

We walk home and drive Karen and Tony to the airport. When we get back, I go in to let the birds out. Duck is on the floor of the cage, barely able to stand. She looks terrible.

"Dick," I say, "something's really wrong with Duck."

Dick comes in, picks Duckie up. She looks like a limp pile of feathers.

"I'll call that vet we went to last fall," I say. I call, only to find out the doctor is leaving soon.

"We gotta go right now," I say to Dick. "We'd better take both birds, just in case."

We get in the car, hit every red light, but somehow get there in time. The doctor examines Duckie, takes her to be x-rayed, returns with bad news. Duckie has swallowed a tiny piece of metal that is now poisoning her. There is an antidote, the bird could pass the metal, but the odds are not good. The doctor thinks Duckie might die.

"How could she swallow metal?" I ask.

"The piece is very tiny," the doctor says. "It was probably on the floor, came in on a shoe, you know how cockatiels peck at everything. It happens." The doctor says Duckie should stay there, the staff will give her food and medicine. We leave Blanco as company for Duckie. Dick and I are quiet driving home.

"Duck's a strong bird," I say. "She survived in the woods when she was a baby, before she found us."

"Yes, but this is a little different. We'll have to wait and see."

We go back to being silent. I'd never had a pet as an adult until Duckie flew into our lives. I didn't want a pet, but then Duckie won my heart, we got Blanco, and both birds became part of our daily lives. I had no idea birds could be so entertaining and affectionate. I'm shocked I might not see Duckie again.

Saturday, April 3

It's nine in the morning. I call the doctor. She tells me Duckie's not doing well, needs to stay there a few days. I give Dick the news.

"The house is so quiet without those guys," I say. "I'm just not prepared. I thought Duckie would die of old age, later, not now. I know she's just a bird, but still, I feel so upset."

"Dogs, cats, birds. Pets are pets," Dick says. "You love them." He's quiet for a moment. "Let's go play tennis, take our minds off all this."

We change into tennis clothes. I put on my knee brace. I play tennis more carefully now.

We zigzag north. There's a public athletic field near the courts, and we often see a soccer game or a softball game in progress when we walk to tennis. Today it's crowded with young children.

"Something's going on," I say.

"Looks like an Easter egg hunt," Dick says. "A day early."

We stop and watch. A lot of the kids look to be quite young, some barely walking. The oldest children are ten, maybe eleven. Other people stop to watch. I ask the man next to me what's going on.

"It's the town's annual Easter egg hunt. This year they hid four thousand eggs," he says. "There's another one going on now at the Flagler Museum. They have a six-foot-tall Easter Bunny over there."

The hunt starts. Parents guide the younger children. Kids run around and find eggs. It's a simple event, everyone seems happy. It's like another snapshot from an earlier era. Finally Dick says, "It's getting close to lunchtime, still want to play tennis?"

"I forgot all about tennis," I say. "No, let's go home."

We walk home slowly. "This town is so curious," I say. "The holiday events here are so simple, there's almost no pomp and circumstance. Yet in other ways there's so much in Palm Beach that is extravagant and showy."

"You mean like the ornate mansions and the expensive cars and the flashy diamonds."

"Exactly," I say. "It's almost like it's simultaneously two different places. Sometimes I think I'm living in a small town in the nineteen fifties. Then a couple of brand new Ferraris zoom by."

We both go quiet for a while and walk on. "Did you and Cam have Easter baskets when you guys were little?" I say.

"Yeah, of course. The Easter Bunny brought them," Dick says. "We'd wake up to a trail of jelly beans that led to a basket with candies and a present or two. I remember I got my first tennis racquet one Easter."

"I got my first bra from the Easter Bunny. I was ten and wanted a bra so badly. Not that I had anything to put in it. I even wore that bra to bed, I was so happy to have it."

"I didn't get my first bra till I was twelve," Dick says.

"You mean you didn't get into your first bra till then," I say.

We continue walking. I see three young girls up ahead. They're maybe six or seven, in pastel dresses with full skirts, bows tied at the back. They've drawn a hopscotch court onto the sidewalk with pink, blue, and yellow chalk. The squares are uneven and the lines a bit irregular. The girls throw their beanbags onto the squares, hopping and squealing with laughter.

"Boy, talk about things being out of another era," I say. "See how funny this town is?"

Sunday, April 4

The weather these early April days is lovely. Nights are in the high fifties. Days are in the mid-seventies and occasionally higher. So far it has been sunny and clear, and it is a joy to keep all the windows open. I hear the sounds of the ocean waves, the cooing of our family of doves, the humming of tree frogs in the early evening.

It's Easter Sunday, almost noon. We're sitting outside with the papers. The tomato seeds I planted are now vines propped up with stakes, heavy with tiny green tomatoes. Two cardinals are splashing in the birdbath.

"I keep thinking about Duckie," I say.

"We can call tomorrow morning," Dick says, "see how the Duckster's doing."

Dick is trying to cheer me up with tidbits from the Shiny Sheet. "They arrested a man on charges of burglary. The police found him asleep in his car with all of the stolen stuff right next to him on the front seat." He looks up. "Burgling must be exhausting work." He puts down the section, and I pick it up.

"Did you see this?" I say.

"What?" Dick says.

"They're renovating Worth," I say. "I don't know how we missed this. It's a big deal. They're going to rip up the entire avenue, replace all the trees, the planting, completely redo the entire street and all the sidewalks."

"Starting when?" Dick asks.

"Tomorrow."

"Tomorrow? How long is it supposed to take?" Dick says.

"Due to be finished in November," I say.

"For the rest of our year in Palm Beach, Worth Avenue will be torn up? There won't be a road there?" says Dick.

"Looks like it," I say. "I wonder if stores will stay open."

"We'd better walk there now, take one last look," Dick says.

We walk to the beach, then walk along Worth Avenue. I've come to take for granted the peace and beauty of the avenue and can't imagine it being overrun with steam shovels and road graders and jackhammers.

Monday, April 5

I call the doctor today. Duckie is neither better nor worse. "Which means what?" I ask.

"It's probably good," the doctor says. "She's fighting the metal."

I feel sorry for Duckie. I want to bring her home and cuddle her on my lap. I give Dick the news.

"So, nothing to do but wait and see," Dick says. "Want to walk over and see if Worth's really being destroyed?"

"Yeah," I say, and we walk over. Sure enough, jackhammers are breaking up the concrete in the first block. The noise is jarring. Workmen are all over the place, there's a big crane, heavy hoses snake along the sidewalk.

"Guess this town won't be quiet again until long after we're back in New Smyrna," Dick says.

We walk home past the town hall, a majestic building that has been meticulously restored. "Did you know," I say, "the Preservation Foundation raised the money to restore the town hall?"

"Makes sense," Dick says. "I see their name in Shiny Sheet articles all the time. They do a lot for this town."

"We use Pan's Garden a lot," I say. "They made that garden. Maybe there's a way we can give something back."

When we get home, I check out The Preservation Foundation of Palm Beach website and discover we can become members for a small contribution. I send in a check.

Tuesday, April 6

Today the doctor calls. Duckie is eating on her own, has gained a little weight. The doctor wants to keep her for another day or two. For the first time, I feel encouraged.

Dick goes to play tennis. I go to Publix for groceries. Up and down the aisles, people greet each other and ask when they are leaving, when they are going north. This is our eighth month in Palm Beach. The time has gone so fast. The holiday crowds and February crowds are long gone. Now the people who spend the whole winter here will be leaving soon. The town is beginning to be empty again. I like how it feels.

I come home from Publix and am putting away groceries. Dick comes home from playing tennis and helps me unload the bags.

Dick says, "Everyone at tennis was asking everyone else when they were leaving, when they were going north. The question was tossed around almost as much as the balls were."

"That's funny," I say. "It was the same at Publix."

Wednesday, April 7
The doctor calls, says Duckie is a little better, we can pick her up late this afternoon. We drive there, go into the office. A nurse appears with the birds in their cage. Blanco looks healthy and greets us with a chirp. Duckie looks almost as bad as she did when we brought her in. I am shocked and can see Dick is, too.

The doctor comes out and explains Duckie is better than she looks. She tells us to give her two medicines by dropper twice a day for the next three days, and to weigh her daily on a kitchen scale to make sure she isn't losing more weight. We drive home. Duckie's on the floor of the cage, looking more like a ball of feathers than a bird. She whimpers occasionally. It's a heartbreaking sight.

"Duckie looks awful," I say.

"Yes," Dick says. "Despite what the doctor said, I think Duckie could be done."

At home, Dick uses the dropper to get the two medicines into Duckie's beak. The medicine is sticky, and Duckie struggles to get away. The little feathers near her beak and all around her throat are already plastered against her face from previous doses of medicine. She eats a little. We keep both birds near us for a while, then put them to bed.

Saturday, April 10

For the next three days, we try to get Duckie to eat and give her the medicine twice a day. Dick and I trade off keeping Duckie with us, periodically putting her back in the cage for food and water.

We are supposed to stop Duckie's medicine today, but she doesn't seem better. She hardly eats and hasn't gained weight. I call the doctor, who tells me to continue both medicines for four more days. Duckie hates the medicine, but continuing with it seems necessary.

Monday, April 12

Now Duckie has virtually stopped eating. She wants nothing to do with her regular food, and I can't entice her with her favorite snacks. She normally loves strands of pasta, and I made a little batch of angel hair. She tried a bite, but that was it.

This evening Dick is trying to get the medicine into Duckie's mouth. Duckie is fussing; she's miserable. By now the whole front of her head is covered with a hardened mask of feathers glued together from the medicine. I start thinking about quality of life.

Dick looks at me. "I hate doing this," he says. "It's been six days. Duckie's getting worse, not better. If we can't save her, she shouldn't have to go through this."

"I agree," I say. "We're making her miserable. Let's see if she's any better tomorrow."

In the night I dream of my father, one of those dreams where he's alive and well and we're talking. I wake up in the dark feeling as if we've just had a visit. My father could be quite stern, but he loved his children, listened well, and was often funny.

My mind drifts to the last week my father was alive. Dick and I flew north, got to my parents' house in the early evening. My father was shockingly pale and thin, unable to get out of bed. He had no appetite. My mother, of course, was distraught.

Soon after we arrived, my father announced he wanted to have "dinner with us at the table." My mother and I were confused, but Dick intuitively realized my father didn't want food, he wanted to experience an elegant dinner, the kind the four of us had had many times over the years.

Dick went to the kitchen, rummaged through the icebox, and quickly assembled four plates with bits of this and that, nicely arranged. My mother and I set the table. Dick then carried my father from the bedroom and sat him at the head of the table, propped up with some pillows. My mother and I took our seats. Dick disappeared into the kitchen and reappeared carrying a chilled wine bucket containing a bottle of Pinot Grigio.

My father's eyes lit up. He said, "Wow! Look at that! What a thing." For the next half hour, we all drank a little wine, mostly left the food untouched, talked and laughed, just like the old days.

It was my father's last real dinner. He died five days later.

Tuesday, April 13

Duckie won't eat at all and is lethargic. I have her on my lap, a few pieces of angel hair next to her. She whimpers occasionally. I rub her neck and tell her the story of how she came to live with us, how she had been lost in the woods as a baby, stared at us for a long time from up in a tree, then flew down to us, determined to be adopted. I tell her she's a brave cockatiel. I think of the people Dick and I have talked to at their bedside, saying good-bye, and I start silently crying.

Then I remember an event with Aunt Jane, who died last year. There was a time a while back when she had pneumonia and was too weak to move. I sat by her bed every day at the nursing home, spoon-fed her, held water to her lips. She got weaker and weaker and then stopped eating, rarely opened her eyes. The nurses told me she was shutting down.

I was sitting by her bed, telling her how glad I was to have known her, reminiscing about this and that, basically trying to say goodbye, when suddenly she sat upright, scaring me half to death. "I'm not ready to go," she said. "I'm hungry." I gave her some applesauce. She lived happily for another five years, and died soon after her hundredth birthday.

I try to wish this idea into Duckie and nudge a little pasta toward her, but she doesn't want it.

Thursday April 15

Duckie still has no energy but yesterday she stared at a piece of pasta for a while and ate a little bit. Throughout the day, she nibbled. Today, she continues to nibble.

As I drive off to my art class, I feel encouraged and allow myself to think maybe Duckie will make it.

When I get to my class, I discover my teacher has left for another job. Harlan is now the teacher. He specializes in abstract art. I'm trying to learn how to paint realistic-looking birds. This won't work, I think. But he gives me good pointers on the bird I am painting.

I hurry home, anxious to check on Duck.

"How was your class?" Dick says.

"Well, the teacher's gone. The new one, his name's Harlan, specializes in abstract painting, something I can't imagine doing. But he helped me with my bird."

"Abstract painting," Dick says. He laughs. "Your birds are beautiful. But maybe it's time for you to start throwing paint around."

Friday, April 16
It's late afternoon. I come back to the cottage after some errands. When I come in the door, Dick calls, "Pam, come into the office."

I rush to the office. "Look at Duckie," he says. Duckie is on Dick's lap, enthusiastically eating a strand of angel hair. "She started to nibble about five minutes ago, then started eating faster and faster. This is her second batch."

"It's almost gone," I say. "I'll go get more."

I return with more pasta. Duckie eats and eats and eats. Then she looks up at Dick and starts chirping. She struts back and forth across Dick's lap, chirping and chirping. She looks like she's happy to be alive. It's hard to believe.

"What do you think happened?" I say.

"I have no idea," Dick says. "But it looks like Duckie may be coming back."

Monday, April 19
Duckie, who is now eating huge amounts of food every day and gaining grams dramatically, is on the top of the cage, preening. Blanco's perched on my shoulder while I work on the computer. It's two o'clock. The phone rings. I hear bits of muffled conversation. I keep working. Dick comes to the door.

"A hundred bucks if you can guess who was on the phone," he says. "No, make it a thousand."

I draw a blank.

"Our landlords," he says. "They're coming for cocktails. Tonight. At six thirty."

"Our landlords?" I say. "They live in Europe somewhere."

"Yes, they do, but they're here now."

I quickly get up and start looking around the house to see if it's presentable, start fluffing pillows and picking up magazines. Dick goes outside and sweeps leaves off the pool area.

At a quarter to six the doorbell rings. Neither of us is dressed for the evening. I give Dick a panicked look. He goes to the door while I run to the bedroom and start changing. He returns with a stunning orchid arrangement, a present from our landlords.

At six thirty the doorbell rings again. This time it's our landlords, a married couple who are much younger than I expected, and quite charming.

Over cocktails they explain they never lived in the cottage but bought it as an investment property a few months before we rented it. They've actually only seen the cottage twice, briefly, and want a tour.

I tell them we had only seen the cottage twice, briefly, before we made the impulsive decision to rent it. It's nice to know other people are as crazy as we are.

Soon they are off to dinner with friends. At the door, they tell us we're welcome to renew our lease for as long as we want. They say they hope we'll stay for many years. We agree to meet again in the summer during their next trip to Palm Beach, before our move back home. They leave.

"Dinner here?" I say to Dick. "We have that pork loin."

"Butterfly and grill it?" Dick says. "Then pile on mushrooms or whatever we have in the icebox."

"Sounds delicious," I say. We go to the kitchen to prep, with Peter Cetera, of course.

"So," says Dick, "that's why nothing was connected when we moved in."

"Right," I say. "Our landlords never lived here. Somebody did a cosmetic fix to sell the house, but nobody ever actually lived in the house afterwards. We were the guinea pigs."

Wednesday, April 21

"I just got our first e-mail from the Preservation Foundation," Dick says. He reads it to me. "The Yale University Whiffenpoofs will be performing in Pan's Garden this afternoon." He looks up. "Remember them?"

I haven't seen the Whiffenpoofs in years, but they were a big part of my childhood. My father worked for Yale, and I dated some Yalies when I was at Bennington. Their a cappella style is such a throwback, I'm surprised they're still around.

In the afternoon, we walk over to Pan's Garden. Chairs and a simple awning are set up, and refreshments are being served.

The Whiffenpoofs are dressed in white tie and tails, with white gloves. I expect them to stick to their traditional repertoire, including their signature number, "The Whiffenpoof Song," the one about tables down at Mory's.

Although they sing the songs I expected, they also go on to do a wonderful job on The Drifters' "On Broadway," switch into Peter Paul and Mary's "Leaving on a Jet Plane," and on to Michael Bublé's "Haven't Met You Yet."

We walk home. Dick says, "I was surprised they did such a variety of songs."

"Me, too," I say. "It was fun."

Thursday, April 22

I go to my art class today and finish up another bird. Most of the students are working on abstract paintings, but one student is copying a Matisse. The idea of copying a painting appeals to me, and I tell Harlan I would like to copy a painting, but I don't know what to copy. He hands me several coffee table books of art. "Find something you like," he says.

I leaf through the books. Eventually I find several Georgia O'Keefe paintings I really like, and settle on *Blue Morning Glories*. I put a blank canvas on my easel, rearrange my paints, put fresh water in a little cup, and start to copy it.

It's quite difficult, but by copying I begin to discover what is actually going on in the painting. I begin to see it in a way I have never seen a painting before. I see the subtle changes of color, the difference it makes when the artist chooses to use a hard line here, a softer line there. I see the painting as made up of many strokes, not as the finished product. The three hours go quickly. I am nowhere near finished with my painting.

Friday, April 23

It's so easy to go dancing in this town. The Chesterfield has live entertainment every night, The Colony five nights a week, and during the season Café Boulud three nights a week, Café L'Europe two nights, and Taboo two nights. The dance floors fill up with people of all ages.

"It's Motown night at the Polo Lounge," Dick says. "Want to go?"

"Great," I say. "Dinner at the Taboo bar around nine? So we get to The Colony before ten?"

I'm not a good dancer but I have fun dancing fast. Dick likes slow dancing (as do I) but he accommodates me and dances fast with me, and even gets silly with me on the dance floor. Now that my knee is better, I dance fast every chance I have.

As we walk into the Polo Lounge, the band Memory Lane begins their version of The Temptations' "My Girl." We find a spot at the bar. The dance floor is pretty full. We join the crowd and dance to the Four Tops' "Reach Out I'll Be There," then Smokey Robinson's "Tracks of My Tears."

There are couples in their twenties, couples in their seventies, and every age in between. The night goes on, and the band keeps playing. We hear the music of the Supremes, Gladys Knight & the Pips, and Marvin Gaye. It is non-stop Motown. Finally, we need to rest, and find our place at the bar. But several couples far older than us keep right on dancing, so we head back to the floor.

"We could've skipped the gym today," Dick says.

Sunday, April 25

Rain is pelting the windows. We're in our bathrobes, curled into the corners of the living room couch, with tea and biscotti, reading soggy sections of *The New York Times* and the Shiny Sheet. Blanco and Duckie, who is back to her old self, settle on opposite ends of the couch and preen.

Dick starts laughing and looks up from the Shiny Sheet. "A man walked up to two women on the public beach and asked if he could pay them forty dollars and expose himself. The ladies declined, and the guy went away."

"Was that forty each, or forty for the two of them?" I say.

The wind picks up. Sheets of rain pound the palm trees outside the windows. Dick gets up and looks out. "The street is a rushing stream," he says. "Remind you of anything?"

"You mean like that day last August when we first saw this house?" I say. "Seems like a long time ago. It hasn't rained like that again until now."

Around one o'clock, the storm dies out, the day turns cool and sunny, and we go out for a walk. We stop and rest on a bench just north of the bridge. It's quiet and the air is thick with the perfume of nearby jasmine. A small boat motors by.

"Want to walk over the bridge to West Palm Beach?" I say. "Somehow, it's never occurred to me before."

"What about your knee?"

"I have my brace on," I say. "And we can always take a taxi back."

We get up and walk to the bridge, follow the bridge's sidewalk to the mainland. We cross Flagler Drive and enter a city canyon, high-rise office buildings on both sides. The traffic is heavy and the noise jarring, even on Sunday.

"We just walked into a different universe," Dick says.

In a few blocks we come to CityPlace, a dense, multi-block group of apartment buildings, townhouses, stores, and restaurants. It's teeming with people of all ages, shapes, and sizes, on the sidewalks, in the central fountain square, in the outdoor cafés.

We window shop and people watch, go into Barnes & Noble, find a couple of books we want plus several cocktail-table books on sale. We carry our heavy load to the checkout counter. Dick says, "We don't have a car."

"Oh, right," I say. "How stupid are we?" We put the books back. "Let's get an espresso."

We walk outside and find a café. "How's your knee?" Dick says. "You okay to walk back?"

"Seems okay so far," I say. "Let's try it."

We make our way back to the bridge and start our walk over to the island. Behind us are tall buildings. Ahead are stately mansions lining the lake shore.

"That was disorienting," I say. "Those tall buildings, all those people."

"All that noise," Dick says. "I didn't like it."

"This is baffling," I say. "How do you think we'd feel if we were in front of our old apartment on Seventy-Second and Third?"

"We went back to New York a year ago and loved it," Dick says, "but now, I don't know."

"Something's happening to us," I say. "I'm not sure what."

Monday, April 26

One side of our pool area now resembles a tomato farm. The tomato seeds Maurizio gave us are now healthy plants. Because we started the seeds at several different times, hoping to avoid that homegrown tomato phenomenon when all possible tomatoes are ready the same day, the plants vary in size. There are medium-size green tomatoes, tiny green tomatoes, and yellow flowers.

The Shiny Sheet continues to amuse us. This morning there's an article on Chateau du Puppy, a dog boutique, which is hosting a gala Champagne night and Italian buffet to thank its loyal customers. The customers may bring their owners if they wish. Also, a lady at Publix reported her wallet missing. But after a little searching it was discovered, money and credit cards intact, in a display of sweet onions.

We walk over to the lake. Two men are loading a Bentley into a van. Dick says, "Isn't that the exact same Bentley we saw them unload in November?"

"Even the cars are going back north now," I say.

"It doesn't seem that long ago when they were bringing them down," Dick says.

We keep walking. A woman startles us as she abruptly pulls her Range Rover over to the curb about half a block in front of us. She opens the door, jumps out, and goes over to a large hibiscus bush in the front yard of someone's house. She picks half a dozen hibiscus blossoms, returns to her car, and takes off.

"That's a first," Dick says.

We find a bench in the shade and take a seat. There are a fair number of empty slips.

"Looks like the boats are going north, too," I say.

Walking back home, we see Barney on his front patio, in his pajamas again, holding court. "I see the Checkers are finally coming home," he shouts.

"No, Barney," Dick says, "it's the Walkers, not the Checkers."

He points at us. "Hah! You are surely the Walkers, but you are also the Checkers. The two of you are out checking on this town day and night, the two Checkers."

There is no point in discussing it because Barney is right, as usual.

Tuesday, April 27

I start to unload the dishwasher. I hate putting dishes away in this house. Our one cabinet is jammed. I happen to love plates, and I think longingly of our uncluttered shelves in New Smyrna, with everything arranged. We left most of the plates there, but still we have too many here. I open the cabinet and study everything.

Cabinets can't get bigger, but stuff can go away. I pick two of my favorite dinner plates, two colorful plates good for around the pool, two sandwich or salad plates, two soup bowls. Everything else I put in a carton. I go find Dick.

"I've solved part of the kitchen space problem," I say. "Come look."

He follows me into the kitchen. I show him the cabinet. "Okay to just live with these? When guests come, we mostly go out. If we stay in, the plates won't match. Who cares?"

"This is good," Dick says. "But are you okay not using the china you love?" Dick says.

"Well, I'll kind of miss it. But I've already learned to live without all the plates we left in New Smyrna. Anyway, it's not permanent. We'll be back there soon."

Thursday, April 29

It's noon. I'm racing to finish up copy for a technical manual. It's been a boring bear of a project. Dick comes into my office.

"How are you doing?" he says.

"I'm just about done, another twenty minutes," I say. Then I say, "Actually, I'm really done. I hated writing that manual."

"So, let's get out of here for a couple of days."

"I have my art class," I say.

"So, we'll go tomorrow morning."

"Go where?"

"I don't know. I'll find a place."

"Actually, that sounds delightful," I say. "But I don't know about leaving Duckie."

"Duckie is fine now. Go to your art class," Dick says. "I'll figure something out."

I go to class, work on my copy of a Georgia O'Keefe flower, come home.

Dick says, "It took a while, but I found a simple place in the Keys; they have room for us for the weekend. Duckie and Blanco have reservations at the vet."

"Where are we going?" I say.

"Island Bay Resort on Islamorada Key." He shows me the website. "I think it's less than three hours from here," he says. "Each room has a little kitchen and a charcoal grill outside. I thought we'd bring our food, make a pasta sauce one night, grill out the next."

"Perfect," I say.

Friday, April 30

We drop off the birds, head south to the Keys, arrive at Island Bay around two. Numerous palm trees create an overhead canopy of palm fronds and lots of shade. Hammocks hang here and there. Ten units are set along a gravel driveway that ends at the bay. We luck out and get the only one directly facing the water. It's a charming single room with a tiny kitchen and two porches.

Unpacking doesn't take long. We have almost no clothes, just food. We take an afternoon walk, sit in a double chaise by the dock and look out to distant flat, green islands. We read together in a hammock.

The evening comes, and Dick puts on Peter Cetera and makes a pasta sauce, opens a bottle of Amarone. I make a salad. We dine on one of our little private porches.

"A walk?" Dick says.

"Lovely idea," I say.

We pour the last of the wine into our glasses, walk across the small beach out to the end of the dock. The bay is inky black and still. There are no people about, almost no lights on along the shore. We sit down, dangling our feet over the edge.

Dick shines a flashlight down into the water, revealing a world of busyness. Schools of small fish swim by. A gangly, long-legged crab makes his way across the bottom. Dick turns the light off and the water goes black. I look up and see a black sky studded with stars. There are so many it's hard to find the constellations. "Look up," I say softly. "It's like one of those Caribbean nights, when the sky is almost completely filled with stars."

We both lie down on the dock and stare up at the sky for a long time.

"Remember that time at Lake Tahoe?" Dick says.

The scene swims into my head. We were at a tiny motel on the north shore of Lake Tahoe. After making dinner, we spent much of the evening sitting outside, alone on the narrow beach, the mountains surrounding the lake a jagged black border to the star-studded sky.

"You mean when we stayed at that little motel on the beach and sat out, just the two of us, like tonight, and watched a sky full of stars?"

"Right." Dick says. "And in the morning, when we checked out, we saw the sign that said, 'Beware of bears, don't sit on the beach in the dark.'"

"Exactly," I say. "Think we should be worried about alligators or something?"

twelve

"YOU DON'T HAVE
THE BULGE."

Monday, May 3

Pam and I spent three days and nights relaxing in the Keys, reading and taking walks during the day, driving to nearby lunch restaurants for fresh fish, and making simple dinners. This morning, we had coffee out on the dock. Then we packed up what little we had left. Our luggage this trip was mostly food and wine, and it's mostly gone. Packing was easy.

Driving back to Palm Beach, I'm thinking about interior space. Pam and I just spent several days and nights, happily, in a tiny motel room. The reason, of course, is because we had almost no stuff with us. I think maybe the relationship between stuff and space could be getting clearer for me.

We stop and pick up Duckie and Blanco and are home by noon. I pull in the driveway. As we get out of the car, Pam says, "Isn't this fun to have almost nothing to unpack?" As we go in the front door, Pam says, "Wow, this place looks much bigger today than it did two days ago."

"After that room in the Keys," I say, "this is a castle."

"It's funny," Pam says. "I guess this space stuff is relative."

I'm pretty sure she's been reading my mind again.

Pam goes to take care of the minor unpacking and to get the birds settled with new food and water. I go into the kitchen and quietly start making Pameleggs, which are fried eggs, over easy, on an English muffin with sliced tomatoes, sautéed mushrooms, and melted provolone. It's one of Pam's favorites, and I'm trying to surprise her.

She walks in the kitchen. "Pameleggs, great. Thank you."

So much for the surprise.

"They're going to start ripping up Worth Avenue even more next week," Pam says. "Did you know the redo is costing over eighteen million dollars?"

"I'd have done it for fifteen," I say, and flip over the eggs.

"After Pameleggs, let's go over and walk the avenue. Maybe do some window shopping, check on things."

This afternoon it is obvious the Worth Avenue Pam and I have known for so many years will be totally transformed in a few months. The first block is now mostly mud.

As we're walking along holding hands, I'm trying to figure out how many days and nights we have actually walked along this avenue. If we've been visiting, let's say ten days a year for ten years, that's a hundred days and probably a hundred nights. And if we've been here around two hundred and forty days since we moved, we must have walked the avenue at least another hundred and fifty days and nights, probably more, maybe two hundred and fifty days and nights in all.

It would be nice if we could get that many days and nights together on the new Worth Avenue.

Tuesday, May 4
Our windows still stay open day and night, but pretty soon

summer will be here, and I'll be turning on the AC. This morning's Shiny Sheet tells of a coconut catastrophe. Apparently, a cluster of ten coconuts came crashing down onto a parked car, causing serious roof damage. Ten coconuts.

We're finishing our espressos when Pam says, "You know, it was in March or April when people started asking each other when they were heading north."

"Right. I heard the question everywhere," I say.

"Well, have you noticed," Pam says, "the people who work in town have started asking us when we're going north."

"I hadn't thought about it, but yes."

"And when you say we're staying here, do you see the way they look at you?" Pam says.

"You mean like I'm kidding, or maybe just nuts?" I say.

"Yes, and what's funny is a lot of people who work in restaurants and stores here go north as well," Pam says. "People who were dining and shopping here this winter will see some familiar faces in the shops and restaurants in Nantucket and Newport and the Hamptons this summer."

It's funny, but it occurs to me that the super rich don't really live anywhere. They may have an apartment in Manhattan, their house in Palm Beach, maybe one in Newport and another in Aspen or Spain, and of course their mega yacht, but in a certain way they don't really live anywhere.

Pam, the lobster queen, also loves soft-shell crabs. Last night we ate at Bice, and she discovered that the soft-shell crab season had begun. Tonight I thought we were staying home, but the idea of another plate of fresh soft-shells is too enticing for Pam. I think she's hoping these crabs are now specials in all the Palm Beach restaurants.

Time to shower, dress, and investigate. Our first stop is

Taboo. We go in the Peruvian entrance to avoid the Worth Avenue mess. We have a drink and a chat with Bobby. Turns out soft-shells won't be on the menu until tomorrow.

Pam suggests we check out the crab scene at Renato's, so to avoid the Worth Avenue construction, we follow Peruvian Avenue to Via Mizner. As we approach the restaurant, Brad opens the door and says, "Mr. and Mrs. Myers, I hope you'll be dining with us tonight. The chef just got a shipment of beautiful soft-shell crabs."

Pam just smiles and nods. Brad takes us to a table in the courtyard. The May breezes are balmy, and the skies are clear. Pam dines on fresh sautéed soft-shell crabs. I stick with spaghetti Bolognese.

We finish and walk out Via Mizner toward Peruvian and see Luciano. He is overseeing the unloading of some fresh fruit for the restaurant out of his Porsche Cayenne. (In another town the fruits might be delivered in a Ford F-150 or an old Dodge pickup. In Palm Beach, it's a Porsche.)

"Luciano, *buona sera*. What are you doing out here?" I say. "Are you stealing fruit?"

He laughs. "No, Mr. and Mrs. Myers. Did you enjoy your dinner tonight?"

"Of course. Everything was perfect," Pam says. "Now we're off to The Chesterfield for a dance."

"Oh, very nice. Wait. Wait, you need some fruit!"

He hands me a bunch, probably eight or nine, of miniature bananas.

"Luciano, what are you, nuts?" I say. "It's ten thirty at night. We're going dancing at The Chesterfield. What'll we do with these bananas?"

I try to give them back.

"You take the bananas. They are good for you. They are a gift from me."

History has taught us one cannot argue successfully with Luciano. So, we thank him and head to the Leopard Lounge, now carrying a bunch of bananas.

Adam is at the piano. Lou is behind the bar. Lou spots us coming in. He approaches us at the bar, expressionless. "So, I guess that'll be two banana daiquiris?" he says.

Saturday, May 8

We're walking back from the lake along Royal Palm Way. As we approach the Palm Beach Recreation Department grounds, I say, "We've fallen through the looking glass again. And landed at a field day out of the fifties."

Ahead, there is a football toss going on, and one by one, boys take their turn. Well-dressed older children and adults stand to the side, politely clapping at each try. There is a girls' soccer game on another field. Parents and children quietly watch from the sidelines.

"You remember these?" Pam says.

"Yes," I say. "My long-term memory is still quite good. I used to love things like this when I was a kid, and when Samantha was growing up."

Everywhere we go in Palm Beach there seem to be snapshots of the past, of simpler times, more civilized times, maybe. A football toss, a soccer game, relay races. Today's field day is sending me some kind of message. I just don't know what it is. Maybe I want to live the simpler Palm Beach life we're living and seeing.

The message Pam is sending me tonight, and as hard as it may be for me to believe, is that she might like soft-shell crabs again. I'm easy. If there were a pasta season, and you could only get pasta out, like, twenty nights a year, I would probably be out eating pasta all twenty nights.

We're back at Taboo's bar tonight. All the seats are taken. Many people are dining at the bar, and in front of just about everyone is Taboo's signature basket of homemade breads and rolls and cheese crisps.

A woman who is by herself at the bar, probably in her fifties, finishes up and asks Hugh, one of the bartenders, for the check. She hasn't touched the bread in her basket.

Hugh begins to clear her plates, but when he touches the basket, she says, "No, wait. Don't take that away. Could you please just put all that in a doggy bag? And maybe add some extra pieces of those delicious cheese crisps? It's for my girlfriends," she continues, "they would be very upset if I came home empty-handed." And out she walks with enough bread for a family of four.

Sunday, May 9

Another civilized Sunday at Café L'Europe. And, possibly, more crabs. As we're walking over, the lyrics are playing again in my head about eating her own weight up in crab meat. I'm thinking maybe Jimmy Buffett knew Pam back when he wrote that song. Lobster or crab, she never gets tired of either one.

About a block away from the restaurant, I can clearly hear David at the piano, which is strange. I never hear his music until I am inside Cafe L'Europe. As we arrive, and I hold the door open for Pam, I notice all the French doors in the restaurant are wide open. Probably against some ordinance, but it transforms the restaurant into an alfresco setting and gives it a Caribbean island feel.

Pam spots fresh sautéed soft-shell crabs as a special on the menu and is, of course, delighted. We order and settle back and relax. Suddenly, I hear an explosion. Bombs? Gunshots? Our table is right next to a set of open French doors, and I see the sky light up with fireworks.

"I'm sure it's not New Year's Eve," I say, "and I don't think it could be July Fourth quite yet."

Bruce is passing our table. "Bruce, what are these fireworks for?" I ask.

"It's the last night of Sunfest," he says. "Surely, you guys have been to Sunfest."

"No," I say. "We've never been, and don't call me Shirley."

He looks at me and laughs. "Ah, I forgot. You guys don't get off the island much. It's a music festival over in West Palm. They always have fireworks the last night. Enjoy. No extra charge."

And we do. Our table offers a full view of the display. We see one burst of color after another, fireworks in red, blue, green, and gold, lighting up the night sky, accompanied by the sound of David at the piano.

Pam says, "New Year's Eve, and now tonight. I can hardly wait until the Fourth of July."

Tuesday, May 11
According to the Shiny Sheet Police Report this morning, a Palm Beach resident reported that he thinks a Rolex watch was stolen from his bureau drawer sometime between the beginning of February and now. Guess it wasn't his favorite watch.

The paper goes on to describe a volunteer squad called the Code Watchers. These people apparently travel around town spotting code violations like "overgrown grass, peeling paint, unsightly debris, and other blemishes that mar the ambiance of Palm Beach." Blemishes that mar the ambiance?

Our tomato plants keep growing taller and taller and have

outgrown their stakes twice. Over the last several days, some of the larger fruits started turning orange, and this morning many are bright red. So much for planting the seeds in batches so we wouldn't have too many tomatoes ripe at the same time.

Tonight we're in the kitchen with Peter Cetera preparing large, very fresh tomato salads, among other things. The phone rings. I look at Pam. I pick up. Pam is listening, but, of course, she can only hear my part of the conversation, which goes something like this: "Van Duzer, when did they let you out?" Short silence. "Are you serious?" Long silence. "Be there or be square." Click.

"Yes?" Pam says.

"Van and Sue are flying into West Palm from LAX on Thursday, spending a night at The Chesterfield, and flying to Connecticut Friday morning. We're meeting them at the Leopard Lounge at seven o'clock Thursday."

"Cool," Pam says.

Wednesday, May 12

In all the years we've been visiting Palm Beach, we have never gone to the Flagler Museum, so today we decide to walk over. We quit work early and zigzag our way north to the museum, which is on the lake, about fifteen blocks north of Worth Avenue. The whole way, we never see another pedestrian. At times like this, Palm Beach feels like our own private town, here just for the two of us.

As we're paying our admission, I pick up a brochure. I start reading it. "This whole place is a museum," I say.

"I see. I didn't quite get that," Pam says.

"Henry Flagler, the Standard Oil and railroad guy, built this as a present for his wife in 1902."

"A nice little gift," Pam says.

"This was the couple's winter residence," I say. "Could have told me it was a hotel and I'd have believed it. It has fifty-five rooms, sixty thousand square feet."

"What's that, about the size of twenty-five normal houses?" Pam says.

"Something like that," I say. "It even makes 'normal' Palm Beach mansions seem insignificant."

We stroll through grand ballrooms, vast hallways, solariums, many sizeable bedrooms, a music room, and a billiards room big enough for three tables. I can't believe that people actually lived like this.

"Look at this," Pam says, "an entire tea service in eighteen karat gold."

"Perhaps a bit extravagant," I say, "but I guess it fits."

Signs in some of the rooms indicate that individual donors have sponsored each restoration. I'm reminded of how much of the conservation of not only this museum, but of the entire Town of Palm Beach, is paid for privately.

My favorite exhibit is Henry Flagler's private rail car. It has beautiful oak paneling, a comfortable bedroom, and bathrooms more modern than those found on today's trains.

In a previous life, I spent two hours a day commuting on a train, six and sometimes seven days a week. If I'd had Flagler's private car, I might not have hated it so much.

Thursday, May 13

Pam's at her art class, and I'm goofing off trimming some palms out by the pool. I'm thinking about seeing Van and Sue tonight. Van and I became friends in second grade. We lived on the same street, played Little League together, and went to the same summer camp (until I was asked to leave). In high school we played on the same championship soccer team and the same bas-ketball team, along with Theo. Van and I even went to the same college. We certainly both see where we are and we both know where we've been. Old friends. Harry Chapin was right.

We all meet at The Chesterfield. The night flies by as we catch up on news and laugh, a lot. They've been in LA for a month visiting their son Bill (mercifully no longer referred to as Van-Van), Bill's wife, and their three grandchildren. Bill is now a television hotshot out in Hollywood. I remember when he was throwing Cocoa Puffs around in his crib.

Van and I reminisce, but the ladies don't mind. They actually expect it. And, not surprisingly, the older the two of us get, the better we were.

Friday, May 14
We're finishing up in the office and Pam says, "Did you see the invitation from the Preservation Foundation?"

"No, what's it for, a tea party?"

"No, actually it's for a garden party, an evening of cocktails, dinner, and dancing," Pam says.

"A garden party?" I say. "You remember what happened to Ricky Nelson? Maybe we should take a pass."

"What about Ricky Nelson?"

"Nothing," I say.

"The party is in Pan's Garden," Pam says.

"Really? Eating and drinking and dancing in Pan's Garden would be fun."

"We won't know one person there," Pam says, "but I don't care. Do you?"

"Please," I say, "call these people up and tell them we'll be there."

Saturday, May 15

The newspapers didn't make it to the driveway this morning. They're out by the road. I sneak over to the hedge and peek both ways. The coast is clear, so I walk over and retrieve the papers. As I'm standing on the sidewalk in my boxers, looking down the street, holding the morning papers, I'm thinking, what a great street. What a great location. What a great hedge.

I walk back inside, struck by how lucky we were to choose this place. We're on a quiet, residential, tree-lined street, and everything we want to do day and night is only a short walk away. We've been here over eight months, and I just finally, really figured this out standing on the sidewalk in my underwear.

After the papers and tea and biscotti, Pam and I walk to the ocean, head south, and soon find ourselves walking along the plywood sidewalks of Worth Avenue, which looks a little like it's been hit by a hurricane. Pam stops to look at some leather purses in a window. "Every one of those purses you're looking at is bigger than our carry-on luggage," I say.

"I don't get it," Pam says. "I'd never be able to find anything. If you asked me for Chap Stick, it could take five minutes of searching to dig it out."

"What about the white leather luggage over there?" I say. "Very practical. They'd be marked and battered after a flight or two."

"I don't think so," Pam says. "Those bags are never going to fly commercial."

"Of course," I say. "The chauffer takes them from the Rolls directly to the jet."

We walk to the lake and then circle back onto Worth. In the distance I notice a group of people on the lawn just outside the Everglades Club dining room, all dressed in white.

"I believe we have fallen through the looking glass once again," I say to Pam. "If I'm not mistaken, that's a formal croquet match on the club lawn."

Sunday, May 16

The front-page story in today's Shiny Sheet is about a daring kitten rescue. It turns out this kitten wedged himself underneath the hood of Vic Damone's Mercedes, which was parked in his driveway. His wife's grandson Krystofer heard the kitty's cries and called the police. A team from the Palm Beach Fire-Rescue Department arrived and, with Mr. Damone's blessing, spent three hours dismantling the engine compartment to free up the kitty. The cat is alive and well and being cared for, and he is now named Crooner after Mr. Damone. As to the car, there is no mention of how it got back together.

I read on. "You know that mansion they're building way south of here, the one that looks like a French chateau?" I say to Pam.

"Yeah," she says. "The one we think some billionaire must be building."

"Well," I say, "it's not being built for anyone. It's a spec house."

"A spec house," Pam says. "Wow. How much is it?"

"Don't know yet, but I'll give you some details. Nineteen thousand square feet of living space, eight bedrooms, five powder rooms. . . ."

Pam starts reading over my shoulder. The grand hall has his and her powder rooms and columned galleries, there's a formal dining room with Marie Antoinette-patterned wood floors, Versailles-patterned floors are elsewhere, a five-car garage, a six-thousand-square-foot raised garden, a twelve-thousand-square-foot motor court, service parking for thirty-five cars (not guests, service people), a powder room for the gardener, a commercial-size elevator, and a two-thousand-bottle wine room, among other things.

"A good starter house," I say. "And here's the asking price. It's eighty-four million dollars."

Wednesday, May 19

Pam and I are dining inside at Bice tonight with George Hamilton and his young son. Well, not exactly. George and his son are about three tables away. We are talking and finishing dinner when I notice a woman at another table staring at us, smiling. She gets up and walks toward us. Then I whisper, "Uh-oh." This woman, cocktail in hand, is now standing at our table.

"I met you in Winter Park," she says. We look at each other. We look back at her and smile. I stand and introduce myself and Pam.

"I know. You are the island people, the romance people," she says. "You signed your books for me. You remember. I was with my daughter, Kimmie."

This woman, who is definitely not holding her first cocktail of the evening, was apparently at a book signing of ours at a Barnes and Noble in Winter Park almost two years ago with her daughter Kimmie.

"Of course, Winter Park. Nice to see you again," Pam says.

"Well, Kimmie is getting married, and she and her husband can't decide where to go for their honeymoon."

"Oh, I think I remember Kimmie," I say. Well, maybe not. "Where are they thinking of going?"

Kimmie's mother drops some resort names and some vowels and may drop her drink at any moment.

"Caneel Bay, Little Dix Bay, and Peter Island are all elegant choices for a honeymoon," Pam says. "If they want to be isolated and swim and hike, maybe Peter Island. If they want to dance every night, perhaps Little Dix, and if they want a choice of seven beaches, then Caneel."

"Thank you. Thank you," she slurs. "Kimmie won't believe this. Can I buy you two a drink?"

"No, thank you," I assure her, "but it is great seeing you again. Please give our best to Kimmie."

We do not get recognized very often and when we do it isn't a problem. I am amused that if we were really famous, Kimmie's mom would probably not have come over to our table. I mean, there are a hundred people in the restaurant who know George Hamilton is here. No one approaches him. There is only one person who knows us.

If you're really a celebrity in Palm Beach, everyone respects your privacy.

Thursday, May 20
The multi-million-dollar renovation of Worth Avenue continues, and the whole scene is a bit surreal. Many sidewalks have been replaced with plywood, there are pipes and pumps everywhere. Despite the usual chaos, when the jackhammers and bulldozers are resting, it is actually quiet, no yelling, no radios. All the workers are deferential and polite.

Pam says, "They must have sent all these construction workers to those Munchkin Manners classes."

"There're no radios playing, no one is yelling. Where do they find these guys?"

"I don't know," Pam says, "but it's quintessentially Palm Beach."

Wednesday, May 26

In a disturbing development, the Shiny Sheet reports that a West Palm Beach man has been arrested for scuffling. First we had rummaging, now scuffling. What's next?

After dinner at home tonight, I suggest a walk to The Chesterfield to listen to Adam and have a dance or two. As we're going in the Leopard Lounge, Pam decides to stop in the ladies' room. I say I'll go find us a couple of seats at the bar. There are two seats on the right side of the bar next to a woman of a certain age. I walk down, nod to the seats, and say, "Pardon me, are these taken?"

"No, they're yours," she says. "Are you taken?"

I smile. "Yes. Quite. My wife just stopped in the ladies' room."

"Well, too bad, but you don't have the bulge anyway," she says.

Don't have the bulge? I'm thinking I should grab my stuff the way Travolta does at the beginning of the movie *Basic*, but I'm an adult. I just smile.

Then she says, "What kind of watch is that, anyway?"

I look at my watch and say, "It's a Skagen."

"Too skinny," she says. "To get the bulge you need a big Rolex or a Piaget. That's what the ladies are looking for in here."

Mercifully, Pamela arrives, and my new friend drifts off in search of the bulge.

Friday, May 27

I've been looking forward to or at least curious about the garden party, and tonight's the night. The gates we usually use to get into Pan's Garden are locked, so we follow some other people into The Preservation Foundation of Palm Beach building, through the library, and out to the garden.

The sounds of people quietly talking mingle with the clinking of glasses and soft music. People are gathered in small groups. Women are in dresses, most men in jackets. It's uncrowded and peaceful. A waiter appears out of nowhere, takes our order, and is back with our drinks in seconds.

"I already like this," I say. "I see at least three bars and waiters are everywhere, carrying drinks and plates of hors d'oeuvres."

"I don't think we'll starve or die of thirst," Pam says. "It's beautiful here at night."

"I agree. Especially since people are bringing us drinks and hors d'oeuvres."

Dance music is playing now, and the buffet and tables are set. Some guests have started eating. Pam and I wander about talking and keeping to ourselves. These are the same paths we walk along during the day. But the night sky, the night sounds transform Pan's Garden into a romantic, moonlit hideaway.

We have a few dances, and Pam says, "Want to join the two couples at that table?"

"Eat with strangers?" I say. "Are you crazy?"

We join the two couples. One is perhaps a few years older than we are and the other, quite a bit younger. The older couple has flown down from New York for this party. I get the impression it was their own plane and wonder if perhaps they have white luggage. The younger couple has been in Palm Beach since Christmas but will be going to Newport in a few days until next Christmas. Both couples seem fascinated, or horrified, that we will be summering in Palm Beach.

We get food from the buffet and eat with our new friends, have a dance or two, and just relax for a while. After coffee and another dance Pam and I decide it is time to go. As we start to walk home, Pam says, "I definitely want to do that again next year."

"Pamela," I say, "you are losing it. We're not going to be here next year."

"I know," Pam says. "But it's a nice thought."

We continue walking. It's a little after midnight, and there's no traffic, no other pedestrians. We slowly amble along in the darkness, enjoying the soft balmy air, the aroma of jasmine, and having the town all to ourselves.

I'm asking Pam how her knee is doing when suddenly, maybe ten feet in front of us, a man pokes his head around a hedge and calls out, "Hello."

I put my arm out in front of Pam.

"Hello?" I say. "You startled us a bit."

"I'm sorry," he says, "but please, can you do me a favor? Can you come into the house and help me?"

I'm looking at this guy. He's got a beard, he's smiling, he's not very tall, and unless he has a gun in his waistband, I don't think he is much of a threat.

"Talk to me," I say. "What's the problem?" I walk a little closer. Pam is behind me now.

The man says, "Can you turn off a light in the bathroom for me? There is water leaking into the fixture."

I look around. "Are we on television or something?" I ask. "Turn off a light switch?" Then I get it. I look at my watch. "It's your Sabbath, right?"

"Yes, thank you for understanding," he says. "Will you help?"

"Of course we will," Pam says.

I look at Pam and then at this guy. "Are you in your pajamas?" I say to him.

He laughs. "Yes, I'm sorry. My wife and I were about to go

to sleep when I discovered the leak."

"Are you a rabbi?" I say.

"Soon, I hope," he says.

We follow him through a hallway and on toward the bathroom. Sure enough, water is leaking into a ceiling fixture. I switch off the light.

"Thank you. Thank you so much," this guy in his pajamas says. "I was worried for my family."

His wife appears out of nowhere and she thanks us, too. She takes Pam's hand, and thanks us again. "Please," she says, "come and share some food with us."

"Thank you, but no. It's late," Pam says.

"You must stay," she says.

"We really can't," I say, "but we're glad we could help."

Walking home, I'm going through some of the other unexpected encounters Pam and I have had since moving to Palm Beach.

Pam turns and says, "Have you heard the one about the rabbi, the light switch, and the weird walking couple?"

Saturday, May 29

I make us a lunch of Pameleggs. Pam gets some pasta for the birds. When we are settled at the table, Pam says, "Last night, the garden party, that was a turning point for me."

"What do you mean?" I ask.

"When we first moved down here, I felt like we were outsiders. We were only renters, only here for a year. I felt intimidated in certain ways."

"The red-headed stepchild, you mean?"

"I guess," Pam says, "but now I feel like we belong here.

"That's because we do belong here," I say.

Monday, May 31

Pam and I are hitting some tennis balls at the Seaview courts. We're the only people here. We finish playing and walk to the lake and then back to the cottage. We almost always take the long way home.

"Is that a note?" Pam says and points to our front door.

"Looks like it. Maybe it's from that plumber," I say.

"Very funny, but who do you think it could really be from?"

I reach and take the note off the door. "It's from someone named Timothy who says he used to live in this house. He missed us today, but he'll be back tomorrow morning."

"He's the one who's been getting all those AARP and Medicare mailings sent here," Pam says.

"Interesting," I say.

"Yeah," Pam says.

thirteen

"CHARDONNAY, AND A BOWL OF CHILLED EVIAN FOR MY PUPPY, PLEASE."

Tuesday, June 1

This morning Dick and I walk to the beach with newspapers and cups of espresso. The day is slightly cloudy, and a cool breeze is coming off the water. The sound of the construction on Worth Avenue, the jackhammers, the beeping of trucks backing up, mingles with the lapping of the waves. Dick starts reading *The Wall Street Journal*. I look at Sunday's Shiny Sheet, which neither of us got around to reading.

"A man told police he left his twelve hundred dollar watch on his beach towel while he went for a long swim," I say. "When he came back, the watch was gone. Wouldn't you think he'd at least hide the watch in his towel?"

"He should have sprung for that waterproof one," Dick says, "the one that guy said cost more than his Ferrari."

I go back to reading and see an ad for pre-owned Bentleys. One only has 112 miles on it. Another, 128 miles. Another, 213 miles. I ask Dick who would drive a car so little.

"Maybe someone with ten cars," Dick says. "Or maybe someone like us."

"Oh, right," I say. "And here, it says Amici is closing this week."

"Well, we knew it was closing soon," Dick says. "Maurizio's opening that gourmet market."

"So our closest neighborhood bar and restaurant bites the dust. And Worth Avenue is all torn up. Funny this all happens the year we choose to live here. It feels like our Palm Beach is dissolving around us."

"I'll miss Amici," Dick says. He looks at his watch. "We'd better go back." We head home and go to work, me to the bird's room, Dick to the yellow room, which still doubles on and off as Dick's office. He commandeered it in March, just to finish up one project, but now, whenever we both have a lot of work, he hijacks the yellow room. It keeps us both sane.

Several hours go by. The doorbell rings. Dick gets there first and opens the door to a large man in a T-shirt and shorts with bare feet.

The man smiles and says, "Hello. I'm Timothy. I used to live here."

Dick says, "Timothy. Your mail still comes here. I think I know how old you are."

"I get those mailings at home, too." Timothy laughs. "I don't mean to intrude, but I wonder if you'd let me take a look around. I have such fond memories of my time here."

"Of course," I say. "Come in."

He walks into the living room. "This room was white," he says. "There was a beautiful mural painted on the ceiling. What a time we used to have."

"We?" Dick says.

"The woman who owned the house was quite elderly, but she liked to have houseguests. And loved to entertain." Timothy walks into the yellow room. "Yep, the bar's still here." He steps over to a set of small yellow doors built into the wall and opens them to reveal our bar. "Every afternoon at five o'clock, she'd throw open these doors and announce to her houseguests, and whoever else was around, that it was officially martini time. People would come and go late into the night. It was wild."

Timothy turns around. "Is that little room still there, past the kitchen?" he says.

"Sort of," I say. "We turned the shower into a storage area and keep clothes and our printers in there. Come see."

Timothy follows us through the kitchen. "You won't believe this, but the maid slept here," he says. "And that was her bathroom."

"This was her entire living space?" I say. "Was she little?"

"Not particularly," Timothy says. "The owner was of that generation when everyone had a maid, no matter what." Timothy laughs. "I can't remember the maid's name, but she was on the phone all day. She'd come out at meal time, cook breakfast, lunch, or dinner for whoever was around, and then come back in here and get back on the phone."

"Want to see the guest cottage?" I say.

"Definitely," he says. "That's where I usually stayed." We walk outside for a look at the guest cottage, and a man about half the size of Timothy comes around the side of the house. He has bare feet, too, and he has no shirt on.

"I'm with Timothy," he says. "I've been at the beach."

"No shirt, no shoes, no service," Dick says. The guy looks at Dick strangely.

"He's just kidding," I say. "Come join the tour." We take them through the guest cottage and back through the main cottage while Timothy reminisces about the good old days. They invite us to lunch, but Dick and I have deadlines and must decline. As Dick closes the door, I hear Timothy say, "Let's walk over to Worth Avenue to eat."

"They're going to be surprised when they get to Worth," I say. "Much of it's mud and boards."

Dick says, "Where on Worth Avenue do you think they can have lunch barefoot?"

Wednesday, June 2

The daytime weather has changed from warm to hot. In the evenings we switch from bumper pool to the swimming pool for cocktail hour, and we almost always sleep with air conditioning at night.

"A frozen drink, to celebrate June?" Dick asks. It's seven o'clock and very warm outside.

"Sounds delightful," I say.

He puts rum, fresh blueberries, frozen strawberries, and lots of ice into the heavy glass pitcher of our retro Waring blender, runs it for a couple of minutes, then fills two glasses to the brim.

We walk outside and dangle our feet in the pool. I slide into the warm water, Dick follows. We stand in the pool, leaning against the rim. I look at the doves, lined up on the cottage roof, not ready for bed yet. The hibiscus bushes around the pool are covered with red, yellow, pink, and orange blossoms. At the far end, the geraniums are bright red. Up above is a square of sky framed by treetops, blue and cloudless. I love this pool, love how private it is.

"This is the last quarter of our year in Palm Beach," Dick says. "The tenth month."

"It's going so fast. Remember when we worried we'd get tired of this town if we moved here?"

"Yeah," he says. "Actually, I think I like the town even more."

"I'm certainly not tired of anything we do here," I say.

"You mean you're not sick of dancing with me?"

"I'll never be sick of dancing with you," I say. "We've danced here more than we ever have in our life, and yet, if a few days go by without dancing, I miss it." I think of the restaurants we go to for dinner, of staying home and grilling, of the cabaret, of lunch at home and out. I think of the gardens and parks and the lake and the beach. How could I get tired of any of this?

"I don't think I've ever felt like this before," I say. "It's like nothing's missing."

"I feel the same way," Dick says. "Funny, isn't it? To be so content even though this cottage still makes us crazy. And even though Worth Avenue is being torn up."

"Also, since we're here for just a year," I say, "I'm probably not paying attention to things I would miss long term. Like our Jacuzzi tub and double shower in New Smyrna. Or our pool table."

"Or doors wide enough that we don't bang our elbows," Dick says. "And driving."

"Yeah," I say. "I miss driving, too. Or think I do, anyway, when I get in a car. But most of the time, somehow, I completely forget about it."

"It won't be long before we have our old life back," Dick says.

Thursday, June 3

I'm asleep, having a nightmare. I'm in a thick forest of tall pine trees, and a giant bulldozer is slowly, relentlessly coming toward me, crushing everything in its way. Broken branches and chips of bark are flying. The noise is terrifying. Frightened, I wake up, but the noise is still there. I sleepily wonder if the town's tearing up our street as well as Worth Avenue. I see Dick getting out of bed.

"What's that noise?" I say.

"I don't know," Dick says, "I'm still half asleep. I'm going to look." He walks out of the bedroom. I get out of bed, grab my robe, and follow him to the front door. The noise keeps getting louder. We both walk out to the sidewalk to see what could possibly be happening.

"Chainsaws," Dick says. "An army of them."

At the far end of the street a bunch of men are busy with power saws, making their way closer to us as they trim the palm trees. A Town of Palm Beach maintenance truck pulls up in front of our house, and a guy gets out.

"What's going on?" Dick says.

"It's June," he says. "Beginning of the hurricane season. We're giving a hurricane cut to all the palm trees on the streets." He points to a big frond. "See that," he says. "A big wind knocks that off, you got a dangerous weapon blowing about."

"Oh," I say, looking at the fronds. I'll probably see them a little differently from now on.

My art class is today. I'm copying another Georgia O'Keefe painting, *Calla Lilly on Grey*. I work on it at home, too, in the guest cottage, where I have taken over a corner and set up an easel and my paints. I learn a lot by copying: how to mix the right colors, and how to see what is there on the canvas. While we're painting, our teacher, Harlan, often reads us things artists have written or said as he walks around looking at our work, giving each of us helpful advice.

I am learning a lot but wonder if I'm hiding behind this copying business, afraid to try my hand at something original or abstract. The other students seem comfortable putting paint on canvas, seeing where it will lead. But Harlan is patient with me and excellent at pointing out exactly what I am missing as I try to copy the O'Keefe painting.

Tonight we stop at Taboo for a drink. We walk in the back way, to avoid the Worth Avenue construction. A big guy, maybe six foot six, two-sixty, is sitting at the bar several seats away. He's wearing a wide-brimmed cowboy hat and intricately-detailed leather cowboy boots. Two young women are sitting near him. He strikes up a conversation. One of the women asks, "What is it you do?"

He slowly drawls, in a very thick Texas accent, "Ahm in oaul an gas."

Then he invites both women to come with him "to hear ole Davey at the pie-anne-o bar at La Ropa." Perhaps that's Texan for "listen to David play the piano at Café L'Europe."

Sunday, June 6
Now that Worth Avenue is being torn up, we spend most of our walking time on the residential streets and only go to Worth to check on the progress being made. The mess is monumental, and sometimes the noise is unbearable, but the construction process is actually interesting. Huge pipes run under the road and they are all being replaced. Much of the sidewalk is now a labyrinth of boards over dirt and mud.

I see workmen installing hurricane shutters on our walk today. Hurricane season is June through November. We'll be here for half of it. I hope we don't have to evacuate. One year, we spent what felt like half the fall packing the car and running from storms.

One time, the hurricane followed us inland, and we spent

three nights at the Lakeside Inn in Mount Dora without electricity. The first night we huddled in our room with Duckie and Blanco, reading with flashlights, trees crashing down outside. The next two days, we walked over fallen limbs to have breakfast, lunch, and dinner in the Lakeside Inn's restaurant, which luckily had a gas stove. The meal choices were simple because the hotel was running out of food, but at night the dining room was lit only by small candles and was quite dark and romantic.

"Palm Beach is beginning to feel as empty as last September," Dick says. "Maybe by August we'll be the only people left here."

Our walk takes us by Bethesda-by-the-Sea. A parade of bagpipers comes marching out the entrance, followed by a bride and groom.

"Our anniversary's soon," I say. "Want to go away for a few days?"

"Absolutely," Dick says. "But right now we need lunch. It's after two."

We walk to Pizza al Fresco and sit outside in the courtyard. The table's umbrella provides welcome shade. I'm thoroughly enjoying the lobster salad, which I could easily eat every day. My husband the sausage lover is working his way through a sausage pizza. A woman with a white miniature poodle cuddled in her arm is at the table next to us. A waitress comes over and asks her what she'd like to drink.

"A glass of chardonnay," she says, "and a bowl of chilled Evian for my puppy." The waitress walks off.

"Did you hear that?" I say.

"Look behind you," Dick says.

I look and see two other dogs have bowls of water. I wonder if it's tap water or bottled, chilled or room temperature.

Sometimes I think everyone in Palm Beach owns a tiny dog and they all travel in carriages and strollers and wear little bows. There's a full-service spa here just for dogs, with a spa menu that includes mud wraps and massages.

"I still can't get used to seeing dogs in stores," I say. "I'll be in Saks, trying on shoes, and the woman next to me will have a dog in her purse or on a leash."

. "I can't get used to the dogs in the driver's seats of cars," Dick says. "Sometimes it looks like a dog is driving."

"Well, sometimes you're right," I say.

Wednesday, June 9

The town of Palm Beach has many regulations for contractors. Construction is monitored, and sites must be kept as acceptable-looking as possible. The other day I walked by a two-story office building, looked in a window, and was astonished to see nothing but rubble on the other side. Workmen were busy hauling it away. The building had been secretly demolished, except for the front wall, which stood like a Hollywood set.

The next day, workmen tore down the façade and hauled it away. The day after that, a sprinkler system was installed, and workmen were laying sod and planting a four-foot hedge around the perimeter of the property. The next day it was a grassy vacant lot surrounded by a hedge. Building to grassy lot in four days.

Saturday, June 12

Caroline and Pete, friends of ours who live in Winter Park, Florida arrive early this morning. They've never been to Palm Beach and know our year is about up and want to visit. Actually, they're golf nuts and the real reason they're here is they want to play the Palm Beach public golf course, which they've told us is one of the best in the country. We don't know. We're cured. They drop off their stuff and continue on to the course. They return in the afternoon, and we take a walk. They can't stop talking about their golf experience.

"Yes, it's a par three, but what a par three," Pete says. "The holes are right on the ocean and the lake."

"They're stunning," Caroline says. "You guys have to start playing again. Well, maybe not here, though. Guess you move back pretty soon?"

"That seems to be the plan," Dick says.

We've been zigzagging along tree-lined residential streets. "A lot of these houses look closed up," Caroline says. "People don't live here in the summer?"

"Well, some do," I say. "But lots of people go to Nantucket or Newport. And some of the people who own these houses only come here for February."

"Oh," Caroline says. "Let's walk to the beach. I haven't walked on sand in a long time."

"It might be crowded," I say.

"How could it be?" Caroline says. "You said nobody lives here now."

"People from the mainland come over for the day," I say.

The four of us walk over to the beach, and it is indeed quite crowded.

We skip the beach and walk over to Worth Avenue, where road graders and jackhammers and thick streams of water gushing out of pipes contrast oddly with the elegant window displays of Ferragamo and Neiman Marcus and Max Mara and Escada.

"What in the hell's going on here?" Pete says.

"Oh, my," Caroline says. "This isn't what I imagined Worth Avenue to be."

"They're redoing the avenue," Dick says. "New street, new sidewalks, replacing all the palm trees, all the planting."

We pick our way carefully along the makeshift boards that serve as Worth Avenue's sidewalk, but Caroline and Pete soon tire of the mud and the mess and we head home to shower and dress. Over cocktails around the pool, the golf talk takes over again and continues through our dinner at Café Boulud. We go the long way home, walking beside the now-empty beach.

As Caroline and Pete walk out to the guest cottage, Pete says, "Great evening. Can't wait to get back on the course tomorrow."

Dick and I look at each other.

Caroline laughs. "Don't worry, we're not staying. We have to drive home right after we play."

Sunday, June 13

Caroline, Pete, Dick and I are sitting out by the pool, reading sections of the morning papers. We're sipping espressos and munching on apples slices and biscotti. Pete has the Shiny Sheet.

"Dick," Pete says. "This says they're going to close South Ocean Boulevard, that's the road by the beach, right?"

"Right," Dick says.

"Well, they're going to close it for a bunch of days in July and August, so two different homeowners can build tunnels to the beach. Tunnels?"

"South Ocean cuts through some peoples' property," I say. "Most of the property's on the west side of the road. That's where they build their mansions. But some of the property's on the east side. That's the beachfront part. The tunnel connects the two."

"That must cost a fortune," Pete says.

"Some people like their privacy," Dick says.

"Sounds like conspicuous consumption to me," Caroline says.

"Well, inconspicuous consumption," Dick says.

Caroline looks at Pete. "Honey, we've got to go if we want to do the par-three again and get home."

We walk them to the car and get back to our papers.

"Another espresso?"

"Yes, please," I say. "I'll get Duckie and Blanco."

He takes my little cup, and after a few minutes, returns with a refill for both of us.

"Our anniversary's getting closer," I say. "Any ideas?"

"I can't decide between beach and city," Dick says. "I was thinking of Anguilla. Or maybe San Francisco."

"Gee, I'd love to go to San Francisco, stay at The Huntington," I say. "I love walking those hills. Maybe we could get tickets to a Giants game. But Anguilla sounds good, too."

"So," Dick says, "which one?"

"I don't know," I say. "Let's think about it."

Monday, June 14

Dick and I are working on separate projects and don't have time to stop for lunch. We barely speak all day. Dick pokes his head into the office around six.

"Want to go to wine night?" he says.

"Did I just work for three days straight?" I say. "Café L'Europe's wine night is Wednesday, not Monday."

"You're right," Dick says. "But I saw in the Shiny Sheet yesterday that Café Boulud is starting a bring-your-own-wine night on Mondays. I just looked in our wine rack. There's a nice bottle of Brunello di Montalcino."

"Sounds wonderful," I say.

We shower, change into something dressy, walk over.

"I feel a little funny carrying a bottle of wine into Café Boulud," I say as we walk in.

"Well, no one else seems to," Dick says. "Look." Several couples ahead of us are all carrying wine bottles.

"The restaurant's full tonight," I say.

"Quite a crowd for a Monday in June," Dick says.

We find two seats at the little bar. Martial, the maitre d' tonight, who we've heard was banned from France for breaking too many hearts, comes over and says he'll have a table for us in about twenty minutes. Just then, a party of six with reservations arrives, and Martial turns to seat them.

"Those people are serious wine drinkers," Dick says. "Looks like they've got nine bottles of wine." He studies their bottles. "Three whites, five reds, and a dessert wine of some kind."

Eventually, Martial leads us to a romantic window table. Outside, fronds glisten with light from the full moon. Mariya, the sommelier, comes over to the table and opens our bottle of Brunello. We order dinner.

"We never got back to what to do for our anniversary," Dick says.

"No, we didn't," I say. "But I've been thinking..." I trail off. "Yes?"

"Well, this is kind of crazy, but what if we spent our anniversary in Palm Beach. At The Chesterfield. We've done it for the past three years and had a great time. We'll just stay the weekend, two nights."

Dick looks at me for a minute. "Well," he says, "aren't you Mrs. Brilliant? I've been dreading the thought of airport lines and going through security."

"So I'll call The Chesterfield in the morning," I say. "See if they have room."

We take the long way home to walk by the beach and end up sitting on a bench for quite a while, listening to the waves, looking at the stars, and watching several lightning shows out on the horizon.

Tuesday, June 15

I call The Chesterfield. They have a special two-night package, so I reserve for the weekend. As I'm hanging up, an e-mail comes into my computer. I assume it's The Chesterfield confirming, but instead it's from our landlords. I read it and go find Dick. "We got an e-mail from our landlords," I say. "They're not coming to Palm Beach this summer. We won't see them again."

"That's too bad," Dick says. "I like them."

"Me, too," I say. "Their e-mail was nice. It said if we change our minds and want to stay here longer, we're definitely more than welcome."

Sunday, June 20

For the first time ever, we walked home from an anniversary escape. Even though we were just a few blocks from our cottage, I felt as if we were miles away. And even though we went to Taboo and Renato's and Bice and The Chesterfield, I still kind of felt like a tourist. And it was so pleasant not to end the trip with airport security lines and hours on a cramped airplane.

We traditionally go out the night we return from a trip, so tonight we start with drinks at Taboo, which is funny to me, since we were just there last night while away on our "trip." The bar is fairly crowded. A couple sitting next to us is chatting with Bobby, telling him they're headed off to Paris tomorrow for their fifth wedding anniversary.

The woman says to Bobby, "We're so excited. We've had so much fun in Paris. We went there for our first anniversary, and then again for our second."

Bobby frowns and is silent for a moment, then says, "Wait, didn't you go to Rome for your second anniversary, and then back to Paris for the third?"

The woman pauses, looks at her husband, turns back to Bobby, and laughs. "Of course. You're right! How did I mix that up?" She pauses again. "And how can you remember my life better than I can?"

Dick looks at Bobby for a second. "Who are you, Carnac the Magnificent?" he says.

Monday, June 21

Today is the longest day of the year. When I lived in New York, I disliked winter, hated the cold and the short days, when it would be dark long before I left my office. Even in Florida, where it can be seventy degrees any given day all winter long, I still like the long days better.

I look forward to the spring solstice, dislike when the clocks go back in the fall, wait out the days of winter darkness. But I have mixed feelings about the longest day of the year. Yes, today has the most daylight, but tomorrow will have a little less, the first sign the short days are on their way.

Today is also the annual International Day of Slowness. The founders suggest taking this day to celebrate the enjoyment of slowing down, looking around, taking time to enjoy the moment. Watch a snail make its way across a leaf. Cook something from scratch. Do nothing. Pretty much the opposite of the world's current obsession with frantic multitasking.

In some ways, Dick and I seem to be incorporating this

slowed-down lifestyle into our year in Palm Beach. We spend much more time here taking walks, looking at stars, and sitting in parks. Ironically, we also get more done in a day than we used to before we moved here. We do more, yet have more time.

Our life here is simpler. Back in April, when I solved the kitchen space problem by boxing up most of our plates, I wondered if I would miss the things I put away. I forgot all about them. It has been surprisingly easy to live with just a few plates.

This, in turn, made using the dishwasher pointless, and I rediscovered the simple pleasure of washing dishes by hand. When I was a child, my father often washed dishes, and I have fond memories of him standing in front of a sink full of suds, carefully rinsing off a glass or a plate. I never understood why he seemed to like washing dishes. Now I think I do.

This afternoon I walk into a tailor's shop to have some pants altered. A woman, probably in her early fifties, is standing in front of the mirror, and a seamstress is pinning the hem of the dress she has on. Behind her is an entire rack of clothes she has just bought that need to be altered. The price tags are still attached. About half the clothes have been fitted.

"I just have to stop now," the woman says. "This is exhausting. It's making me way too tired." She makes a date to come back and finish another day. I guess that's her version of how to celebrate the International Day of Slowness.

Friday, June 25

Ritey and Ron, friends of ours who live outside Ocala, called yesterday and asked if we'd be around tonight. He's an oral surgeon, and they're both headed to a conference in Miami tomorrow. We've only known them a few years, and just recently, Dick and Ron discovered they played against each other in a college soccer game. Ron was in the goal for Emory. Dick was in the goal for Rollins. Neither can remember who won.

They arrive about seven, and we have cocktails around the pool.

"So, Ron," I say, smiling, "aren't you sorry you got here too late to shop Worth Avenue?"

Ron is not a shopper. He laughs. "Right. Not my thing."

"We might have time in the morning," Ritey says.

Ron says, "You girls can go. I'll be here, in the pool."

We discuss various restaurant possibilities, decide on Renato's. We avoid Worth Avenue because it is so torn up and head in the back way to Renato's. Parked on Peruvian is an old Rolls-Royce roadster, probably from the late 1930s. It looks to be in mint condition. The top is down, and a white pullover sweater is casually tossed across the black leather passenger seat.

"Look at that old Rolls," Ron says.

"The keys are in it," Ritey says.

Indeed, in the ignition is the key, with a little gold keyring hanging from it.

"Boy, that's out of another era," I say. Tempting, I think.

We dine outside in Renato's enclosed courtyard, bougainvillea subtly lighted against the stucco walls, the stars above. Then we walk over to The Chesterfield to dance and end up staying until the band packs up.

We head home on Peruvian and walk by several art galleries. A cop is standing inside one of the galleries, and Ron waves at him. Dick and I share a knowing glance. The cop doesn't move. Ron waves again. We get closer. Ritey says, "Oh, my God, he's not real! Or is he?" She looks carefully at the cop. "He's not alive, right? I mean, is he? Look at his skin. This is creepy."

We all gather around the window. Indeed, the cop is a

sculpure but an unnervingly lifelike one. Dick and I were completely fooled the first time we saw him. We actually stood at the window for quite some time, periodically convinced that the guy was alive but just being still, like the Buckingham Palace guards.

Saturday, June 26

I wake late and walk out to the living room. Dick is looking at his laptop but there's no sign of Ron or Ritey. Just then, the front door opens. Ritey and Ron walk in carrying, of all things, shopping bags.

I look at Ritey. "Ron went with you while you shopped?"

"No," Ritey says. "Actually, Ron went shopping. There must be something weird in the water here. He bought designer jeans, a belt, a shirt."

Ron smiles sheepishly.

"Worth Avenue's a mess," Ritey says. "Anyway, we gotta go." We do hugs all around, and they're out the door.

"Ron went shopping?" Dick says. "There *must* be something in the water."

Sunday, June 27

Duckie and Blanco are in their cage, out by the pool with us. Duck is back to her old self and actually weighs more than she did before she swallowed the metal.

Dick says, "The Shiny Sheet says a resident called the police because a delivery truck drove over the grass at the edge of his driveway and damaged the lawn." We may have to notify Interpol again.

"Such problems these people have," I say. "Time for a walk?"

"Good idea," Dick says.

I take the birds back inside, and out we go. The sun is strong, the temperature's in the eighties, but there's a light breeze and puffy white clouds create patches of welcome shade. As is usual on a Sunday, tiny open signs are in front of some houses that are for sale. The Town of Palm Beach requires these signs be discreet: no bigger than eight inches by five inches, no words other than "open," and hung on a thin black post.

We almost miss a sign tucked into the end of a forty-foot-long, ten-foot-tall ficus hedge. The gate is open and a brick driveway leads to a two-story frame house, painted white, with black shutters.

"Want to go in?"

"Sure," Dick says. "It looks like a Norman Rockwell-type of house, only bigger." We walk up the driveway. As we get to the door, a woman opens it.

"Hello," she says. "My name's Frances. Please sign in." We do, and she leads us through a foyer into a formal living room. "You can easily have cocktails for seventy in this room," she says.

"Good, let's have one," Dick says.

Frances is silent. I look around. The room is a riot of floral prints, from the wallpaper to the silk-upholstered furniture to the pillows and drapes. Hanging on the walls are what look to be original oils by eighteenth-century masters. I move close to one to inspect it.

"Watch out," says Frances. "There's an alarm system. Don't touch."

I hadn't intended to touch, but I do move a respectful distance away.

Frances leads us into an adjoining room and says, "And this is for your more intimate gatherings."

"No," Dick says. "We've walked through a time-space warp. This is The Huntington Hotel bar in San Francisco." He looks around. "Where's Ty? Must be time for a beer."

Frances looks puzzled, which I think she often might.

I say, "This looks remarkably like a bar we love in San Francisco. Ty Sanders has been the bartender there for years."

Dick and I have had good times at The Huntington's Big Four Bar, and this room brings back memories. It's dark, with mahogany-paneled walls and leather chairs framing a large wood-burning fireplace. There's also an L-shaped mahogany bar with leather-covered stools and a brass foot rail. Behind the bar, mirrored shelves sparkle with liquor and glasses. The only thing missing is The Huntington's piano.

"Come see the kitchen," Frances says. We follow her. Although it's state of the art, it seems modest given the size of the house.

"This kitchen looks kind of small," I say.

"Oh, this is just the family kitchen," Frances says. "The chef prepares some family meals here, but his kitchen is down the hall."

"Oh," I say. "Of course."

"The owners entertain quite a bit," Frances says. "When they're in town, they often have parties for fifty to a hundred people, so they built their chef his own kitchen."

We follow Frances to a kitchen almost as big as the one in Henry and Michelle's restaurant. A giant hood covers a wide griddle and eight gas burners.

As we leave the kitchen, four people walk in, and Frances's cell phone rings.

"We'll leave," I say. "This house is way too big for us. These people might be customers." Frances mouths the word "thanks" and we find our way out.

It's not too long before we pass a brand-new house with a

discreet open sign by the newly planted front hedge.

"Shall we?" I say. In we go. The real estate agent meets us at the door.

"I'm George. This house is brand new, never lived in," he says. "Fifty-five hundred square feet of luxury living space. Come," he says, "follow me."

We walk across a polished marble floor from the foyer into the living room. The ceiling is two stories high. A grand fireplace is at each end of the room, and although there is no furniture in the house, a flat-screen TV hangs next to each fireplace.

George takes us through a formal dining room, a breakfast room, an enormous kitchen. Every room has a flat-screen TV. George shows us the full-size elevator, takes us up the wide curved stairways. Flat-screen TVs are in every room upstairs, too, including the bathrooms and dressing rooms and a long hallway.

As we go back downstairs, Dick says, "George, this house has more TVs than a sports bar."

George smiles. "People can't be without TV these days. This house is the future." ·

I say nothing, thinking of our TV-less cottage a few blocks away.

"This is a smart house," George says. "It's electronically state of the art." He walks to a control panel on the living room wall. "Every room has one of these panels," he says. "It controls the air, the music, the lights." He puts on his reading glasses, studies the panel, starts moving switches. Lights flash on and off: a massive chandelier, sconces, indirect lighting along the edge of the floor, pinpoint ceiling lights.

I look carefully at the control panel. Sixteen switches can be placed in multiple positions. Tiny notations under each indicate its purpose. "Ah, a cheat sheet," I say.

"Yes, but in no time you'd know what was what," George says.

Dick looks doubtful, but George's enthusiasm is not to be dampened. "Not only is this house wired for sound, it's also wired to be wireless. You can change the air conditioning settings from your car or even from your plane."

That does it for Dick. We thank George, explain this is too much house for us. Back out on the street, grateful to be walking to our little cottage, Dick says, "Let's see. We're in our private jet flying back from Paris and want to make sure our bedroom in Palm Beach is cool when we arrive. If we owned that house, wouldn't we have a butler to handle that?"

Wednesday, June 30

It's eight in the morning. I'm in the pool, lying on a float. The sun is creeping across the north end but much of the pool is still in shadow. The circulation system is on, taking me on a slow journey around the edge. The trees above frame a cloudless deep blue sky. I relax, try to think about nothing, but also I follow my thoughts, see where they go. This is one of my forms of meditation.

This week my art class was switched from Thursday to Wednesday. This afternoon I go to my class and decide to tackle abstract painting for the first time. I set a blank canvas on my easel and put paint on it, some of this and some of that, experimenting with different brushes, different strokes, different colors.

I ask Harlan for help, but he just smiles and says to keep on going. I get into this loose style of painting a bit and realize it's not dissimilar to the way I felt this morning, letting go and then observing where I'm going. I suddenly understand this is one of the things Harlan means when he talks to us about painting.

I find I can't stay with the completely loose feeling for long, and after a while I take a second canvas and get out a photograph I have taken of a red hibiscus. I start to paint the flower. But the letting go feeling must still be with me because this time I start to paint my version of the hibiscus, the hibiscus as I see it, or maybe as I want to see it. Or want to paint it.

The painting becomes mine. I can do what I want. I don't have to make the petals look the way they do in real life. I can focus on what I like about the petals. I make the petals flashier than they really are, exaggerate the size of the stamens. It is a liberating feeling, and I paint faster. The class is over long before I am ready to leave.

fourteen

"WE FINALLY JUST STOPPED COUNTING AT NINETY-SIX."

Thursday, July 1

I'm standing in the pool with a frozen drink resting on the pool's edge. Pam's lying next to me on a float. It's almost ninety degrees. I say, "Mike and Maggie will be sailing in tomorrow. Do you think there are fireworks somewhere on Sunday?"

"Have to be," Pam says. "We've already seen two shows this year. They have to have fireworks on the Fourth."

I'm really into the ease of living here in the summer, the flow of the days and weeks. Summer has a different pace than the other seasons. Summer has always said to me, "Chill, slow down, kick back." Summer here is no different. No Bentleys honking and blowing through stop signs this time of year.

Friday, July 2

Mike, a man of few words, and Maggie, a woman of many, are due this afternoon. Pam and I have known Mike since we were first married. Maggie arrived in the picture about two years ago. They escaped from Manhattan last year and now live in Sea Island, Georgia. Maggie's sister used to live in Palm Beach, and

Maggie has informed Pam she has a very specific to-do list: she wants to spend her days "shopping and enjoying the beach, the nights eating, drinking, and staying out late." Pam and I have been resting up.

At about two o'clock, Mike pulls in the driveway in a vintage British racing green Triumph TR-4, spoked wheels, chrome luggage rack. "Nice ride," I say.

"Thanks. It's a lot of fun," Mike says. He looks at the Corvette in the driveway. "Maybe we should drag for beers later."

"Oh, please, Mike," Maggie says.

I take their stuff back to the guest cottage, and Maggie declares it is time to shop. Pam says, "You guys are on your own till around five o'clock. Dick and I have to work. Go spend all your money, and we'll see you when you get back."

Later, Pam walks out of the office and says, "I think I hear Maggie."

"Me, too," I say, "but she could still be just a block or two away."

"Be nice," Pam says and goes to the door to let them in.

"Maggie," I say, "Pam was kidding when she said 'spend all your money.' You look like a bag lady."

Mike is just shaking his head.

"Well, you'll want to see what I got. And I didn't even do the avenue today, just the vias," Maggie says. "The town is really torn up. Worth is a mess, but I didn't mind."

Maggie begins her show and tell, pulling things out of shopping bags. "I got these two dresses from Biba, this tunic and purse from Marley's Palm Beach Collection, and this pair of slipper shoes, aren't they silly, from Stubbs and Wooten. And look, I got these Limoge plates from Sherry Frankel's Melangerie. That's my favorite shop in Palm Beach."

I look at Mike and say, "You know, I think some of the stores are still open. Maybe you guys could take another run at it."

Mike, who is behind Maggie, gives me a look and apparently has some kind of hand cramp or something. One of his fingers is sticking up. "I think we're okay for today," he says.

"For today, we're fine," Maggie says. "Tomorrow, it's Armani, Saks, Neiman Marcus, and Trillion. Can we do Motown tonight?" Maggie asks. "I want to wear one of my new dresses."

"Take a breath here, Maggie," I say. "How did you know there is Motown tonight?"

"I've done my homework," she says.

"Not well enough, I'm afraid. You and Mike are way too old for Motown. It's a young crowd," I say.

"We are?"

"Maggie, he's kidding you," Pam says. "Of course, we can go. There'll be people from twenty-two to eighty-two."

"So that means there'll be people from your age, Maggie, right up to Mike's age," I say. I think Mike should have that hand problem looked into.

"You have any place you want to go for dinner?" Pam says.

"We're going to Bice," Maggie says.

"We are?" Pam says. "Well then, we'll change, have a cocktail by the pool, and then we'll go to Bice."

Saturday, July 3

Pam and I are up before Mike and Maggie and walk to the beach. When we get back, Mike and Maggie are sitting by the pool. The four of us decide on a breakfast of espresso, biscotti, and fruit.

"Well," Mike says, "last night Dick and I proved once again there is nothing much sillier than two old white guys trying to dance fast."

"Stop. You guys were great," Pam says.

"You were," Maggie says. "Now we're going to the beach, and then we'll take you guys to lunch, and then we'll do some more shopping. It's dancing at the Leopard Lounge tonight."

Mike looks at me and shrugs.

"You two go to the beach," I say. "We'll all meet for lunch, and then you can shop till you drop."

They're back from the beach at about one o'clock; we walk to lunch at Pizza al Fresco. We're sitting in the courtyard next to a bed of flowers. Maggie points to a stone in the flowers and says, "What does it say on that stone?"

"Actually, it's a gravestone, and it reads 'Johnnie Brown the Human Monkey,'" I say.

"A gravestone for a 'human monkey,' in a restaurant?" Maggie says.

"It's a long story," Pam says, "that building used to be Addison Mizner's house, and he had a pet monkey named Johnny Brown. When the monkey died, it was buried there."

"That's a little strange," Mike says.

Walking back from lunch, I'm thinking how strange Palm Beach really is. There is a monkey buried on the island, and next to him a dog, but no humans. Palm Beach has no graveyards, no funeral homes, no hospitals.

Sunday, July 4

Pam and I sleep in this morning. I discover the Sunday papers out by the pool, but Mike and Maggie are nowhere to be found. I'm not unhappy.

Pam comes out of the bedroom and I say, "Anything you want to do before Maggie comes back with today's itinerary?"

"A quiet espresso and the papers by the pool with just you would be fine with me," Pam says.

"I think the stores on Worth Avenue are closed today, so they're probably at the beach," I say.

Around noon, Mike and Maggie find us by the pool. "The beach is beautiful today," Maggie says, "but Mike and I were thinking about going to the Gardens Mall for lunch, maybe some shopping. I checked. The stores there are open on the Fourth. It's not very far, is it?"

"No," Pam says, "it's about a half hour, straight up US 1 or I-95."

"Good. Then we're going. They have a California Pizza Kitchen. You guys want to come?"

"No thanks," I say. "We're good. We'll see you when you get back."

"Okay, tonight's a big night, maybe Echo and the Palm Beach Grill," Maggie warns us. This means we'll be heading about a mile north tonight to Royal Poinciana Way, near Publix. This is quite a journey for us at night.

Monday, July 5

Not surprisingly, last night went as planned, by Maggie. Since Maggie wanted to go to Echo and the Palm Beach Grill, we had to drive. Driving home, I figured out the last time I drove a car at night was in January.

This morning has gone as planned, by me. We have just waved goodbye to Maggie and Mike. Walking back to the house, Pam says, "How long was she here for, a week?"

Exhausted, we walk back into the house and I see this morning's unread newspapers. I pick one up. "Today's July fifth," I say to Pam.

She laughs. "You mean we missed the fireworks last night?"

"It's the Maggie factor," I say.

In our year in Palm Beach, Pam and I have seen two great, completely unexpected fireworks displays, and missed the only fireworks we'd planned to see. Humans plan. The gods laugh.

Tuesday, July 6

We're just wandering and end up walking through the construction on Worth Avenue. The scene is now familiar, a jumble of heavy machines. There are cranes lifting long sections of pipe, backhoes digging up the street, jackhammers tearing at the sidewalks. The process and the progress continue to be interesting to us. It is extremely well organized. "It's quieter in the middle of all this construction than sitting by our pool with Maggie," I say.

"She certainly can talk. And shop. Anyway, it was nice seeing them," Pam says.

Well, I was happy to see Mike, but the jury may still be out on Maggie.

Today, traipsing through the construction, Pam and I start laughing. Pam says, "Wouldn't you know they'd pick 'our year' in Palm Beach to redo Worth Avenue."

"Yes," I say. "The winter people are going to come back and see a new avenue but they'll have no idea the mess that went on while they were away."

"I like seeing the construction," Pam says. "It's quite an undertaking. I like being here for all this."

I'm happy today it's just the two of us, out together. We cross Hibiscus and are walking on Peruvian. Ahead, there's a building that's been going up for quite some time. It is obviously going to be a commercial building. Today, the contractor and some other men are looking at a blueprint right by the sidewalk.

I say, "Excuse me, what kind of business is going in here, do you know?"

The contractor looks up and says, absolutely straight-faced, "A McDonald's. We're putting up the golden arches today."

Before he's even finished his sentence, everybody starts laughing. The idea of a McDonald's anywhere in the Town of Palm Beach is, of course, preposterous.

"That, my friend, is an excellent choice," I say. "My wife and I are building a waterslide on the Preservation Foundation property and," I say, pointing to a parking lot, "turning that space into a go-cart track."

"Well, I guess we'll all get rich," the contractor says. "Or arrested."

Pam and I leave the future home of what is anything-but-McDonald's and head home. We come to The Invisible Man's driveway where, for almost eleven months now, we have seen a car parked in virtually every possible position but have never seen a person other than the gardeners.

An attractive gray-haired woman is standing there. She says, "Good morning. You're the authors, in the little cottage, right?"

I'm looking at The Invisible Woman, amazed that she has managed to remain invisible for eleven months, and wondering how this woman knows where we live and what we do for a living. I say, "Yes, we're both writers," and we all introduce ourselves.

"How are you liking Palm Beach?" she says.

"We love it," Pam says. "I can't imagine living anywhere else."

I've got to find out about the invisibility thing, so I say, "Do you live here full time?"

She smiles. It's a sad smile, or maybe just a wistful smile. "My husband and I have lived in this house full time for over twenty years. He's not doing so well the last year or two, so full time has taken on a whole new meaning for us."

Pam says, "I'm sorry. Can we help in any way?"

"No, thank you." She smiles. "We're doing okay. I usually sneak out very early in the morning to do errands and get supplies. Then we sit together on the back porch or by the pool. He still enjoys reading and his oldies music. We're doing okay."

"Well, Pam's offer was serious. You know where we are if there is ever anything we can do to help," I say. "And it is a pleasure to finally meet you."

When we get back home, Pam says, "I feel terrible. We've been making jokes about The Invisible Man for almost a year. And it isn't funny. He is sort of invisible."

"We didn't know." And it's not funny. It's scary. Stuff does happen. And the older I get, the less I am concerned about dying and the more I am terrified of becoming a burden to Pam or Samantha. As far as I know, I'm healthy at the moment, but the thought of becoming Pam's invisible man haunts me a bit. Some things we can control, some things we can't.

Thursday, July 8

First I hear the doorbell and then, a moment later, several authoritative knocks on our door. I open it and am greeted by a police officer. I put my hands up.

He shakes his head and says, "I'm wondering if you've seen anyone that looked suspicious in the neighborhood today."

Pam has joined me at the door. We look at each other. "Actually, we were out walking earlier," Pam says, "and not only did we not see anyone suspicious, we didn't see anyone at all."

"I can believe that," he says. "I've knocked on every door on this block and you guys and one lady down the street are the only ones who answered. Anyway, somebody knocked on a woman's door the next block over, and she called us because she didn't recognize him. When we got there, he was gone. It's probably just a mistaken address, but we're checking anyway."

Even though the Palm Beach Police do investigate stolen sunglasses and the occasional unknown knocker, and they'll give you a ride home on New Year's Eve, they are not Keystone Kops. This is a thoroughly trained, professional modern police force. They are the reason this is such a safe place to live.

Sunday, July 11

We're in Café L'Europe for another civilized Sunday. David is working his usual magic. I'm realizing how much I'm going to miss things like our civilized Sundays, dancing any night we want, going to the Royal Room Cabaret. Back in New Smyrna, the closest thing to cabaret is probably karaoke. But the truth is, unless Pam's done something she hasn't told me about, we haven't been banned from returning to Palm Beach to visit. We only live three hours north. Still, I'm feeling like September is coming at me way too fast.

David starts his rendition of "Happy Birthday." The wait-staff comes out carrying Café L'Europe's signature sparklers, and Pam and I both turn to see who the birthday person is.

At the table is a father and, next to him in a booster seat, a tiny, precious-looking little girl. In front of her is a decorated cup-cake with a single candle on it. Pam says, "Not a bad place for your first birthday."

I raise my glass. "May all her birthdays be as elegant."

Norbert and Lidia, the owners, have walked over and are talking to Pam. Norbert is German, Lidia from Brazil. I'm looking around the restaurant at various employees we have gotten to know. This is not Café L'Europe, this is Café Le World, I'm thinking. Rainer is from Germany, Damir from Croatia, Noureddine from Morocco, Marco from Brazil, Sergio from Argentina, Francesco from Nicaragua, Milton from Brazil, Greg from Philadelphia, Monsieur Jean from Haiti, Sylvaine from Monaco, Billy from Peru, Clarissa from Miami, Bruce from Maine, John from Brooklyn, Ayhan from Russia, and Ramsey from North Carolina, and these are just a few people from the front of the house. Café Le World.

Monday, July 12

It's getting hotter. Some nights the temperature doesn't go below eighty, but if there is a breeze off the ocean it's still quite pleasant. Even this far south in Florida, I'm struck by the changing of the seasons. Every month so far has been different from the last, at least in subtle ways. And, of course, certain seasons down here in Palm Beach are marked by the comings and goings of people, not the falling of leaves or snow, or the sprouting of crocuses like up north.

Duck and Blanco are reading the papers with us this morning. Pam says, "Today's Shiny Sheet reports that police were called to a shop in Via Parigi. Overnight someone removed a terracotta flowerpot from outside a shop."

"That's funny," I say. "I mean it's not funny, but it's unusual that storekeepers and restaurants here close up and leave flowerpots, chairs and tables, potted plants, and other stuff outside."

"You mean, and this is the first time we've ever heard of anything being taken?" Pam says.

"In most towns, store owners bring everything inside at night or lock it up, or it's gone."

Pam and I eat outside tonight with early Sinatra and then slip into the pool for a swim. After a few minutes, we dry off and go around to the front yard to do a little stargazing. It is a very clear and dark night with no moon, and we are sitting in our beach chairs on the grass, talking and looking at the night sky.

"Did you see it?" Pam says.

"Yep," I say. "A big one." My head knows shooting stars are only bits of cosmic dust hitting the earth's atmosphere, but my heart knows they're magic.

Pam says, "Do you remember Antigua?"

"No," I joke, then add, "yes, of course I remember. Who could forget that night?"

Pam and I were alone on the beach one December night in Antigua. The entire sky was filled with shooting stars. We were laughing and pointing and counting. We finally just stopped counting at ninety-six, even though the show continued on.

Whether it's one hundred or just one, I love seeing shooting stars with Pam. As long as we have been together, Pam and I have been stargazers. From Connecticut to the Caribbean to California and all over Florida, we have gazed into the night sky.

Saturday, July 17

Pam and I are checking out a sale at Polo Ralph Lauren. Pam is looking through some sweaters. A man next to her is buying several jackets that need altering, and the saleswoman asks, "Which address would you like me to have these sent to?" She obviously knows the guy has several houses.

A moment later, a different salesperson asks another customer the same question. Pam whispers, "You think everyone who shops here has two addresses?"

"The truth is most of the customers here probably have more than two," I say. An alternate universe.

We have only one address at the moment. Fortunately, it is near the Colony's Royal Room, and tonight we're going to see Jennifer Sheehan.

Ms. Sheehan's show is a celebration of the *Great American Songbook*, and she is brilliant. I have socks older than Ms. Sheehan, but she is poised and confident and hugely talented.

After the show, we go into the Polo Lounge for Rob Russell's cast party. Pam says, "I think we just saw a woman who is about to be a big star."

"I think you're right," I say.

We order a late supper and dance to the Switzer Trio, which is a duo tonight. Rob Russell takes the stage and gets the crowd going with a few songs. Then Wayne Hosford, a former headliner, makes a surprise appearance and does a few Peter Allen songs. To cap off our evening, Jennifer Sheehan does two more numbers and then puts on a dancing exhibition with Rob.

As Pam and I are walking home barefoot on the beach, I am struck yet again by what a wonderful evening we're having. I'm very happy, but also aware that evenings like this won't be possible in six weeks or so.

Sunday, July 18

I put a CD into the Bose to listen to some music while I read in the living room. I hit the AM radio button by mistake, so instead of Robin Spielberg's piano, it sounds like a Red Sox game.

Pam comes around the corner and says, "Is that a baseball game?"

I start changing stations, figuring if the Sox are on down here, the Yankees probably are, too. Bingo. "Yep," I say. "I think we're listening to a Yankee game now. Yep, Robbie Cano just hit a double."

Pam shakes her head. "Talk about simpler times," she says. "This takes me back almost a half a century."

"Remember those transistor radios with the single earplug? I used to snake the wire under a long-sleeved shirt and listen to games in school."

"My first summer boyfriend was a baseball nut," Pam says. "We used to sit on his parents' porch all the time and listen to games holding hands."

"You held hands with someone before me?" I say. "Was this that Willy cad?"

"I don't think you can be a cad at twelve, but yes, it was Willy," Pam says. "Now, can we listen to the game?"

After the Yanks hold on to win it, Pam and I head out for the evening with our umbrella in a light rain. We stop and have a glass of wine at Pizza al Fresco. The skies clear and we head over to Bice for dinner. Halfway through our salad, Pam says, "Do you have the umbrella?"

"Nope," I say, "I forgot it." Just then, Javier walks over to the table with our umbrella.

"Anna called and said you left it, so I just went up and got it for you guys."

"That was very, very nice," Pam says. "You really didn't have to do that."

Javier just smiles and shrugs.

Wednesday, July 21

"Did you know there were German submarines off the coast of Palm Beach during World War Two?" I ask Pam. I'm reading the Shiny Sheet.

"I think those were rumors," Pam says. "I don't think they were, like, shelling the beach here."

"They weren't shelling the beach, but at least twenty American ships were attacked in Florida waters, some just off of Palm Beach."

"I didn't know the war got that close to home," Pam says. "Your father was in the South Pacific, mine was in the North Atlantic, and the Germans were a few hundred yards east of Saks?"

"Well, sort of."

The phone rings, and I pick up. "Dicky Boy, it's the reigning Palm Beach bumper pool champion," Henry says.

"Madam, I think you have the wrong number," I say.

"Ha. How're you guys doing? Look, I'm working out August's schedule. What day are you moving back?"

I say, "We're not coming back. Pam's been elected mayor. We're staying here."

"Okay, but just in case you decide to move back, what day should I drive the truck down?" Henry asks.

"Enrique, I think you and Michele already did your part for our year, using your truck, moving us down. You guys are off the hook."

"Stop. Stop. Stop," Henry says. "Look, my other line is ringing. Figure out the day and let us know. We're on it."

Pam comes in. "Who was that?"

"Henry. He and Michele want to help us with the move back."

"That's too much. They've done enough," Pam says. "We can rent a truck down here."

"I agree. We'll figure it out next week."

Saturday, July 24

In the summer, Palm Beach is definitely on island time. It is warm. It is empty. Those of us who are here year-round are not in a rush. And there aren't many of us. I love it.

Today we are walking back home from the dry cleaners when Pam says, "It's warm but much too beautiful a day to go back inside. Let's just leave the dry cleaning inside the door and walk on to the beach."

We go to the beach. Both of us take off our shoes and walk south for a while, then double back, leave the sand, and start walking aimlessly, enjoying the day and the scenery.

Café Boulud appears in front of us. "Lunch seems like a good idea," I say.

"Lunch always seems like a good idea to you," Pam says, "but I agree. A nice treat."

And it is. Afterwards, we waddle out and walk west toward the lake.

Pam sees a small "open" sign on one of the few houses on the island that could be smaller than our cottage. A man in the front yard says, "I'm James. Please come on in. It's an open house and nobody's been here yet. You two are the only people I've seen."

The house is immaculate and professionally put together, but it looks more like an exhibit than a house you could live in. Everything appears to be in three-quarter scale: the doors, windows, the rooms, the coffee table and couch, even the beds. It makes our cottage look spacious.

I bend through a doorway and say, "James, I don't mean to be rude, but are adult humans supposed to live in this house? Aren't these rooms a little on the small side?"

"Well, yes, this tiny cottage was built in 1912. The current owners bought it four years ago and did a complete remodel but didn't want to change the size. I can see the house might pose some problems for you," James says.

"For me? This house would pose space problems for Tom Cruise or Danny DeVito," I say.

James walks us outside. We thank him for the tour, wish him luck, and continue our walk.

"Maybe he could advertise that house at the Munchkin Manners dinners," Pam says.

"You mean and find an extremely wealthy fourth grader."

The sky is still deep blue and cloudless. The town docks are mostly empty. Pam and I amble north, then head east to the ocean. We have not seen another person since leaving the open house. We take off our shoes and walk toward home on the sand, occasionally stopping to get our feet wet in the surf, and then on to our cottage. I unlock the front door.

"Oh, the dry cleaning," Pam says. "It seems like a different day when we picked it up."

I look at my watch and realize it's four o'clock. "Well, it was five hours ago."

Sunday, July 25

When an expensive mansion is sold on Palm Beach, it makes the front page of the Shiny Sheet. This morning is no exception. Pam says, "James Patterson and his wife have just bought a house on South Ocean Boulevard."

"Do we know where?"

"Just a mile or so south of us," Pam says. "It's next to a house John Lennon and Yoko Ono used to own, and it hasn't been lived in for a decade or so. It's not finished."

"It's a fixer-upper, a handyman's special, Palm Beach style."

"Well, yes," Pam says. "Palm Beach style for sure. Not many places you can find a handyman's special for seventeen million."

"There aren't many places you could find a spec house like

that eighty-four-million dollar spec chateau either," I say.

"Here's some more news you don't want to miss," Pam says. "A store on Worth Avenue is having a special fashion show today, for dogs. The dogs are encouraged to wear their fanciest outfits."

"There is something really strange about this town and all the dog stuff," I say. "And real dogs look like dogs. They're not smaller than cats, and they don't wear clothes."

Wednesday, July 28

The French doors are open to the pool, but the screens are closed because Duckie and Blanco are sitting on our shoulders, preening. Suddenly, the birds go nuts. They start jumping and shrieking and running around like crazy birds. Duck puffs herself up and starts making growling noises like she's going to attack someone or something.

"What is going on?" Pam says.

"I have no idea." I start looking around for the problem. Blanco has run behind the couch, still screeching. Duck is puffed up, flexing, I guess.

"I see," Pam says. "There's the fox again, standing on the guest cottage roof."

Mr. Fox is staring at us indifferently. "I'll get a broom and save the day," I say. By the time I'm back with my weapon, the fox has moved on.

I laugh and say to Pam, "Three months ago, Duck was knocking on death's door. This morning she was ready to take on that fox. The Duckster."

Friday, July 30

July is almost over. Trillion, an exclusive men's and women's clothing store on Worth, is having a big sale. Pam and I decide to check it out.

When we arrive, the front door is wide open, a UPS guy is walking away, and two women are struggling with a cardboard box that is disintegrating as we watch. Water begins to leak out onto the entrance floor, and the two women lower the dissolving box to the ground to try to open it.

A gentleman comes to the front of the store, smiles at us, and says, "Oh, sorry, just step over here."

We step around the mess and into the elegant space. "What kind of clothes did you order that leak water?" I say.

He looks vaguely embarrassed and says, "It's pasta sauce."

Behind us, the two women, both laughing, rescue two plastic tubs of what looks exactly like a tomato-y pasta sauce from the soggy box, which recently held ice. "David, I'm going to put these in the refrigerator," one of them says, "and then we'll clean up the mess at the entranceway."

The gentleman leads us to a rack of slacks on sale.

Behind us we hear a woman (Tatiana, the co-owner of the store, we later learn) burst out laughing again. She's back in front of the store, trying to clean up the mess. She cries out, "David, the hose bib just broke," and she walks back into the store from outside, barefoot, dripping wet from head to toe, and leaving a trail of wet footprints as she heads to the back.

The gentleman (who, it turns out, is David, Trillion's other co-owner) is trying not to laugh because he is with customers he doesn't know, but finally he loses it and dissolves into laughter. Soon we are all laughing.

It's July, business is slow, the store is a mess, and everybody is happy.

288

fifteen

"IT'S A PERFECT EXAMPLE OF THE LAW OF UNINTENDED CONSEQUENCES."

Monday, August 2

It's the last month of our year in Palm Beach, our last four weeks. It is hot, but there's the ocean breeze to keep us breathing. As much as I was happy and excited to pack up and move down, I don't feel as excited to be packing up again. I guess that's always the case. It's more fun heading towards an adventure than it is heading back. The one thing I am looking forward to is taking Pam's paintings home. They will go perfectly in our house.

Pam's reading to me from the Shiny Sheet. "Some guy was arrested in town yesterday driving his car on three good tires and a rim. He apparently didn't know his car was missing its rear left tire."

"Maybe it's the heat," I say.

We're floating lazily in the pool when an evening thunderstorm chases us from the pool to the bumper pool room. As I'm drying off, I say, "When this table arrived last December, we didn't know how much we'd use it."

"I admit I wasn't sure about that purchase," Pam says, "but it was a great decision."

"You mean if we divide the cost of the table by the hours we've played, it's about ten cents a dance," I say. "And if we can figure out where it would fit in New Smyrna, that ten cents will become five."

I rack up the balls and we play a few games. "Remember when we first found the sculpture garden, found Winston and FDR?" Pam says.

"And when we first joined the gym and started playing tennis?" I say, "And Theo's chicken-walk thing at The Chesterfield, and the Ferraris, and our friend, the iguana."

"And John Pizzarelli, Jennifer Sheehan, and the Royal Room?" Pam says.

"What are we doing here, a year-end retrospective?"

"I guess," Pam says. "This is the last month. The year's gone too fast."

"Well, one more month here," I say. "Let's make it our best one."

Tuesday, August 3

Pam and I are at the Leopard Lounge. The bar is fairly empty, and Adam is at the piano and singing. The restaurant is also empty except for a group taking up a handful of tables at the back of the dining room. It looks like they're having a celebration of some kind but the room is dark and it's hard to see.

Lou brings us a drink and a joke. "You hear the guy who owned the movie theatre across the bridge died? His funeral is Wednesday at 2:10, 4:20, 6:30, and 9:00."

Adam starts playing "Second Time Around," so Pam and I head out to the dance floor. About halfway through our dance, the music changes to "Here Comes the Bride."

Pam says, "Let's go back to the bar. That must be a wedding

party back there. We'll let the newlyweds have the floor."

Back at the bar, we watch and wait. And wait. And wait.

"The newlyweds are a bit older than we thought," Pam says, nodding, "over there."

I turn and see them slowly, very slowly, making their way over for a wedding night dance. The bride, Lou tells us, is a young ninety-eight, the groom an even younger ninety-five. They make quite a couple, dancing slowly on the Leopard Lounge dance floor.

"'Cougar Town', Palm Beach style," Pam says.

The odds are against Pam and me dancing cheek to cheek together at The Chesterfield in thirty years. But wouldn't that be something?

Thursday, August 5

It's almost seven o'clock. Pam and I have been hitting tennis balls, and now we're walking home. Out of the blue, Pam says, "You know, it doesn't seem that long ago when we weren't supposed to trust anyone over thirty."

"I can't even remember thirty," I say.

"Even Samantha's looking back at thirty now. It goes so fast. I don't want to waste a moment of the time we have left," Pam says.

"Where did that come from?"

"I don't know," Pam says. "What's the James Dean quote?"

"'Dream as if you'll live forever. Live as if you'll die today.'" I say. "That one?"

"Yes," Pam says. "Let's try to live some version of that."

We cross South County and Barney yells, "Mad dogs and Englishmen!"

"Barney, check your watch. This is hardly the noonday sun,"

Pam says.

"Don't care what time it is. Old coots like you two shouldn't be running around in this heat," he laughs.

We wave and walk on to the cottage.

At the door, I look at Pam. "Old coots?"

Friday, August 6

I wake up this morning remembering Barney's "old coot" remark. Today is my birthday, but I don't feel like an old coot. I feel pretty good. The birthday does, however, remind me that if I live as long as my mother, I have three years left, as long as my father, five. Not a long time, but who knows, maybe I have twenty.

Birthday or not, it's a regular workday. We do quit early for a long walk and then have a celebratory cookout and a bottle of champagne. Pam gets my walker for me and helps me into bed.

Sunday, August 8

This morning I read in the Shiny Sheet that a woman from Houston informed the Palm Beach police she is missing a bracelet she had with her during her Fourth of July visit to the island. I can't help wondering if she knows the Greenwich woman who lost a bracelet back in November.

I have decided for the Worth Avenue transformation we should appoint ourselves the official Worth Avenue Renovation Excavation and Construction Kibitzers and Supervisors. The town WRECKS. We're on duty wandering Worth, checking on the renovations. The sections that are almost finished are beautiful. The resurfaced, widened sidewalks give us a glimpse of how nice everything will be when it's finished.

Pam and I are reminiscing again. Pam says, "Remember

when you were looking for a hardware store when we first moved down? All you could find were boutiques and shoe shops and galleries."

"Seems like last week, not almost a year ago."

Pam says, "Let's walk and do a tally of what the different shops sell."

About an hour later we have our results.

Places to purchase a bottle of aspirin, zero.

Number of shops selling ladies' clothing, fifty-three.

Number of shops selling bread, zero.

Number of shops selling jewelry, thirty-seven.

Number of shops where you can buy a six-pack of beer, zero.

Number of shops where you can buy antiques, twenty-one.

There are five shops that sell ladies' shoes and seven shops that just sell purses.

As we discovered soon after we moved to Palm Beach, shops on Worth Avenue have nothing people need, but just about everything people want.

Tonight after our survey, Pam and I are catching the end of a Yankee game at Bice. A guy comes in the side door and looks around. All the stools are occupied except two. These two are being occupied by a huge purse and a shopping bag.

The man says politely to the woman sitting next to these items, "Excuse me, are these your bags?"

She turns her head. "Yes, I'm waiting for a friend." And she turns back.

After a few beats, the man asks, "Is your friend really, really fat?"

The young woman's head snaps around. "Excuse me?"

"I asked if your friend is extremely fat."

"She most certainly is not!"

"Good. Then do you think it might be possible for me to use one of the two stools you seem to be saving for her?"

Tuesday, August 10

Today's mail has a reminder from a local insurance agent urging Palm Beachers to review their insurance coverage. This particular agent specializes in coverage such as a one hundred million dollar personal liability umbrella, twenty-five thousand dollars' worth of coverage for the hiring of a PR firm to protect your reputation in case of a scandal, insurance for your staff, and, of course, special insurance to cover kidnapping expenses.

It reminds me of the call Pam got last fall regarding our staffing needs. Anyway, I don't need insurance today. I need boxes and to start organizing our move back.

It looks like another Chesterfield night. We didn't get out of our offices until late, and it's now almost nine thirty. Time for the Leopard Lounge bar menu, specifically Bea's chicken soup for me and a plate of lobster salad for Pam, and then a dance or two. I'll miss being able to walk over and get Bea's soup and a dance after working late, or even after not working at all.

Ricky and Lucy are the servers in the dining room, and Lou and Candy are behind the bar. Lou comes over. "Let me ask you this," he says, pointing to the dining room. "If Ricky and Lucy are working the dining room, where are Fred and Ethel?"

After a quiet dinner, it is time to walk home. The hotel lobby always has a small jar of jelly beans near the front desk, and I usually stop by to spoon out a few. Tonight the jar is not there.

"No jelly beans tonight," I say to Pam.

We are almost half a block from the hotel when the night auditor catches up to us with a small plastic cup of jelly beans.

"We always have jelly beans," he laughs. "You just have to know the right person." I thank him.

"You know how often something like that has happened to us this year?" Pam says.

"I'll bet I could list a couple dozen of these random acts of kindness," I say. "It is not going to be easy to leave this island."

Thursday, August 12

I hit some tennis balls with Todd. It's only eight thirty, but the temperature is in the high eighties, and there's not much breeze. After about twenty minutes, I say, "Todd, I feel a little weird. I'm gonna sit down for a minute."

I walk over to a bench. Todd follows. "You okay?" he asks.

"Yeah, yeah, I'm just going to sit for a minute." I fade off to some other planet for a few seconds. I'm brought back by the sound of sirens.

Todd is putting a wet towel around my neck. "Thanks," I say. "Are those sirens for me?"

"Yeah, you worried me. Better to be safe," he says.

Two trucks from the Palm Beach Fire-Rescue Department arrive, and suddenly six EMT professionals and Mary Flynn, the facility supervisor, are marching onto the courts with enough medical machinery to open up a mobile hospital.

I am extremely embarrassed, but I'm also a little scared, so I'm not unhappy to see a six-pack of trained professionals. One of the paramedics begins by checking my blood pressure and pulse, then they hook me up to a portable EKG machine that is printing stuff like a stock ticker.

Todd hands me a cup of water. The paramedics are still checking me out ten minutes later when I see Pam walking onto the court. I look at Todd. He shrugs.

Pam looks scared, so I smile and give her a thumbs-up to let her know I'm okay.

"He's absolutely fine," one of the paramedics says as she approaches. "He should take it easy and stay out of the sun for the rest of the day, but everything seems normal."

Pam has several questions, actually more than several questions, but after four or five minutes she seems convinced it's okay to take me home.

I thank everyone, and as Pam and I are walking to the car, I say, "Our first day in Palm Beach we were met by the police. Then the firemen came to the cottage, and now, as our year is ending, I get a visit from the paramedics."

"Well, I'm glad we weren't arrested, I'm glad we didn't burn down the neighborhood, and I'm glad you're okay," Pam says.

As she's driving home, Pam says, "I was really scared when Todd called."

"I know. I'm sorry," I say. "Thankfully, there's nothing to worry about."

But I know Pam is still worried, and it is not lost on me that I just had a birthday, or that when my father got off a plane at La-Guardia and was walking to the baggage area, there was "nothing to worry about" then either. He dropped dead of a heart attack before he ever got his bag.

Saturday, August 14

I felt fine yesterday but took it easy. It was Friday the thirteenth, after all, and the tennis court incident scared me a little more than I let on. Today, as Pam and I are coming home from an early morning walk, I see a young couple in the driveway of the house next door. No one has been at that house since we first arrived.

Pam and I walk over and introduce ourselves. Fabrizio and Maddalena live in Italy and are here for two weeks to check on the house, which Fabrizio's family owns. We chat for a while, then continue home.

Tonight I'm on a mission to have one more burger-and-dog cookout at our cottage before our year is up. The burgers, dogs, salad, potato salad, and all the trimmings are sitting in the icebox.

Pam and I are sitting in the pool. Peter Allen is entertaining us. I haven't started the coals yet, but I'm looking over at my little forty-nine dollar Smokey Joe grill. I remember the firemen joking about it. Our house could easily be the only house on this island with a funny little grill like this. The truth is, it is just perfect for us.

Sunday, August 15

I read in this morning's Shiny Sheet that the mayor of South Palm Beach has had a dustup at a local "gentlemen's club." The mayor's been in a dustup in a strip joint. I'm wondering if he has some of that special PR insurance for these difficult times.

The renters of our New Smyrna house have moved out. I'm wondering if we should go up and check it out. It seems like a waste of time. We'll be moving back in two weeks, anyway. Why waste a trip? Why waste a night in Palm Beach? I run my thoughts by Blanco and the Duck. We all decide not to drive up.

Tuesday, August 17

Yesterday, Pam brought up the idea of checking on the New Smyrna house. She thought we should see it before sending back the security deposit. As usual, she's right. She also pointed out that it's only three hours away. The birds and I changed our minds.

So today we are driving up I-95 blissfully unaware how this trip may be changing our lives. We haven't made the trip for almost a year, but it is familiar and uneventful. As we leave I-95, head east on SR-44, and cross over the bridge to New Smyrna Beach, Pam says, "This is quite a different picture."

I've also been looking at the surf shops, sandwich shops, and T-shirt shops. "This is a great beach town," I say, "but a very different beach town from Palm Beach.

As I turn in our driveway, Pam says, "I'd forgotten how beautiful it is here."

I park, fumble with some keys, and we go inside.

"Coming here from the cottage," Pam says, "is like when we came back to the cottage from that little motel room in the Keys."

"It's not the Flagler Museum, but the space feels wonderful," I say.

Pam puts the contents of our cooler in the icebox and then we both start our house inspection. The place looks to be in perfect condition.

"Isn't this a nice surprise?" I say. "If the rent checks hadn't been coming in every month, I might not believe there were renters here."

We both start to wander around for a closer look. I go out and check on the garage, and when I come back in, I find Pam sitting at her desk in her office. "What're you doing?" I ask.

"I'm imagining having this office in Palm Beach," she says.

"It'd be nice," I say, "but pretty tough to move it there. And we certainly couldn't afford to buy or rent a house like this in Palm Beach.

"You're right," Pam says. "I know."

"You want to check the outside and the double deck with me?" I say.

We walk out to the end of the property by the wetlands. "Everything looks great out here," I say. "It's almost seven. Shall we have a glass of champagne in the tub?"

"I'd love that," Pam says. "I've missed our baths together."

Inside, I fill an ice bucket and find a half bottle of Veuve. Pam starts filling the tub. After about a half hour of sipping and talking in the tub, we're rinsing off in the two-person shower. I laugh. "This shower is about the same size as the third bedroom of the cottage. The one we turned into a closet," I say.

"The tub and the shower are great," Pam says. "I've missed them. And I want to cook in this kitchen tonight. It'll be a nice change."

We brought dinner with us: arugula, carrots, peppers, garlic, an onion, tomatoes, a box of penne, and a couple of hot and sweet Italian sausages. I have also, of course, brought Peter Cetera.

Pam creates the salad, and I, the pasta sauce. There is plenty of room for both chefs. Not even a near-collision throughout the entire prep. I'm beginning to think we don't even really need all this room.

Pam says, "This kitchen is huge. It's almost too big."

"You're reading my mind again. It's creepy."

"A game of pool while the sauce simmers?" Pam says.

"Excellent," I say. "The table's going to seem like a football field."

It takes us a game or two to adjust, but it appears we're now bilingual, pool and bumper pool. After several more games, we cook the pasta and have a candlelit dinner in the dining room.

"I love this table," Pam says. "And I love these plates. The cabinets are full of stuff I'd really like to have in Palm Beach."

"If we had room, you mean?" I say. "Anyway, we'll be back

here in less than two weeks and there's plenty of room here for everything."

We play another game of pool, then go to bed.

Wednesday, August 18

Lying in bed in New Smyrna this morning, I'm thinking about houses. In particular, I am thinking about the house I grew up in with my brother—my childhood home, "my house." That's what I called it, but even then, it wasn't really mine. Other families lived in it before we did, and certainly other families lived in it after we left.

This house in New Smyrna is Pam's and my house, but it's only our house now. Different people have owned it and lived in it before and will again. Anyway, I've lived in this house and the house I grew up in for almost the same number of years. Pretty soon, I will have lived in this house longer than any other house in my whole life.

After espressos, we find ourselves turning out of the driveway around nine thirty in the morning, having no reason to stay. As I'm pulling onto I-95, Pam says, "That was fun last night. What a luxury to have all that space."

"Yep, it was fun," I say, "but it was also a little strange."

"You mean like we were sneaking into somebody else's house?" Pam says.

"Exactly."

"Weird, isn't it? We've lived in that house for over ten years," Pam says.

We're both quiet on the drive south and both happy when we get to the Palm Beach bridge. Back home, I gather the newspapers and Pam lets the birds out. They've survived happily without us.

We're reading the papers with the birds. Pam says, "It's nice to be home."

"I thought we were home when we were in New Smyrna," I say.

"It's confusing, isn't it?"

We walk over to Victor's for lunch. Pam and I are both quiet, a little zoned out, or perhaps zoned in. We are the only ones in the courtyard. Well, the only humans. A heron wanders over to join us. He walks toward us on his spindly legs. Then he has a sudden change of mind and swoops gracefully up to the sky in the opposite direction.

Thursday, August 19

Today we pick up cartons at Scotti's, and when we get home, we find a note tucked into our door. Our new neighbors, Fabrizio and Maddalena, want to know if we would like to come for a drink this evening. Pam calls and says we'd love to.

We walk over around six with a small bouquet. Chairs and a table with light hors d'oeuvres are set up by their pool. There is also a brass tub filled with ice, two different Italian whites, and a selection of beers. These are good neighbors.

Over pinot grigio and Peroni, sopressata and mixed olives, we learn that Fabrizio's family has owned the house for almost twenty years, and that Fabrizio actually lived in it for four years when he was in college here. Maddalena is a model in Italy and this is her first visit to the States. After about an hour, I look at Pam and she nods.

"Why don't you two come over to our house for dinner," I say. "We're just going to grill some shrimp and chicken and make a green salad. There's plenty of food."

"No, we can't do that," Maddalena says. "We are the ones

who invited you."

"Look, it's no big deal," I say. "We'd love to have you, but we certainly understand if you have other plans. No pressure."

They look at each other, Fabrizio says, "We accept, but I'll bring the wine."

The four of us spend the rest of the evening by our pool sharing conversation, laughter, and three outstanding bottles of Italian Sauvignon Blanc, which we learn the Italians simply call Sauvignon. It is almost midnight when we say *buona notte.*

"We shall do this every August," Fabrizio says.

"That is an excellent plan," I say, "but unfortunately our lease ends this month."

"Well, then you must sign a new lease! We expect you for dinner at our house one year from tonight."

Friday, August 20

We walk home from Scotti's this afternoon loaded down with a second batch of cartons for the move. Back in the cottage, we stack the new ones with the others in the yellow room. There are probably a dozen or fifteen cartons now, all empty. We have promised ourselves we will start packing today. No excuses.

"You want to start packing?" I say.

"Not really," Pam says.

"Want to take a walk to the beach?"

"Maybe a short walk to the beach."

We walk over and drop down in the sand. We're both quiet.

"We don't want to leave Palm Beach, do we?" Pam says.

"No," I say, "I don't think we do."

"We don't want to move back to our house," Pam says. "Our dream house."

"You mean the one we've been perfecting for ten years? The

one with two great offices? A perfect kitchen? All that space in-side and out?"

"That house is great," Pam says.

"I know it is," I say. "It's not that we don't want to go back there. It's that we want to stay here."

For the next hour, sitting in the sand, Pam and I talk. Then we're both quiet for a while. We came down here basically on a lark. We had sort of been captive in New Smyrna because of Aunt Jane, and when she died, we were free in a certain way and wanted an adventure. Now we don't want the adventure to end.

What's more, if we hadn't gone back on Wednesday to check on the house, we'd probably just be packing up in a week or so and moving. And then what would have happened? All this stuff is a perfect example of the law of unintended consequences.

Pam stands up and stretches. "I think somewhere in the back of my brain I've known this for a while," she says.

"We both have. But it's like when we first fell in love and couldn't admit it to ourselves or each other," I say, "because we both knew it could never work out."

"Well, it did work out. Quite well," Pam says. "Can staying here work?"

"Why not?" I say. My answer surprises me.

"Why not?" Pam says. "Let me count the ways."

Back at home, we both get on floats in the pool. "This is an-other fine mess we've gotten ourselves into, Ollie," Pam says.

I laugh. "Ten days left on our lease, and now we decide we don't want to leave."

"It might have been easier if we'd figured this out a little sooner. I don't see how we can make it work."

"We can make it work if we really want it to, but right now about the only certainty in this equation is that the landlords want us to stay," I say.

"So first we have to find out if we can rent our house in New Smyrna again."

"Alex'll have a pretty good idea," I say. "I'll give him a call."

I come back out to the pool. "Alex sounded confident that he could rent it and maybe even sell it. He's going to do some research, make some calls, and get back to us."

"Sell it?" Pam says. "Oh, my."

Sunday, August 22

Pam, Duckie, Blanco, and I are reading the Sunday papers in the air-conditioned living room. It's already in the mid-eighties outside. The phone rings and Pam picks up. It is obviously Alex. Pam seems quite happy with whatever he's telling her. She says, "Thanks," and hangs up.

She then picks up the Book Review section and pretends to read.

"What, are you crazy?" I say. "What did Alex tell you?"

"Oh, that," she says. "Well, he says he knows he can rent it unfurnished on an annual basis, but he also said we should hold off renting because he showed it once this morning and has two clients who want to see it early this week."

"Two clients who, what, may want to buy it?" I say.

"That's what he says."

"And he knows he can rent it?"

"That's what he says."

"Scary stuff," I say.

"We should probably check with Bob," Pam says "and go online. See if there are any new rentals on the market down here."

"Good idea. We should know what's out there," I say. "But it's got to be in town."

"For sure," Pam says.

"I can't call him now, and tomorrow I know you've got to finish that project," I say. "So I'll do the research tomorrow and report to you at cocktail hour."

Monday, August 23

It's evening, almost seven o'clock. I'm out by the pool with the Mamas and Papas. Pam comes out. "I just e-mailed that article. Do you have any news for me?"

"I've got a real estate report for you," I say. "You want the short version?"

"Definitely."

"There are seven comparable rentals available at this time. Four we saw when we were looking last year and we hated them. There's one that's almost okay, but it doesn't have a pool. Then there are two that are possible but they're almost as far north as the Breakers."

"I think that's too far out of town," Pam says.

"I agree," I say. "Whoever said 'location, location, location' was absolutely right."

"In fact, if I had to pick an exact street and an exact block," Pam says, "it would be exactly where we are right now."

"So, if we're going to stay here, we're going to stay here."

"So, why don't we see if we can really stay here," Pam says. "Let's dry off, take the Mammas and Papas inside, and go through this cottage room by room, closet by closet, drawer by drawer, and see if we actually want to live in this space, this cottage."

We start our tour in our bedroom. We decide the room is small, the closet space smaller, but agree we both like the room a lot. It's cozy and relaxing.

Pam heads into the living room. "I love this room," she says.

I'm following her in. "The pink took me a while to adjust to," I say, "but I do like the room. It works for us."

"We call it coral, not pink," Pam says, "and the tray ceiling, the fireplace and the bookcases make it my favorite room."

Moving though the swinging door to the kitchen, I say, "Well, it's small."

"And it's ugly," Pam says. "But, you know, since it's a galley kitchen, it works."

"A galley kitchen," I say, "remember the galley on the boat? What happened to us?"

"What do you mean?" Pam asks.

"We lived on a boat for two years that was about the size of the little guest cottage. Yet somehow we had plenty of space. Then what happened? Where did we get all this stuff? Why do we need it?"

"You're right," she says, "and we have three times this much stuff back in New Smyrna." Pam walks over next to me, tilts her head, and looks up. She says, very slowly, "You know, all the stuff that made this year special, all the stuff that makes our life in Palm Beach special, that makes our life together special, well, none of it is stuff."

Well, that was easy. It only took us fifty-one weeks to figure out we want to live here, in this cottage, and that we have way too much stuff that we don't know what to do with. I guess we're not what you would call "quick studies."

Tuesday, August 24
The stuff discussion continues over breakfast and soon turns into a specific "things" discussion. "If we sell the house or rent it unfurnished," Pam says, "do we just get rid of all the furniture and things?"

"We don't want to store it. Samantha doesn't want it," I say. "So the answer is probably, if it doesn't fit in this cottage, it's history."

"My aunt's bureau? Your dad's desk? The pool table? How can we do that?"

"What do you think I was thinking about last night instead of sleeping?" I say. "The bureau and the desk will fit in the cottage. The pool table won't."

"The dining room table won't, either," Pam says. "Do we really want to do this?"

"Let's take a walk, see if we can answer that question," I say.

We walk over to the lake and sit under one of the giant banyan trees. We talk for almost an hour, and it's helping. We are getting clearer. Pam and I are coming to the same conclusion. Finally, Pam says, "We do want to move down here. We both love living here. It's okay to get rid of those things in New Smyrna."

"I think it is okay, and it's probably time," I say. "To paraphrase what you were saying last night, the best things in life aren't things. And yes, we both love living in Palm Beach."

"Okay," Pam says, "there's just one more question, and we should think about it today and sleep on it tonight. It's the big one."

"You mean, do we really want to walk away from our dream house?" I say.

"That's exactly what I mean. That would be a huge step."

Wednesday, August 25

We didn't exactly "sleep on it." In fact, we didn't exactly sleep. But we're now sitting together on a chaise out by the pool, and it's getting light. The birds are still asleep, the newspapers still in the driveway.

"We agree we have too many things, too many clothes, too many books, too much furniture," Pam says.

"And we agree that our house in New Smyrna is a better living space for us than this cottage," I say.

"That's right," Pam says, "but it's not about the house or the stuff or the things or the space. It's about our life together, and our life has been better in Palm Beach."

"For whatever reasons," I say, "what is outside our house in Palm Beach is more important to us than what is inside our house in New Smyrna."

"So, we'll be okay if we sell the house?" Pam says.

"Better than okay."

"Gee, what a struggle to figure this out," Pam says. "Want to e-mail the landlords?"

"Yes, I do," I say. "And then I want to take the day off, eat lunch out, and walk around our town."

I e-mail the landlords and tell them we would love to stay for another year, then Pam and I spend the day wandering around Palm Beach. We have a quiet dinner by the pool with Jamie Cullum, and for the first night in close to a week, we both sleep.

Thursday, August 26

No answer from our landlords. Pam assures me there's nothing to worry about.

Friday, August 27

No answer from our landlords again today. I assure Pam there is absolutely nothing to worry about.

Saturday, August 28

We are having tea and grapefruit juice with the birds in the yellow room. We all go to the office. Pam checks her e-mail and says, "Good, our landlords answered." She pauses. "No, not good."

"What?"

Pam reads, "'Sorry, do not wish to extend lease as requested. Will call Monday to explain.'"

I slump down on the couch. "What the hell does that mean?"

"I don't know. I don't get it," Pam says. "They said we could have the cottage forever. They practically begged us to stay. They said they weren't going to rent it to anyone else. What could have changed that?"

"It could be anything. Sickness, divorce, something to do with their kids," I say. "But the wording is weird. What does 'do not wish to extend lease as requested' mean?"

"I don't know," Pam says, "but it's going to be a long forty-eight hours before we talk to them and find out."

Tuesday, August 31

It has been three days since our landlords' baffling e-mail, and about twenty-four hours since we had a very long conversation with them and found out what their e-mail meant.

This is our last night of our "year in Palm Beach," night 365. Pam and I want to end our year the way it began: A drink at Taboo, dinner at Renato's, and a dance at The Chesterfield.

Taboo is so quiet you can almost hear the fish. We watch our favorites as they cavort around the tank. We have a drink and chat quietly for a while. The Yankees are up six to three in the eighth. We finish and walk slowly down to Renato's. Dinner at Renato's is as sophisticated and special as always. Uncharacteristically, we are the last to leave. Only an hour and a half left before our year in this alternate universe is over.

After a glass of champagne, a toast, and a few dances at The Chesterfield, it's time to head home. As we did three hundred and sixty-five nights ago, Pam and I do not head to the elevator. Instead, we walk through the lobby and the courtyard and out onto the street.

Our year in Palm Beach, the one-year lease on our cottage, will end in twenty minutes or so—and then our new three-year lease will begin.

EPILOGUE

Our landlords' e-mail "sorry, do not wish to extend lease as requested" turned out to be a misunderstanding about the terms of the lease. Pam and I had asked for a one-year extension. They wanted three years. Three was fine with us.

We hope to sign another lease and another and another. Perhaps some day in the distant future, Pam and I can both be laid to rest in Via Mizner next to "Johnnie Brown the Human Monkey."

Despite all of our initial uncertainty and our fears about the rather rash decision to leave our house and move down to Palm Beach for a year, it turned out to be the right decision at the right time.

For us, Palm Beach is a wonderful two-sided coin. One side is a beautifully maintained small town with quiet, safe streets, plus the ocean, and the lake. The living is easy, and the people are friendly. Life is simple.

The other side of the coin is the civilized and sophisticated opportunities usually found in a big city, the parks and galleries and museums, the dining and dancing and cabaret. We love both sides.

Our year here taught us that our dream house, the house we renovated and refined to fit our life, was just a house. It was a great house on two beautiful acres, but that house, those acres, were on the wrong island for us at this time in our lives.

Do we miss that house? Yes. Do we miss the custom kitchen? The two-person tub and shower? The pool table? The space? Yes. But it's okay, because if we moved back to that house, we would miss living in Palm Beach much more.

I don't know about the acorn and the oak thing or if the teacher always arrives when the student is ready, but our year in Palm Beach has been a great learning experience. Pam and I learned we are definitely not as smart or as wise as we thought. We knew we could never live here. We knew we couldn't afford to live here. We knew that the magic of Palm Beach would fade. We were wrong on all counts.

Before our move, we were very happy with our life on two secluded acres that backed up to hundreds of acres of wetlands. We were happy in a large house we owned, filled with books and art and fine china. We were happy having two offices, a pool-room, a great swimming pool, a bocce court, and driving thousands of miles a year.

In Palm Beach we are still bruising our elbows on doorways and having the occasional space crisis, but we are even happier now on our not-so-secluded fraction of an acre, in a small cottage we rent, slowly shedding our possessions and walking hundreds of miles a year. We are also enjoying the process of downsizing and simplifying.

And it is not like we've taken a vow of poverty. Our cottage is not a tent, and we're not subsisting on canned soup and crackers. Our life is very comfortable. It's just getting a little simpler than it was. A little less cluttered.

Pam and I know we're only dancing on this earth for a short time, and our year here, from The Invisible Man, to Pam's knee, to my visit from the EMT people, to the addition of another birthday each, reminded us our time for dancing is getting even shorter. So we're trying to focus more on the moment, the moments, we have left together, trying to do what we really want to be doing on any specific day or night.

Pam is painting more than ever and loving the process. I have returned to work on a novel I abandoned a decade ago. When we have a choice, when the decision is ours, we want to be sure we're actually doing what we want to be doing.

We know we are very lucky to have had a chance to live in Palm Beach. And we take some perverse pleasure that, while living in what some consider the Mecca of Excess where too much is never enough, we are learning the pleasures of living with a little bit less. Our cottage may be getting emptier in Palm Beach, but our life is fuller here.

And Life Goes On . . .

The Worth Avenue renovation has been completed and it is magnificent. Everyone in the town is still nice. We now have two foxes that visit often, and our birds don't seem to mind.

We've had no further visits from the firemen, the EMTs, the police, or the iguana. We have not seen Jimmy Buffett again (we don't think).

Mike, the man of few words, and Maggie, the woman of many, have gone their separate ways. Henry and Michele visit regularly, as do many of our other friends. Ron has never gone shopping again. Theo is still doing the chicken-walk.

Duckie and Blanco have a new companion, Fluffy. Pam and I are selling a car if we can ever decide which one. Pam recently sold her first painting. Samantha and Jason have set up housekeeping in Manhattan and are very happy. Pam's sister Sophie has sent us another collapsible vase. Lou still thinks he's Henny Youngman.

We're still walking and still finding new houses to name. Pam's knee isn't perfect, but it's pretty close. We're back to traveling to revise some of our other books and taking an occasional road trip. We still haven't hooked up our television.

"And the truth is we're not getting any younger,
And the years are getting hard to pursue,
In our youth we are driven by a hunger,
For the big important things we will do,
But today I'm not dreaming of tomorrow
Cause the future is so clearly in view,
All I see is one more moment with you."

—from "One More Moment"
lyrics by Johnny Rodgers and Lina Koutrakos

ACKNOWLEDGMENTS

Thanks to Carmen, who, on a weekly basis, helped us reclaim our cottage from the chaos of paper.

Thanks to Jon (Jon Corhern of Imagecraft) for immediate and professional help with various technical and software computer emergencies.

Thanks to Arlene and Terry, who put us on another road.

Thanks to Sophie for the lovely box of little notepaper we used up writing down middle-of-the-night thoughts.

And, as always, thanks to Samantha—from North Street to Bourbon Street to Wall Street to South Baptist Street—still the best kid ever.

ABOUT THE AUTHORS

The husband and wife writing team of Pamela Acheson and Richard Myers escaped from Manhattan over two decades ago and headed south. Since then, they have contributed to many editions of *Fodor's Caribbean*, *Fodor's Virgin Islands*, and *Fodor's Florida*, and dozens of national and international magazines, including *Caribbean Travel + Life* and *Travel + Leisure*.

They have coauthored a number of books together, including *The Best Romantic Escapes in Florida, Volume One*; *The Best Romantic Escapes in Florida, Volume Two*; *The Best of St. Thomas and St. John, U.S. Virgin Islands*; and *The Best of the British Virgin Islands*.